# HTML, XHTML & CSS
## QuickSteps

# About the Author

**Guy Hart-Davis** is the author of more than 50 computer books, including *PC QuickSteps, Second Edition, Mac OS X Leopard QuickSteps*, and *How to Do Everything: iPod, iTunes & iPhone, Fifth Edition*.

# HTML, XHTML & CSS
## QuickSteps

**GUY HART-DAVIS**

New York  Chicago  San Francisco
Lisbon  London  Madrid  Mexico City
Milan  New Delhi  San Juan
Seoul  Singapore  Sydney  Toronto

**The McGraw·Hill Companies**

Cataloging-in-Publication Data is on file with the Library of Congress

1234567890   CCI CCI   019

ISBN    978-0-07-163317-8
MHID        0-07-163317-0

**SPONSORING EDITOR /** Roger Stewart

**EDITORIAL SUPERVISOR /** Patty Mon

**PROJECT MANAGER /** Vasundhara Sawhney, Glyph International

**ACQUISITIONS COORDINATOR /** Joya Anthony

**TECHNICAL EDITOR /** Jennifer Kettell

**COPY EDITOR /** Lisa McCoy

**PROOFREADER /** Carol Shields

**INDEXER /** Claire Splan

**PRODUCTION SUPERVISOR /** Jim Kussow

**COMPOSITION /** Glyph International

**ILLUSTRATION /** Glyph International

**ART DIRECTOR, COVER /** Jeff Weeks

**COVER DESIGN /** Pattie Lee

**SERIES CREATORS /** Marty and Carole Matthews

**SERIES DESIGN /** Bailey Cunningham

This book is dedicated with thanks to Roger Stewart.

# Contents at a Glance

Chapter 1 **Creating Your First Web Pages with HTML and XHTML**....1
Begin and organize your website, choose HTML tools, create web
pages, and describe and check your web pages.

Chapter 2 **Choosing a Web Host and Getting Your Own Website** ... 27
Understand the basics of the Web; choose a web host or ISP; plan,
design, and create your site; and transfer it to the Web.

Chapter 3 **Structuring Web Pages and
Applying Manual Formatting**............................... 45
Apply manual formatting, create lists, apply indents and alignment,
use inline styles, and work with the style attribute.

Chapter 4 **Adding Graphics to Your Web Pages**.................... 67
Create or acquire graphics files, add and format inline graphics,
place background graphics, and create an HTML signature file.

Chapter 5 **Adding Links** ....................................... 81
Link to another web page or the same page, create links that download
files or send e-mail, create imagemaps, and add audio and video.

Chapter 6 **Creating Tables** .................................... 97
Create a table, add rows and columns, format table borders, format
and group cells, and create nested tables.

Chapter 7 **Creating Frames** ................................... 119
Create frameset documents and component documents, lay out the
frames, add alternative text, and create inline frames.

Chapter 8 **Applying Formatting
Using Cascading Style Sheets**........................... 135
Create style rules; create embedded and external style sheets; set
alignment, indents, margins, and line height; and create floating
two-column and three-column layouts.

Chapter 9 **Creating Web Pages
Using the Microsoft Office Applications**............. 159
Configure web options, insert hyperlinks, and create web pages
using Word or from your spreadsheets and presentations.

Chapter 10 **Using Forms and Scripts**................................... 183
Create forms to collect information, create a login form, and use
scripts in your web pages.

Index ................................................................. 201

# Contents

Acknowledgments..................................................................................xv

Introduction ..................................................................................xvii

Chapter 1   **Creating Your First Web Pages with HTML and XHTML**................................................1
  🔋 Understanding Tools for Creating HTML.......................................2
  Understand HTML, XML, XHTML, and HTML 5.............................2
    HTML...............................................................................2
    XML................................................................................3
    XHTML.............................................................................3
    HTML 5 ...........................................................................3
  🔋 Organizing Your Site ...........................................................4
  Which Version of HTML Should You Use?.......................................4
  Get Started with Your Website...................................................4
    Create a Folder for Your Website..............................................4
    Open Notepad ..................................................................5
  🔋 Understanding the DOCTYPE Declaration ...................................6
  Create a Web Page and Adding Content to It...................................6
    Create the Page's Structure.....................................................6
  🔋 Understanding the Header and the Body .....................................8
    Add Header and Body Tags.....................................................8
    Add Content to the Page .......................................................9
    Apply Formatting ..............................................................14
    Add a Picture...................................................................14
  Add Hyperlinks and Tags, and Reloading Pages ..............................16
    Add a Hyperlink................................................................16
    Create Linked Files ...........................................................18
    Describe Your Pages with Meta Tags ......................................20
    Reload a Page Automatically .................................................20
  🔋 Understanding How Search Engines Work ...............................21
    Redirect the Browser to Another Page.....................................21
  Validate Your HTML and Checking Your Pages .............................22
    Validate Your HTML with the W3C Markup Validation Service.............22
    Check Your Pages with Other Browsers....................................23

Chapter 2   **Choosing a Web Host and Getting Your Own Website**...........................27
  Understand Web Basics ..........................................................27
  🔋 Understanding IPv4 and IPv6 ..............................................28
    Understand Web Clients and Servers .......................................28
    Access a Web Page............................................................29
  🔋 Understanding URLs ..........................................................30
  Choose a Web Host ..............................................................30
    Assess Your Requirements ...................................................30

🖋 Understanding Intranets and Extranets ...................................................31
    Choose an ISP or Web Hosting Service.............................................31
    Decide on Web Hosting Features .......................................................31
🖋 Running Your Own Web Server .............................................................33
🖋 Understanding Domains .........................................................................34
    Evaluate an ISP..................................................................................34
    Evaluate a Web-Hosting Service........................................................34
    Register a Domain Name....................................................................34
Plan, Design, and Create Your Site.............................................................36
    Plan Your Site's Contents..................................................................36
    Make Your Site Effective ...................................................................37
    Keep Your Web Pages Small Enough to Download Quickly ...................39
    Check Your Website ...........................................................................40
    Update and Maintain Your Website ...................................................40
Transfer Your Site to the Web.....................................................................41
    Get the Information Required for FTP................................................41
    Transfer a Site Using an FTP Client..................................................42

<table>
<tr><td>**3**</td><td>Chapter 3</td><td>**Structuring Web Pages and<br>Applying Manual Formatting** ............................ 45</td></tr>
</table>

🖋 Using Proportional and Monospaced Fonts.............................................46
Understand Considerations for Web Formatting..........................................46
Use Paragraphs, Divisions, Breaks, and Hyphens........................................47
    Create Paragraphs..............................................................................47
    Group Paragraphs into Divisions.......................................................48
    Control Breaks...................................................................................48
🕲 Inserting Special Characters....................................................................49
    Keep Text Together with Nonbreaking Spaces....................................49
    Control Hyphenation with Optional Hyphens ...................................49
Create Headings, Lists, and Indents ...........................................................49
    Create Headings.................................................................................49
    Create Numbered, Bulleted, and Definition Lists..............................50
    Apply an Indent .................................................................................55
Align Elements...........................................................................................56
Use Preformatted Text................................................................................57
Apply Formatting Tags and Attributes ........................................................57
🖋 "Physical" and "Logical" Style Tags .......................................................58
    Apply Boldface...................................................................................58
    Apply Italics.......................................................................................58
    Apply Underline.................................................................................58
    Apply Strikethrough ..........................................................................59
    Apply Monospaced Font ....................................................................59
    Apply Subscript and Superscript .......................................................59
Control Font Formatting and Styles............................................................60
🖋 Understanding Other Formatting ...........................................................60
    Control Font Formatting....................................................................60
🖋 Working with Fonts ................................................................................62
    Change Style Using Inline Styles.......................................................62
🕲 Catch the Eye with Moving Text .............................................................65

**Chapter 4  Adding Graphics to Your Web Pages** .............. 67

   *Creating or Acquiring Graphics Files* ...........................................68
Add an Inline Graphic ..............................................................68
   Insert a Graphic............................................................68
   Use Suitable Alternative Text.....................................68
   Choose Where to Locate the Graphics File ................69
   Add a Long Description URL .......................................70
   Align a Graphic.............................................................70
   Change the Size of a Graphic ......................................70
   *Using Graphics to Control How Text Appears*............72
   Apply Borders to a Graphic ........................................72
   Add a Title to a Graphic..............................................72
   Position a Graphic with Spacers..................................73
   *Understanding GIF, JPEG, and PNG* ...........................74
Add a Background Graphic .......................................................74
Add a Horizontal Rule..............................................................75
Create an E-mail Signature Containing a Graphic ..................76
   *Laying Out Your Web Pages*........................................77
   Create an HTML Signature File ...................................77
   Use an HTML Signature File in Windows Mail ...........78
   *Keeping Down Graphic Size to Make Pages Load Faster* .......79

**Chapter 5  Adding Links** ....................................................... 81

Create Links...............................................................................81
   *Understanding Absolute and Relative Links* ..............82
   Link to Another Web Page...........................................82
   Link Within a Web Page...............................................84
   Link to a Particular Point on a Web Page...................85
   *Making Your Site Navigable* .......................................86
   Open a Link in a New Window ....................................86
   Create a Link to Download a File.................................86
   Display a ScreenTip for a Link ....................................87
   Create Links to Send E-mail ........................................88
   *Making Your Imagemaps Useful and Intelligible* ......91
   Create Two or More Links in a Graphic ......................91
Add Audio and Video to Your Web Pages ...............................93
   Understand Audio and Video Formats .......................94
   Understand Audio and Video Delivery Methods.......94
   Create a Link for Downloading an Audio or Video File ...........95
   Create a Link to Play an Audio or Video File .............95
   *Embedding a Video File in a Web Page*......................96

**Chapter 6  Creating Tables** ................................................. 97

Understand How Tables Work and When to Use Them...............97
   Plan a Table.................................................................98
   Create the Table's Structure......................................98
   Add Rows and Columns to a Table.............................103
   Add Table Borders ......................................................103
   Group Cells by Rows and Columns.............................105
   Set Table and Cell Width.............................................108

Setting Table and Cell Height .................................................................109
Add Padding and Spacing .......................................................................109
Align a Table, Row, or Cell ....................................................................110
Make a Cell Span Two Columns or Rows .............................................114
Apply a Background Color or Picture ...................................................115
Create a Nested Table..............................................................................115
Create a Vertical Line..............................................................................117

## Chapter 7   **Creating Frames** ............................................... 119

Understanding Frames and Their Alternatives.......................................120
Understand How Frames Work..................................................................120
Plan a Web Page That Uses Frames.........................................................121
Define Frame Height and Width .............................................................121
Create the Component Documents .........................................................123
Create the Frameset Document................................................................123
Lay Out the Frames .................................................................................124
Add the Component Documents to the Frameset .................................126
Adding Alternative Text to a Frame Page ..............................................127
Change a Frame's Borders and Margins .................................................127
Control Whether a Frame Scrolls............................................................129
Prevent Visitors from Resizing the Frame..............................................129
Nest One Frameset Inside Another.........................................................130
Create Inline Frames................................................................................130
Create a Link That Changes the Contents of a Frame ..........................133

## Chapter 8   **Applying Formatting Using Cascading Style Sheets** .................................. 135

Understand CSS Essentials........................................................................136
Understanding the Style Cascade ............................................................137
Create a Style Rule...................................................................................138
Understanding Other Ways of Creating Style Rules ..............................139
Create an Embedded Style Sheet.............................................................139
Understanding CSS Versions ...................................................................140
Create and Apply an External Style Sheet .............................................140
Use Special Selectors ...............................................................................142
Apply a Style to Part of an Element .......................................................145
Override Style Sheets ...............................................................................146
Control Font Formatting..........................................................................146
Set Alignment, Indents, Margins, and Line Height ...............................148
Prevent a Background Graphic from Being Tiled or Scrolling...............150
Create a Floating Layout with CSS .........................................................151
Creating a Three-Column Floating Layout.............................................154
Overriding Style Sheets in Your Browser................................................155

## Chapter 9   **Creating Web Pages Using the Microsoft Office Applications** ................. 159

Get Ready to Create Web Pages in the Office Applications .........................159
Configure Web Options in the Office Applications ...............................160
Understanding How the Office Applications Use HTML ......................161
Adding the New Web Page and Web Page Preview Commands
to the Office Applications ...................................................................166

Create Web Pages in Word ................................................................................166
  Start a New Web Page in Word ...............................................................166
  Create Hyperlinks....................................................................................168
  Check How a Page Will Look ..................................................................173
  Remove Sensitive Information from the Document .................................173
  Save Word Documents as Web Pages ......................................................175
  ✏ Choosing Suitable Web File Formats ....................................................176
  Remove Office-Specific Tags from a Word Document ...........................177
  ✆ Using Word to Create HTML Elements.................................................178
Create Web Pages from Excel and PowerPoint .................................................178
  Create Web Pages from Excel Workbooks...............................................178
  Create Web Pages from PowerPoint Presentations..................................181

## Chapter 10 **Using Forms and Scripts** ................................... 183

**10**

Create Forms ....................................................................................................183
  Understand the Basics of Forms ..............................................................184
  Define the Form Structure .......................................................................184
  ✏ Understanding the method Attribute....................................................186
  Add Fields to the Form ............................................................................186
  Complete a Form .....................................................................................192
  ✆ Letting Visitors Upload Files................................................................193
  Create a Form That E-mails Its Contents to You ....................................194
Use Scripts in Your Web Pages.........................................................................195
  Understand the Different Categories of User Events ...........................195
  ✏ Dealing with Script Threats.................................................................197
  Show When a Page Was Last Updated .....................................................197
  Redirect the Browser to Another Page.....................................................198
  Verify That a Form Is Filled In ................................................................198

Index ...............................................................................................201

# Acknowledgments

My thanks go to the following people, who put in a huge amount of work on this book:

**Marty Matthews**, series editor, developed, shaped, and improved the first edition of the book.

**Joya Anthony**, acquisitions coordinator, organized the acquisitions end of the project.

**Jenn Kettell**, technical editor, reviewed the book for technical accuracy and made many helpful suggestions.

**Lisa McCoy**, editor, edited the book skillfully and with good humor.

**Glyph International** laid out the book with great skill, turning the raw manuscript and graphics into a highly polished book.

**Carol Shields**, proofreader, caught widely varied inconsistencies throughout the text.

**Claire Splan**, indexer, created the index for the book with speed and precision.

**Roger Stewart**, editorial director and grand hierophant at McGraw-Hill, helped create the series and pulled strings in the background throughout the process.

# Introduction

*QuickSteps* books are recipe books for computer users. They answer the question "how do I..." by providing a quick set of steps to accomplish the most common tasks with a particular operating system or application.

The sets of steps are the central focus of the book. QuickSteps sidebars show how to quickly perform many small functions or tasks that support the primary functions. QuickFacts sidebars supply information that you need to know about a subject. Notes, Tips, and Cautions augment the steps, presented in a separate column so as to not interrupt the flow of the steps. The introductions are minimal rather than narrative, and numerous illustrations and figures, many with callouts, support the steps.

*QuickSteps* books are organized by function and the tasks needed to perform that function. Each function is a chapter. Each task, or "How To," contains the steps needed for accomplishing the function along with the relevant Notes, Tips, Cautions, and screenshots. You can easily find the tasks you need through:

- The Table of Contents, which lists the functional areas (chapters) and tasks in the order they are presented

- A How To list of tasks on the opening page of each chapter

- The index, which provides an alphabetical list of the terms that are used to describe the functions and tasks

- Color-coded tabs for each chapter or functional area with an index to the tabs in the Contents at a Glance (just before the Table of Contents)

# Conventions Used in this Book

*HTML, XHTML & CSS QuickSteps* uses several conventions designed to make the book easier for you to follow. Among these are:

- A ⊕ in the Table of Contents and in the How To list in each chapter references a QuickSteps sidebar in a chapter, and a ⬦ references a QuickFacts sidebar.

- **Bold type** is used for words or objects on the screen that you are to do something with—for example, "Click the **Start** menu, and then click **Computer**."

- *Italic type* is used for a word or phrase that is being defined or otherwise deserves special emphasis.

- Underlined type is used for text that you are to type from the keyboard.

- SMALL CAPITAL LETTERS are used for keys on the keyboard such as **ENTER** and **SHIFT**.

- When you are expected to enter a command, you are told to "press" the key(s). If you are to enter text or numbers, you are told to "type" them.

- Red font (for example, "the opening <title> tag") distinguishes HTML code terms that appear within body text.

- Code lines show examples of HTML code—for example:

```
<html>
<head>
    <title>Acme Virtual Industries: Solving Your Problems
in Moments
</head>
```

## How to...

- ⬪ *Understanding Tools for Creating HTML*
- • *Understand HTML, XML, XHTML, and HTML 5*
- ⬪ *Organizing Your Site*
- • *Create a Folder for Your Website*
- • *Open Notepad*
- ⬪ *Understanding the DOCTYPE Declaration*
- • *Create the Page's Structure*
- ⬪ *Understanding the Header and the Body*
- • *Add Content to the Page*
- • *Apply Formatting*
- • *Add a Picture*
- • *Add a Hyperlink*
- • *Create Linked Files*
- • *Describe Your Pages with Meta Tags*
- • *Reload a Page Automatically*
- ⬪ *Understanding How Search Engines Work*
- • *Redirect the Browser to Another Page*
- • *Validate Your HTML with the W3 Markup Validation Service*
- • *Check Your Pages with Other Browsers*

# Chapter 1

# Creating Your First Web Pages with HTML and XHTML

Hypertext Markup Language, or HTML, is the formatting language in which most web pages are built. It lets you specify the contents of a web page and control how it looks in a web browser. All modern computer operating systems have browsers, so pages created using HTML can be displayed on almost any computer.

An HTML file consists of plain text with *tags* (formatting codes), so you can create an HTML file quickly and easily using only a text editor and a browser. This chapter shows you how to start creating web pages using only the Notepad text editor and the Microsoft Internet Explorer browser, both of which are included with Microsoft Windows.

This book assumes that you are using Windows, because Windows has the bulk of the computer market. The examples use Windows Vista with Service Pack 1, the latest version of Windows at this writing. If you use a different operating system, such as Mac OS X or Linux, you will be able to follow along easily using similar tools on that operating system.

# Understand HTML, XML, XHTML, and HTML 5

Part of what makes creating web pages confusing is the number of technologies you can use. HTML is the general, overarching technology—but then there are XML, XHTML, and HTML 5.

Here are some key definitions to get things straight from the start.

## HTML

HTML (Hypertext Markup Language) is the formatting language in which web pages have been written from the start of the Web. HTML tags describe how a web page should look, but they don't describe what kind of contents it has. (More on this in a moment.)

HTML is flexible and "forgiving": Many web pages contain coding errors, and most browsers have been built to tolerate the errors and display a malformed web page as best they can rather than stopping with an error. Generally, it's better to see the web page, even if it doesn't appear exactly the way it's supposed to, than to quibble over technicalities such as a missing tag (or a missing character from a tag).

The definition of HTML is an ongoing process involving various standards. Most current HTML uses the HTML 4 standard, but is gradually moving ("transitioning") toward XHTML and the HTML 5 standard that is in development.

## XML

XML (Extensible Markup Language) is a language that lets you create structured data, data that describes its own content as well as how that content should appear.

For example, if you need to transfer details about different components of a car, you can create custom XML elements that describe the different components. For instance, you can create an element called "brakepad" that contains the information about a brake pad: its part number, the vehicles with which it's compatible, its dimensions, its cost, its documentation, and so on. A program can then read your XML document, recognize the information as describing a brake pad, and pull it into a database or manipulate it in another way.

## XHTML

XHTML (Extensible Hypertext Markup Language) is HTML that is written in XML syntax.

At this point, you may feel like holding your head in your hands or banging it against your desk. But the benefit of writing HTML in XML syntax is straightforward: XHTML lets you check quickly that a web page is correctly formed and doesn't contain any coding errors. This helps you to ensure that the web page will appear correctly in any browser that conforms to these standards.

## HTML 5

HTML 5, the fifth revision of HTML, is currently in draft form and is expected to remain so for several years while the final details are worked out. This means that there won't be a sudden move to HTML 5. Instead, what's likely to happen is that some browsers will implement some parts of the HTML 5 draft standard, and then others, leading gradually to a migration to the standard when it is finished.

HTML 5 has a "classic" variant called (confusingly) HTML 5 and an XHTML-based variant called XHTML 5.

## ORGANIZING YOUR SITE

Even the smallest site quickly grows far beyond the size and complexity originally intended—so even if you're planning a "small" site, organize it carefully. Careful organization is yet more important if you know from the outset that you'll be creating a larger site.

Use these three techniques to organize your site.

- **Separate content by folder**   Create a separate folder for each different type or category of content: graphics, different text topics, scripts, and so on. For example, for a family site, you might create folders such as html, pictures, music, and recipes. Keep the folder names short for ease of use. Create subfolders as necessary within the main folders.

- **Use naming conventions**   Develop naming conventions for the files that make up your site's content so that you can figure out easily what a file would be called and where to locate it if you've forgotten its name or location. Short, descriptive names using lowercase letters are usually best. When you need to use multiple words in a name, separate the words with underscores rather than with spaces. This is because Internet programs have to substitute codes for spaces, which makes for confusing-looking addresses.

- **Document your site**   Create a short document that explains how the site is structured, how files are named, and which content goes in which folder. You don't need to be excessively formal, but this document will help you and anyone else who assists you in creating and managing your site. Keep updating the document as you go along.

## Which Version of HTML Should You Use?

At this writing, the most sensible approach is to create your web pages using the "transitional" version of XHTML. This allows you some flexibility in creating your HTML code while keeping it more or less within a straitjacket of proper form that will let you move it easily to the HTML 5 standard when it is finally approved.

# Get Started with Your Website

To get started with your website, you'll need to create a folder to contain in, and then open Notepad or another text editor to create files.

## Create a Folder for Your Website

You will typically store your website on your local computer while you create it and then transfer it to a web server when it is ready for public consumption. Many HTML tools let you create and edit web pages directly on a web server, but creating the site locally has three advantages.

- You can create the site more quickly if it is stored locally. You can work on your site without an Internet connection if necessary.

- You can keep each page on your final website (on the Web) in a finished state rather than in an intermediate state. You can upload a new copy of any page as soon as you've updated it.

- Your local copy safeguards your site even if your Internet service provider (ISP) or web host has a server disaster; once the server is back up, you can simply upload your site again.

Start by creating a folder (if you do not already have one) on your computer for your website (if you do not already have one) and such subfolders within that folder as you need for the content. See the "Organizing Your Site" QuickFacts for suggestions on how to organize your website.

1. Click the **Start** button, and then click **Documents**. The My Documents window opens.

**2.** Click the **Organize** menu button, and then click **New Folder**. You can also right-click in the document area (the main part) of the Windows Explorer window and choose **New | Folder** from the shortcut menu. Windows creates a new folder with the default name "New Folder" and displays an edit box around the name so that you can change it.

**3.** Type the name for the folder (for example, Website), and press ENTER to apply the name.

**4.** Double-click the new folder to display its contents.

**5.** Repeat steps 2 and 3 to create as many new folders as needed within the main folder.

**6.** Click the **File** menu, and click **Close** to close the Windows Explorer window.

## Open Notepad

To open Notepad, click the **Start** button, click **All Programs**, click **Accessories**, and then click **Notepad**. A Notepad window opens, containing a new, blank text document.

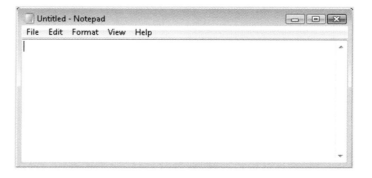

**QUICKFACTS**

## UNDERSTANDING THE DOCTYPE DECLARATION

Normally, each XHTML document begins with a Document Type Declaration, or DOCTYPE for short. The DOCTYPE tells the browser which Document Type Definition (DTD) the web page uses so the browser knows how to interpret the web page's tags.

To make your documents comply with HTML and XHTML standards, you'll normally want to add a DOCTYPE at the beginning. Table 1-1 explains the most widely used types of DOCTYPE as of this writing. Each DOCTYPE consists of two parts.

- **Public identifier** The *public identifier* is the text that appears in double quotation marks after the PUBLIC keyword—for example, PUBLIC "-//W3C//DTD XHTML 1.0 Transitional//EN" is the public identifier for the XHTML 1.0 Transitional DTD. This identifier gives the name of the public version of the DTD and always uses exactly the same text shown in the table.

- **System identifier** The *system identifier* is a Uniform Resource Locator (URL) that provides the location of the DTD. This can be either the reference DTD on the World Wide Web Consortium (W3C) website, as shown in the table, or a copy of the DTD on your own website.

# Create a Web Page and Adding Content to It

To create a web page, you first set up the HTML structure for the web page. You can then add content to the page and apply formatting to it.

## Create the Page's Structure

HTML is a set of tags that identify the elements of your web pages. A *tag* (or *markup tag*) is a name contained within angle brackets (<>) and usually comes in pairs (an opening and a closing tag). The tags may enclose a page element, such as text or a graphic, that you want to format. The closing tag has a slash preceding the tag name to identify it as the closing tag. Tags may also have *attributes* that further define the formatting or function of the tag.

The following sections show you how to create the structure of the web page.

### ADD THE DOCTYPE

To start your web page, insert the appropriate DOCTYPE definition from Table 1-1. This example uses the XHTML 1.0 Transitional DOCTYPE.

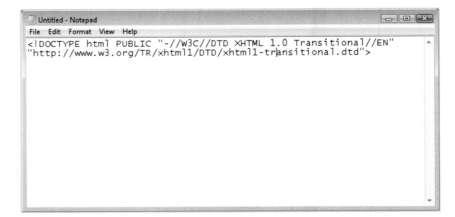

| DOCTYPE | DOCUMENT TYPE DECLARATION | COMMENTS |
| --- | --- | --- |
| XHTML 1.0 Transitional | `<!DOCTYPE html PUBLIC "-//W3C//DTD XHTML 1.0 Transitional//EN" "http://www.w3.org/TR/xhtml1/DTD/xhtml1-transitional.dtd">` | Widely used by web-authoring tools. Allows some flexibility in coding. |
| XHTML 1.0 Strict | `<!DOCTYPE html PUBLIC "-//W3C//DTD XHTML 1.0 Strict//EN" "http://www.w3.org/TR/xhtml1/DTD/xhtml1-strict.dtd">` | Ensures strict adherence to the XHTML 1.0 standard. |
| XHTML 1.1 | `<!DOCTYPE html PUBLIC "-//W3C//DTD XHTML 1.1//EN" "http://www.w3.org/TR/xhtml11/DTD/xhtml11.dtd">` | Ensures strict adherence to the XHTML 1.1 standard. |
| XHTML 1.0 Frameset | `<!DOCTYPE html PUBLIC "-//W3C//DTD XHTML 1.0 Frameset//EN" "http://www.w3.org/TR/xhtml1/DTD/xhtml1-frameset.dtd">` | Used for web pages laid out in different areas (frames) rather than a single area. |
| XHTML 2.0 | `<!DOCTYPE html PUBLIC "-//W3C//DTD XHTML 2.0//EN" "http://www.w3.org/MarkUp/DTD/xhtml2.dtd">` | This is a draft DOCTYPE and is best avoided as of this writing. |
| HTML 5 | `<!DOCTYPE html>` | Used for the HTML variant of the HTML 5 specification (still in draft as of this writing). |

*Table 1-1: **Document Type Declarations and When to Use Them***

**ADD THE <HTML> TAGS**

All web pages have a basic set of tags that identify the page as an HTML document, with all the major sections defined. These tags state the page is written in HTML so that the browser knows that it should use HTML rules for displaying the page. (Other markup languages have different rules from HTML.) The tags may also give the version of HTML used, the language (for example, "en" for English or "es" for Spanish), or other information.

1. In Notepad, on the next line of your text document after the end of the DOCTYPE statement, type the opening HTML tag. Because we're using the XHTML 1.0 Transitional DOCTYPE, we also need to include details of the XML *namespace*, the area of XML to which the tag applies. So type <u>&lt;html xmlns="http://www.w3.org/1999/xhtml"&gt;</u> and then press **ENTER**. This tag indicates the beginning of the HTML section of the document.

### UNDERSTANDING THE HEADER AND THE BODY

Each HTML web page consists of a header and a body.

- The *header* (also called the *document head*) typically contains the title for the web page and information about the document, including terms for search engines, information on links, and information about the style and scripts used.

- The *body* is the rest of the HTML web page. The body contains the text that appears when you display the web page as well as instructions for other objects (for example, pictures) to be included in the web page.

## NOTE

You use HTML to create the content and structure of a web page. For example, you can add headings, body paragraphs, and images to create a straightforward page. You can also apply formatting to the page, either by using HTML (which is the old way that's now looked down upon) or (better) by using Cascading Style Sheets (CSS). CSS formats your HTML content so that the web page looks the way you want.

2. On the next line, type the closing tag, <u></html></u>. This tag indicates the end of the HTML document. The remainder of the HTML document goes between the <html xmlns="http://www.w3.org/1999/xhtml"> tag and the </html> tag.

## Add Header and Body Tags

The header of an HTML web page starts with a <head> tag and ends with a </head> tag. Similarly, the body starts with a <body> tag and ends with a </body> tag. Type these into your web page between the existing <html> and </html> tags:

```
<head>
</head>
<body>
</body>
```

```
Untitled - Notepad
File  Edit  Format  View  Help
<!DOCTYPE html PUBLIC "-//W3C//DTD XHTML 1.0 Transitional//EN"
"http://www.w3.org/TR/xhtml1/DTD/xhtml1-transitional.dtd">
<html xmlns="http://www.w3.org/1999/xhtml">
<head>
</head>
<body>
</body>
</html>
```

The elements that make up the header go between the <head> and </head> tags, and the elements that make up the body go between the <body> and </body> tags.

*what info goes in the header?*

## TIP

Always give each web page a descriptive title so that anyone viewing it can grasp immediately which page it is. It's best to include the name of the site and a brief description of the contents of the page. Keep the description brief so that it fits in the title bar in a small window, on a tab in a tabbed browser window, or on the Favorites menu or a Bookmarks menu. If a web page doesn't contain a title, the browser displays the file name instead. Even if the file name is long and descriptive, it is unlikely to be as easy to grasp as a title.

## TIP

Instead of choosing All Files in the Save As Type drop-down list, you can put double quotation marks (" ") around the file name. This prevents Notepad from adding its default .txt file extension to the filename (which would give a name such as *index.html.txt*).

## CAUTION

If a directory doesn't include a default file (such as index. html or default.html, depending on the server technology), the server may display a page that contains a full list of the files in the directory. This is often a security risk, because it enables other people to view all the files in the directory rather than just the files that you want them to see. You should always include an index file in each directory to make sure that nobody can view the full list.

# Add Content to the Page

After creating the structure for the web page, add content to it, as described in this section.

### ADD THE TITLE FOR THE PAGE

Most web pages begin with a title—the text that appears in the browser's title bar when the web page is loaded, and that is used as the default text for a Favorite or bookmark created for the page. Create your title by placing an opening <title> tag, the title text, and the closing </title> tag between the <head> tag and the </head> tag, as shown:

*appears in Tab*

```
<head>
<title>Acme Virtual Industries - Home Page</title>
</head>
```

### SAVE THE PAGE

Save the page so that you can view it in your web browser.

1. Click the **File** menu, and then click **Save**. The Save As dialog box appears.

2. Navigate to the folder for your website. (Note which folder it is, because you'll need to access it again in a minute.)

3. Open the **Save As Type** drop-down list and choose **All Files** instead of Text Documents.

4. Select the contents of the File Name text box, and type index.html over the selection, replacing it.

5. Click **Save**.

### VIEW THE PAGE

Open the web page you're creating in Internet Explorer so that you can see the effects of the HTML tags you enter.

1. Click the **Start** button, and then click **Documents** (Windows Vista) or **My Documents** (Windows XP) to open your Documents or My Documents folder, respectively.

*How to include an index file?*

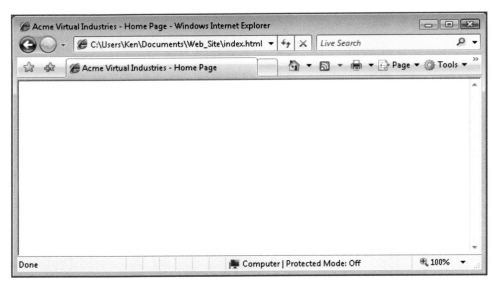

**Figure 1-1:** *Use your browser to see the progress in the page you create. At first, only the title is visible.*

2. Double-click the folder in which you stored your website.

3. Right-click the **index.html** file, click **Open With**, and then click **Internet Explorer**.

Figure 1-1 shows the page open in Internet Explorer. All you see is the title in the title bar because the body of the web page is blank.

### ADD A HEADING

Add a level-1 (top-level) heading to your web page by entering the heading text inside <h1> and </h1> tags within the body section (between the <body> and </body> tags). For example:

```
<body>
<h1>Welcome to Acme Virtual Industries!</h1>
</body>
```

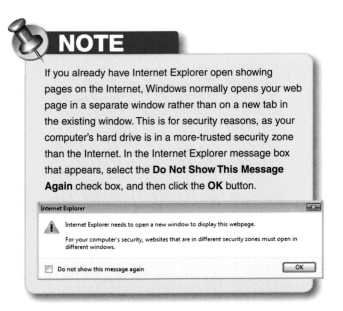

**NOTE**

If you already have Internet Explorer open showing pages on the Internet, Windows normally opens your web page in a separate window rather than on a new tab in the existing window. This is for security reasons, as your computer's hard drive is in a more-trusted security zone than the Internet. In the Internet Explorer message box that appears, select the **Do Not Show This Message Again** check box, and then click the **OK** button.

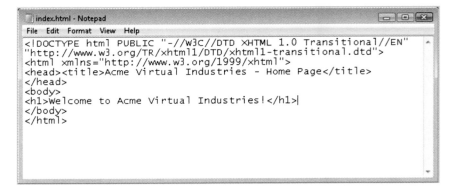

Save the web page (click the **File** menu and then click **Save**), then switch to Internet Explorer, and click the **Refresh** button to force Internet Explorer to read the web page again. Figure 1-2 shows the page.

*Refresh button*

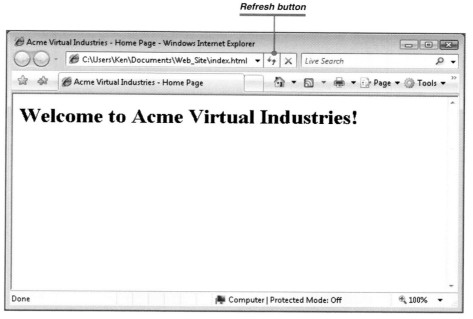

*Figure 1-2:* **To see the effect of the changes you make, click the Refresh button to update the display after each change you save to the page.**

### ADD TEXT PARAGRAPHS

To add a text paragraph to the body of the web page, enter the paragraph's text between an opening `<p>` tag and a closing `</p>` tag.

1. Immediately below the heading, add two or more text paragraphs to the page, putting each paragraph within `<p>` and `</p>` tags. For example:

```
<p>Acme Virtual Industries is the premier provider of
virtualized office space in the United States and Canada.</p>
<p>Contact us to learn how we can help you by providing virtual
staff and premises that allow your business to grow at the
touch of a button.</p>
```

2. Save the page, switch to your browser, and then refresh the display so that you can see the change. Figure 1-3 shows the example page with the text added.

**NOTE**

Browsers ignore line breaks and automatic text wrapping in HTML documents, so you must explicitly tag each paragraph mark that you want the browser to display in a page.

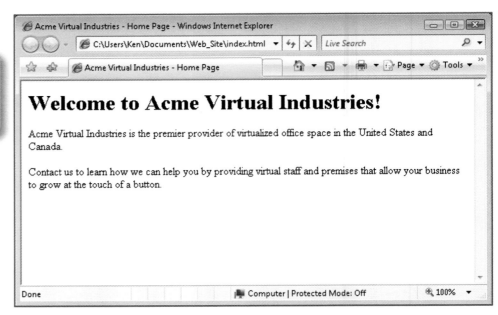

Figure 1-3: *Paragraphs without specific attributes appear in the browser's default font.*

**NOTE**

The <br/> tag is *self-closing*—it doesn't need a closing tag. The forward slash before the closing angle-bracket indicates that a tag is self-closing.

**ADD A LINE BREAK**

Most browsers accept only one paragraph tag at a time, figuring that multiple <p> tags in sequence are an error. To put space between paragraphs, use a line-break tag, <br />, instead of multiple <p> tags.

**1.** Add a <br /> tag before "virtualized" in the first paragraph:

```
<p>Acme Virtual Industries is the premier provider of <br />
virtualized office space in the United States and Canada.</p>
```

**2.** Add a <br /> tag between the two text paragraphs:

```
<br />
```

**3.** Save the page, switch to your browser, and then refresh the display so that you can see the change. Figure 1-4 shows the example page with the breaks added, making the words "virtualized office space" appear at the start of the second line of the first paragraph and adding extra space between the first and second paragraphs.

**Line break providing extra space between paragraphs**

**Line break breaking a text paragraph**

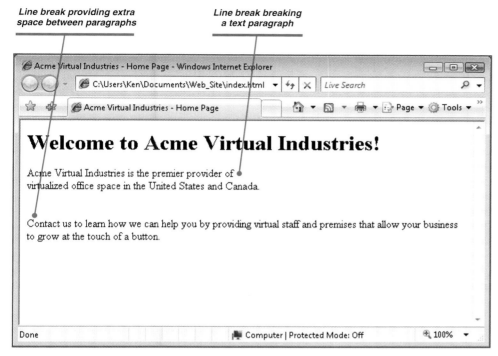

*Figure 1-4: Use a <br/> (line-break) tag to add extra space between paragraphs.*

Use the View Source command (or the equivalent in your browser) to examine any page that contains interesting effects that you want to understand.

## ADD A COMMENT

*Comments* are text that the browser is instructed not to display. You can add comments to a web page to note a change you need to make, explain an effect you're trying to achieve, or add other information for yourself or others helping you to create and manage your site.

To add a comment, use the <!-- --> tag, placing the comment between the two pairs of dashes. Put a space between each pair of dashes and the comment.

**1.** Add a comment to the line after the line break you just inserted, together with a new text paragraph below it:

```
<br />
<!-- Insert the picture here -->
<p>Virtualized office space is an
exciting and fast-moving market
sector.</p>
```

**2.** Save the page, switch to your browser, and then refresh the display so you can see that the comment is not displayed, while the new paragraph is displayed.

## VIEW THE SOURCE CODE

Although browsers don't display comments when they display the web page, anyone who can view your pages can view the comments by examining the source code for the pages. Most browsers include a View Source or View Source Code command (often on the View menu) for displaying the source code.

To view the source code for the page currently displayed in Internet Explorer:

**1.** Click the **Page** drop-down menu, and then click **View Source**. Windows opens the page in Notepad (or your default text editor).

**2.** When you've finished examining the source code, click the **Close** button (the X button) to close the Notepad window.

## Apply Formatting

HTML lets you apply formatting in several ways. The most basic way is by applying direct formatting to the text that needs it. This is an old-style formatting technique that is "deprecated" in both current HTML standards and the forthcoming HTML 5 standard. ("Deprecated" here means the standards-setting body wishes it would go away—but it won't.) But direct formatting still works, and you'll see it used widely, so it's a good idea to understand how it works even if you use CSS—the preferred formatting method—for your web pages.

**NOTE**

A better way to apply formatting consistently is by using Cascading Style Sheets, which are discussed in Chapter 8.

To apply direct formatting using HTML, you use tags. In this example, you'll quickly apply centering to a paragraph by adding the align attribute to the paragraph tags that contain it.

1. Click before the closing angle bracket of the `<p>` tag at the beginning of the paragraph you want to center. In the example, the paragraph is "Virtualized office space is an exciting and fast-moving market sector."

2. Press **SPACEBAR** and then type align="center" before the closing angle bracket, as in this example:

```
<p align="center"> Virtualized office space is
an exciting and fast-moving market sector.</p>
```

3. Save the page, switch to your browser, and then refresh the display so that you can see the change.

## Add a Picture

Add a picture to the page by using an `<img>` tag. The `<img>` tag uses an src attribute that specifies the source file used for the image and an alt attribute that specifies alternative text to display if it is missing.

1. Choose the picture you want to display.

2. Copy it to your site's folder.

3. Type the tag on the line below the line break (<br/>) tag, substituting your picture's name for "open_plan_office.jpg" and a description for the alt text.

```
<img src="open_plan_office.jpg" width="500" alt="Open-plan
office" />
```

4. Save the page, switch to your browser, and then refresh the display so that you can see the change. Figure 1-5 shows an example of a page with an image added.

5. If the picture appears at an unsuitable size for the page, adjust the width value to make it wider or narrower, save the file, and then reload the page in your browser.

*Figure 1-5: **Adding a picture is a quick way to give impact and life to a web page.***

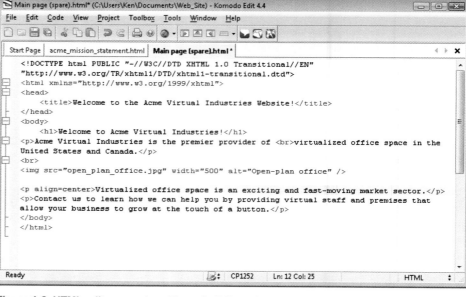

Figure 1-6: *HTML editors, such as Komodo Edit, make the process of inserting and checking codes easier. Some include an integrated browser for viewing pages as you work.*

**NOTE**

You have two options for making a picture appear at the right size. If the picture is about the right size, you can simply set the picture's display width (as you did here) and height to the dimensions you need. But if the picture is far bigger than it needs to be, you'll do better to create a smaller version of it in a graphics editor and then use that version. This helps keep your web page from becoming bloated and taking ages to download.

# Add Hyperlinks and Tags, and Reloading Pages

With your page's content in place, you can add hyperlinks to other web pages and web sites, and add tags to describe the page's contents to search engines. You may also want to reload a web page automatically to keep it fresh, or redirect the browser to another web page.

## Add a Hyperlink

A *hyperlink* is a link in a web page that leads to another page or to another point on the same page. You click the hyperlink to switch the browser to the hyperlink's target or destination. Hyperlinks are usually implemented as text or graphics.

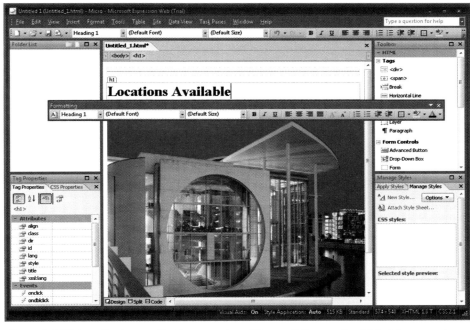

Figure 1-7: *Web-authoring applications, such as Microsoft Expression Web, let you apply formatting graphically rather than by entering the HTML codes manually.*

**TIP**

If you want to have two or more files open in Notepad at the same time, you need to run an instance of Notepad for each file. To launch a new instance of Notepad, use the Start menu as usual (for example, choose Start I All Programs I Accessories I Notepad or click the **Notepad** icon you've pinned to the Start menu).

Add hyperlinks from this page to another page by using a pair of anchor tags, <a> and </a>, with the href (hypertext reference) attribute and the path and name of the linked file.

1. Position the insertion point where you want the hyperlink—for example after the last </p> tag in the file—and press **ENTER** to create a new line.

2. Create any heading or other text that you want to immediately precede the hyperlink. For example, type a new level-2 heading using <h2> and </h2> tags, as shown:

   ```
   <h2>Acme Virtual Industries Locations</h2>
   ```

3. Type the actual hyperlink. This example creates a link to a page named west_coast. html that uses the words *West Coast* as the object the user clicks to use the hyperlink:

   ```
   <a href="west_coast.html">West Coast</a>
   ```

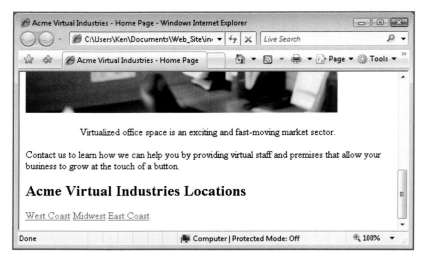

*Figure 1-8:* **Text hyperlinks provide an easy way of letting visitors access other pages on your website.**

**4.** Type additional hyperlinks as needed—for example:

```
<a href="midwest.html">Midwest</a>
<a href="east_coast.html">East Coast</a>
```

**5.** Save the page, switch to your browser, and then refresh the display so that you can see the change. Don't click any of the links, however, because there are no linked files yet.

Figure 1-8 shows the bottom of the page with the hyperlinks added. Notice that even though the hyperlinks appear on separate lines in the text editor, they appear on one line in the browser because there are no paragraph tags or line-break tags between them. If you want the hyperlinks to appear one above the other, put paragraph tags around each like this:

```
<p><a href="west_coast.html">West Coast</a></p>
<p><a href="midwest.html">Midwest</a></p>
<p><a href="east_coast.html">East Coast</a></p>
```

# Create Linked Files

Create the files that are referred to by the hyperlinks you just created.

**1.** Create a new text file by clicking the **File** menu and then clicking **New**. Notepad automatically closes the index.html file because it can work with only one file at a time.

**2.** Type the structure of the new file and any contents that can be common to each of the hyperlinked pages, such as a hyperlink back to the index.html page. For example:

```
<!DOCTYPE html PUBLIC "-//W3C//DTD XHTML 1.0 Transitional//EN"
"http://www.w3.org/TR/xhtml1/DTD/xhtml1-transitional.dtd">
<html xmlns="http://www.w3.org/1999/xhtml">
<head>
<title></title>
</head>
<body>
<h1></h1>
<a href="index.html">Back to Acme Virtual Industries home
page</a>
</body>
</html>
```

**3.** Click the **Edit** menu, and then click **Select All** to select all the contents of the file.

**4.** Click the **Edit** menu, and then click **Copy** to copy the structure of the file to the Clipboard.

**5.** Enter the unique contents of the page using the techniques discussed earlier in this chapter to add a title, a heading, some text, and perhaps a picture. This example shows the HTML for a short page (shown in Figure 1-9) that contains those items:

```
<!DOCTYPE html PUBLIC "-//W3C//DTD XHTML 1.0 Transitional//EN"
"http://www.w3.org/TR/xhtml1/DTD/xhtml1-transitional.dtd">
<html xmlns="http://www.w3.org/1999/xhtml">
<head>
<title>Acme Virtual Industries - West Coast Locations</title>
</head>
<body>
<h1>West Coast Locations</h1>
<p>Please click your nearest city:</p>
<p><a href="redding.html">Redding</a></p>
<p><a href="berkeley.html">Berkeley</a></p>
<p><a href="los_angeles.html">Los Angeles</a></p>
<p><a href="san_diego.html">San Diego</a></p>
<br />
<p><a href="index.html">Back to Acme Virtual Industries Home
Page</a></p>
</body>
</html>
```

**NOTE**

HTML files use the file extensions .htm and .html more or less interchangeably. When you're browsing the Web, you'll often enter an address that ends with one or another of these extensions, but you'll often use other extensions as well, such as .php, .asp, and .mspx. These file extensions indicate technologies used by the servers to provide dynamic web pages (web pages that change as the user interacts with them).

Figure 1-9: *Use the techniques discussed earlier in this chapter to create a short page that includes a hyperlink back to the index.html page.*

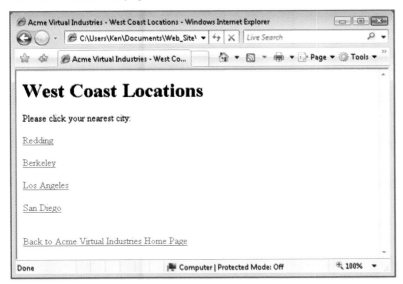

**6.** Save the file under the filename you assigned to the first hyperlink you created in your site's folder. Remember to use double quotation marks to force Notepad to use the .html extension rather than the .txt extension.

**7.** Switch to your browser and then click the first link at the bottom of the page. Your browser displays the page you just created. Click the link on the page to return to the home page.

**8.** If you have additional hyperlinks, create a new text document for each, paste in the document structure and common elements that you copied, and then add the unique elements desired. Save each file under the name used for the hyperlink, and test the links from the index.html page to each file and back to the index.html page.

## Describe Your Pages with Meta Tags

To enable search engines to determine the contents of your web pages and catalog them correctly, you can use meta tags with the appropriate information. You place these tags inside the head of a web page, where they're read by search engines, but not displayed in the browser.

The main attributes for the meta tag are the name attribute and the content attribute.

- name specifies the name of the meta tag you want to create. HTML supports a wide variety of names for recording details such as the author, editor, purpose and rating of the page, and more. When describing your pages, you'll typically want to use the description name and the keywords name because search engines typically concentrate on these tags.
- content specifies the content of the meta tag.

To add meta tags to a page:

1. Position the insertion point within the header of the web page you want to affect.
2. Type the first meta tag, making it a description tag and assigning it a brief description of the page—for example:

   `<meta name="description" content="virtualized office space"/>`
3. Type the next meta tag, making it a keywords tag and assigning it the keywords you want to use for the page, separated by commas—for example:

   `<meta name="keywords" content="virtual, office, services"/>`
4. Type further meta tags as required—for example:

   `<meta name="author" content="Acme Virtual Industries"/>`
5. Save the page.

Unlike most of the tags discussed in this chapter, meta tags don't have a closing tag.

## Reload a Page Automatically

Sometimes you may need to create a web page that automatically reloads itself without the user's intervention so that it can display the latest information

**NOTE**

You can place the meta tags anywhere in the header, but you'll probably find it best to choose a standard location for all your pages. For example, you might decide always to put the meta tags after the page's title.

**TIP**

Often, you may want to use meta tags to describe your site (or an area of your site) rather than simply the content of the page to which you're adding the tag. This will help increase your site's presence in search engines, but you will need to ensure that users can easily navigate to the other areas of your site to find the contents that have drawn them to it.

**TIP**

There's a special meta tag called robots that you can use to request search engines *not* to scan a page or follow links on it. You might do this if you want to avoid having a page appear in search engines—for example, if it's private or if you're still testing your site. It's not 100 percent effective, as search engines can disregard it, but it's still worth doing. Add this tag to the header area:
`<meta name="robots" content="noindex,nofollow"/>`.

available. For example, you might need to update a page of sports events with the latest statistics.

To update a page automatically, use a meta tag with the http-equiv attribute set to refresh.

1. Position the insertion point within the header of the web page you want to affect.

2. Type the meta tag in the following format, assigning to content the number of seconds after which you want the page to be refreshed:

```
<meta http-equiv="refresh" content="60"/>
```

3. Save the page, switch to your browser, and refresh the display.

4. Wait the specified number of seconds, and the page will automatically reload itself.

## Redirect the Browser to Another Page

If you've used the Web much, you'll be familiar with being redirected from one page to another. You'll often need to use redirection in your pages as well. For example, you might need to redirect browsers from your old website to your new one or from an alternate domain (such as .org or .net) to your main domain.

To redirect the browser, use an http-equiv meta tag with the url attribute set to the destination URL.

1. Position the insertion point within the header of the web page you want to affect.

2. Type the <meta> tag and specify the http-equiv attribute with the refresh value:

```
<meta http-equiv="refresh"
```

3. Add the content attribute with the number of seconds to wait, followed by a semicolon (;), and then the URL that you want to use—for example:

```
content="2;URL=http://www.acmevirtualindustries.com"/>
```

The entire tag should look like this:

```
<meta http-equiv="refresh" content="2;url=http://www
.acmevirtualindustries.com"/>
```

Save the page, reload it in Internet Explorer, and you will be whisked to the specified site after the delay you set.

**NOTE**

You can also redirect the browser to another web page using JavaScript. Chapter 10 shows you how to do this.

**NOTE**

If your redirect sends Internet Explorer from a web page on your computer to a web page on the Internet, Internet Explorer opens the redirected page in a new browser window rather than in the same browser window. This is because the pages are in different security zones. But if you redirect from one website to another, as you will normally do, Internet Explorer uses the same window. The same is true if you redirect from one page on your computer to another page on it.

**NOTE**

The Markup Validation Service lets you validate a document online by providing its Internet address, by uploading a file, or by "direct input"—simply typing or pasting code into a box in a web page. We'll use the direct-input method here.

# Validate Your HTML and Checking Your Pages

Before you put a page on the Web, you should validate it to make sure the HTML code is correct. You should also view the page in various browsers to make sure it looks as you intend.

## Validate Your HTML with the W3C Markup Validation Service

You've now written a couple of web pages in HTML, and they work okay in Internet Explorer. But are they technically valid so that they will display properly in all browsers? The easiest way to check is to use the Markup Validation Service at the World Wide Web Consortium (W3C) website.

1. Open your index.html page in Notepad.

2. Select all the code and copy it to the Clipboard. The easiest way is to press **CTRL+A** and then **CTRL+C**. Alternatively, right-click in the code and choose **Select All**, then right-click again and choose **Copy**.

3. Open Internet Explorer and go to http://validator.w3.org. You may want to bookmark this site so that you can access it quickly in the future.

4. Click the **Validate By Direct Input** tab to display its contents.

5. Right-click in the **Enter The Markup To Validate box**, and choose **Paste** from the shortcut menu to paste in your code (see Figure 1-10).

6. Click the **Check** button. The Markup Validation Service chews through your code and lets you know how it tasted. Figure 1-11 shows the result of a successful check.

If you get a red "Errors found while checking this document" message, scroll down the page and read the details. You can then fix the errors one by one and click the **Revalidate** button to try your code again.

Don't worry if the Markup Validation Service shows a huge number of errors: It may mean only that you're missing a couple of codes that, in turn, trigger other errors. For example, if you've typed a <head> tag instead of a closing </head> tag, you'll get nine or so errors—but inserting the missing slash will fix them all.

*Figure 1-10:* **The W3C Markup Validation Service lets you quickly check that your code is correct.**

## Check Your Pages with Other Browsers

As of this writing (June 2009), Internet Explorer still has the lion's share of the browser market, with an estimated 60–70 percent share, depending on which market-research organization you believe. After Internet Explorer come Firefox (www.mozilla.com), with market share in the 20–25 percent range, and Safari (www.apple.com/safari), in the 7–10 percent range.

Figure 1-11: *A green bar indicates that the code checked out successfully. A red bar indicates there are errors; you'll find the details further down the page.*

| BROWSER | OPERATING SYSTEMS | SOURCE |
| --- | --- | --- |
| Internet Explorer | Windows | Included with Windows |
| Safari | Mac OS X, Windows | Included with Mac OS X; www.apple.com/safari |
| Opera | Windows, Mac OS X, Linux | www.opera.com |
| Mozilla Firefox | Windows, Mac OS X, Linux | www.mozilla.com |
| Camino | Mac OS X | www.caminobrowser.org |
| Konqueror | Linux | www.konqueror.org |
| Google Chrome | Windows, Mac OS X, Linux | www.google.com/chrome |

Table 1-2: *Web Browsers, Their Operating Systems, and Where to Get Them*

**TIP**

If you already have both a PC and a Mac, you'll be in a good position to check how your web pages look on both platforms. If you have just a Mac, consider either running Windows under Boot Camp or getting a PC-emulation program so that you can run Windows (and perhaps other PC-based operating systems, such as Linux) within Mac OS X on your Mac and check how your pages look. The main PC-emulation programs for the Mac are VMWare Fusion (www.vmware.com/products/fusion), Parallels Desktop (www.parallels.com), and VirtualBox (www.sun.com/software/products/virtualbox). You can get a 30-day evaluation version of VMWare Fusion or Parallels Desktop; VirtualBox is free. There are currently no PC-based emulators for Mac OS X, so if you use a PC and want to check how your pages look on Mac OS X, you'll need to use an actual Mac.

After these come other browsers with 1 percent of the market or less. Table 1-2 summarizes current Web browsers, the operating systems they run on, and where to get them. All these Web browsers are free.

This means it's vital to use Internet Explorer as your primary browser for testing your web pages, because you want the majority of visitors to see the site exactly as you intend it to look. It's also a good idea to check your web pages with Firefox and Safari, because most of the visitors who aren't using Internet Explorer will be using one or other of these browsers.

Beyond this, you may want to check your web pages with other browsers for the sake of completeness. But unless you know that a significant part of your website's audience uses a particular browser other than Internet Explorer, Firefox, or Safari, it is not normally worth checking your pages with every browser just in case minor discrepancies occur.

Figure 1-12 shows Mozilla Firefox, the second most widely used Web browser as of this writing.

When you've installed a browser, you can run it from the Start menu in Windows or from the Applications folder in Mac OS X. If you need to use this browser often, pin it to the Start menu or add it to the Quick Launch toolbar in

**Welcome to Acme Virtual Industries!**

Acme Virtual Industries is the premier provider of virtualized office space in the United States and Canada.

Virtualized office space is an exciting and fast-moving market sector.

Contact us to learn how we can help you by providing virtual staff and premises that allow your business to grow at the touch of a button.

**Acme Virtual Industries Locations**

West Coast Midwest East Coast

*Figure 1-12: **Most browsers, such as Mozilla Firefox, have similar interfaces and controls.***

Windows; in Mac OS X, launch it, **CTRL**+click or right-click the **Dock** icon, and then choose **Keep In Dock**.

You're almost certainly familiar with the basic way of accessing a web page.

1. Start the browser, if it's not already running. For example, click the **Start** button, click **All Programs**, and then click the browser's entry on the Start menu.

2. Select the address in the browser's address bar by dragging across it or by pressing a keyboard shortcut. For example, press **ALT+D** for Internet Explorer or Firefox on Windows, or press **COMMAND+L** for Safari, Firefox, or Camino on Mac OS X.

3. Type the URL of a web page on the Internet or the path and filename of the web page on a local drive, and then press **ENTER**.

## How to...

- 🪐 *Understanding IPv4 and IPv6*
- *Understand Web Clients and Servers*
- *Access a Web Page*
- 🪐 *Understanding URLs*
- *Assess Your Requirements*
- 🪐 *Understanding Intranets and Extranets*
- *Choose an ISP or Web Hosting Service*
- *Decide on Web Hosting Features*
- 🪐 *Running Your Own Web Server*
- 🪐 *Understanding Domains*
- *Evaluate an ISP*
- *Evaluate a Web Hosting Service*
- *Register a Domain Name*
- *Plan Your Site's Contents*
- *Make Your Site Effective*
- *Keep Your Web Pages Small Enough to Download Quickly*
- *Check Your Website*
- *Update and Maintain Your Website*
- *Get the Information Required for FTP*
- *Transfer a Site Using an FTP Client*

# Chapter 2

# Choosing a Web Host and Getting Your Own Website

To make the web pages you create available to your potential audience, you put them in a folder on a web server; the web pages make up the website. This chapter discusses how to assess what type of website you need, how to choose a web host, how to design and create a site, and how to transfer your website from your local computer to the web server.

## Understand Web Basics

The *Internet* is the umbrella term for the worldwide network of computers that are connected together and use the Transmission Control Protocol/Internet Protocol (TCP/IP) protocol suite of controlling standards. The Internet uses several different forms of communication, including e-mail, file transfer, and the Hypertext Transfer Protocol, or HTTP. The World Wide Web (hereafter, simply *the Web*) is that part of the Internet that uses HTTP to transfer information.

## UNDERSTANDING IPV4 AND IPV6

There are two main versions of the Internet Protocol: Version 4 (usually called IPv4) and version 6 (usually called IPv6).

### IPV4

IPv4 is the older version of the Internet Protocol. IPv4 uses a 32-bit address space, which gives around four billion possible addresses. This seemed plenty of addresses when the standard was approved in 1980, but now, IPv4 is rapidly running out of different addresses for computers.

IPv4 is still used most widely in much of the world, so this book uses IPv4 for most of its examples that show IP addresses.

An IPv4 address consists of four groups, called *octets,* written in "dot-decimal notation"—for example, 192.168.1.212 or 216.54.31.255.

### IPV6

IPv6 is the newer version of the Internet Protocol. IPv6 uses a 128-bit address space, which gives around $3.4 \times 10^{38}$ addresses—340 undecillion, if you like to brandish the terms for absurdly large numbers. This seemed like plenty of addresses when the standard was approved in 1998, and it still does today.

IPv6 is increasingly used in China and other rapidly developing economies, and will eventually take over from IPv4. Apart from the extra addresses, IPv6 provides other improvements over IPv4, but few businesses and even fewer customers are yet prepared to move from IPv4 to IPv6 unless forced to do so. This is because moving to IPv6 involves both expense and technical upheaval.

*Continued . . .*

# Understand Web Clients and Servers

If you have an Internet connection, you're probably already familiar with the Web from the consumer's end—using a web browser, such as Microsoft's Internet Explorer, to view the contents of a website and navigating from one web page to another by following hypertext links. The mesh of links among pages gives the Web its name. (Another name considered for the Web was "the Mesh.")

Websites (a *site* is a collection of linked web pages) are stored on *servers,* computers that provide data to other computers (*clients*) on request. Web servers can run almost any TCP/IP-capable operating system, such as UNIX, Linux, Solaris, Windows, or Mac OS X. Likewise, Web clients can run almost any operating system, although most run client operating systems rather than server operating systems.

Figure 2-1 shows a web client requesting a web page from a web server across the Internet.

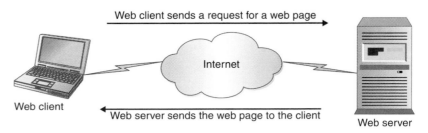

Web client sends a request for a web page

Internet

Web client

Web server sends the web page to the client

Web server

*Figure 2-1:* **A web client (using a browser) typically connects to a web server across the Internet. You can also use a browser to open an HTML document on your local hard drive or network.**

## Access a Web Page

Every computer directly connected to the Internet has a unique address called its *Internet Protocol address,* or *IP address,* that enables the computer to be identified. If you enter that address in a browser, you will access the public web page on that computer (provided that it has one).

Since an IPv4 address is a complex series of up to 12 digits, most web servers have a domain name associated with that address that is simpler to remember and use. For example, the IP address 198.45.22.173 is registered to the computer associated with the domain host name "mhprofessional.com," home of McGraw-Hill Professional, publishers of this book. To access their website, you can also enter their domain name using their URL, or Uniform Resource Locator, http://www.mhprofessional.com, in your browser (see Figure 2-2). Your browser consults a Domain Name Service (DNS) server (usually at your ISP) to resolve the URL to the appropriate IP address. See the QuickSteps "Understanding URLs," in this chapter.

Long URLs tend to be hard to remember, so most companies try to keep them as short as possible. For example, on the back of this book, you'll see the URL www.mhprofessional.com for the McGraw-Hill Professional website. To access the McGraw-Hill website:

1. Click the **Start** button, and then click **Internet**.

2. Type www.mhprofessional.com into the address bar of your browser, and then press **ENTER**.

*Figure 2-2: **When you enter a host name, your browser resolves the IP address and displays the appropriate website.***

## UNDERSTANDING URLS

A typical full URL looks like this: http://www .acmevirtualindustries.com/services/phones.html.

The first part of a URL, http://, tells the client and the server that the site uses HTTP as opposed to another protocol. If the URL begins with https://, it uses encryption to secure the data transmitted between the client and the server. For example, if you connect to your bank via the Web, the connection will almost certainly use HTTPS rather than unsecured HTTP so that your sensitive data is secured in transit.

The next part of the URL, www, indicates that the server being contacted is a web server. This part appears in most URLs, but is not always required. For example, URLs such as http://store.apple.com do not use www.

The next part of the URL identifies the domain name or IP address of the server to which to connect. Typically, the URL uses the domain name—in the format acmevirtualindustries.com—because domain names are easier for people to remember and to type. Sometimes, the URL uses the server's IP address instead of the domain name—for example, http://216.239.37.99.

The last part of the URL is the address of the file that's being opened—for example, /services/phones.html. The address consists of the filename (phones.html) preceded by the folder path (/services/). The folders are divided using forward slashes (/) rather than backward slashes (\) because much of the Internet is based on UNIX (which uses forward slashes to denote directory divisions).

When you enter a URL like this, your browser automatically adds *http://* to the beginning of the address, because most websites use HTTP rather than another protocol. The request doesn't include a filename, so the web server supplies the default file for the website. The default file is usually named index.html, but may also be named index.htm (without an L) or default.html, depending on the server technology used. You may or may not see this filename after the URL in the browser's address box when you access the website.

# Choose a Web Host

Before you can put up a website, you'll probably need to choose a web host or ISP. This section discusses how to assess your requirements, decide whether to run your own web server, establish which features your need, and choose a web host.

## Assess Your Requirements

First, assess your requirements for an ISP or web host and a website.

- If you're planning to build your own website, you'll need to find an Internet location to host your site, unless you have a location already. Follow the instructions in this chapter to choose an ISP or a web hosting service and create your own website.

- If you're creating pages for your school, organization, or company, however, that body will probably have set up a hosting arrangement for the site, so you'll put the pages either on an existing website or on an intranet site (an *intranet* is a web network similar to the Internet but contained within and limited to a single organization; see the "Understanding Intranets and Extranets" QuickFacts later in this chapter). In this case, you can skip most of this chapter, provided that you learn the details of the server that will contain your web site.

- If you're creating HTML content for pages on a special site (for example, eBay or Blogger.com), you won't need to get a website, but the site may have specific constraints on the tags you can use and where you can place them.

## Choose an ISP or Web Hosting Service

If you're looking for web space, your main choices are your ISP or a web hosting service. You can research your options on the Web by visiting ISPs' websites, web hosts' sites, and host-finding sites, such as TopHosts.com (www .tophosts.com) and HostSearch (www.hostsearch.com), but you should also ask your friends and coworkers. In particular, if you're part of a company or a school, ask its system administrator or webmaster for suggestions, because they should be able to steer you toward suitable ISPs or hosts.

## Decide on Web Hosting Features

When choosing an ISP or web host for your site, decide which features you will need.

### AMOUNT OF SPACE

The web host rents you a certain amount of space on its web servers for your site. One hundred megabytes (MB) is enough for a small site; as soon as you add more than a handful of pages with graphics or post one or more of your musical compositions (even in a compressed format, such as MP3), you'll need to get more space. To start with, look for 1 gigabyte (GB) or more; even if you don't use anything like that amount of space, it's good to have room to expand as needed.

### AMOUNT OF TRAFFIC

The web host allows you a certain amount of *traffic,* or data transferred, usually measured in gigabytes per month. (Avoid any web host that offers less than a gigabyte.) If your site exceeds your allowance, the web host charges you extra for each gigabyte.

How much traffic you need depends on how many people visit your site and what they do when they're there—for example, viewing pages consisting of compact files generates far less traffic than downloading your audio or video files. Even if your site fits comfortably within, say, 100MB, you may need many

### UNDERSTANDING INTRANETS AND EXTRANETS (Continued)

Having a valid tracking number establishes you as a bona fide customer; without the tracking number, you can't (for example) learn the delivery information about hundreds of packages on the off-chance of finding one that interests you. At other extranet sites, users must log in using a password.

From the customer's point of view, an extranet works in the same way as a website except that it provides more useful information and may require logging in. The difference lies in how the extranet provides information to the customer from inside the firewall instead of simply providing the set of information available on the web server.

In addition to being used to make information available to customers on the Web, as in the examples given here, extranets can be used to provide information securely to the employees of another company without the information being available to users of the Web as a whole. This type of extranet is sometimes called a *business-to-business (B2B) extranet*.

## TIP

The easiest way to get a domain registered and hosted is to have the web host or ISP handle the registration for you. If this is what you need, check whether your intended host or ISP offers this service.

---

gigabytes of traffic if your site is busy. To start with, look for around 25–50GB per month; more is better, providing it doesn't cost too much.

Some hosts have creative accounting policies for traffic, such as excluding the heaviest-traffic day of the month from the total calculation, which allows your site to ride out brief surges of visitor interest without incurring extra cost. Other hosts are less generous and deduct all data transfer from your allowance.

### NUMBER OF E-MAIL ACCOUNTS

Most web hosts include some e-mail accounts with the web space. Make sure that your host offers enough e-mail accounts and that you can add accounts at reasonable rates should you need them.

If you don't already have an e-mail account, you'll want one for yourself, of course—and one for each family member who will use the Internet. But it's sensible to split your e-mail among a main account that you protect vigorously against spam and other accounts that you use for more public purposes. This means it's good to have extra accounts that you can set up as needed and dispose of if they become polluted. (You can also use web-based e-mail, such as Microsoft's Windows Live Hotmail or Google's Gmail, for this purpose.)

You may also want to have a separate e-mail account for administering your website, allowing visitors to write to the webmaster without exposing your main e-mail address.

### YOUR OWN DOMAIN NAME

For impact and ease of access, you'll probably want your website to have its own domain name (for example, www.acmevirtualindustries.com) rather than a name that includes your ISP's name or web host's name (for example, www .earthlink.net/~acmevirtual). All web hosts support domain names, but some ISPs do not.

### INTERNET CONNECTION SPEED AND UPTIME

Check that the web host has a fast connection to the Internet's *backbone*, the main lines of connection of the Internet, so that would-be visitors will be able

## RUNNING YOUR OWN WEB SERVER

Instead of renting space from an ISP or from a web hosting service, you may be tempted to run your own web server, especially if you have both the main items needed.

The first thing you need is web server software, which you may already have as part of your computer's operating system.

- Windows Vista Business Edition and Windows Vista Ultimate Edition include a stripped-down version of the Internet Information Services (IIS) web server that permits up to 10 connections at a time. (The Home versions of Windows Vista don't include IIS.)
- Mac OS X includes Apache, a full-bore web server.
- Most Linux distributions also include Apache.

The second thing you need is a reliable broadband connection to the Internet.

If you've got both these things, you could run your own web server. But in most cases, running your own web server makes sense only for a medium- to large-size company, because you must keep your web server running all the time so that the site is always accessible and provide enough bandwidth for however many users choose to visit the site. Even minor outages, such as those caused by having to restart your computer after installing software, can cost you part of your audience.

Worse, most residential broadband Internet connections are *asymmetrical*, delivering fast download speeds but slower upload speeds, so your site will not respond speedily to multiple visitors. In addition, many ISPs specifically exclude running a server from residential and small office/home office (SOHO) service agreements and will notice—and object—if you try to run a popular website on such a connection.

---

to access your website quickly. Most serious web hosts will have multiple Gigabyte Ethernet (GigE) connections to the backbone, usually through separate carriers, such as AT&T, Sprint, and Verizon.

A good web host will publish statistics for its *uptime*—the percentage of time that its servers and network are typically available. Look for an uptime above 99.9 percent.

### SUPPORT FOR ANY WEB TOOLS

Some ISPs and web hosting services limit you to using their custom tools for building and maintaining your website. Some of these custom tools consist of online templates and wizards that walk you through the process of creating a site; others are executable programs that you download and install on your computer.

Many of these custom tools enable you to put together a good-looking website with minimal time and effort, but they do not provide the flexibility that you will need to create a full-featured website that meets your needs. Make sure that you can use your preferred tools as well as any tools that the host provides.

### AUDIO AND VIDEO STREAMING

If you plan to place audio or video files on your website for streaming rather than for download, make sure your host offers streaming. *Streaming* is a way of splitting up an audio or video file so that it can be played as it is being transferred. Streamed files are usually not permanently saved on the computer that plays them. By contrast, downloaded files are permanently saved, unless the user chooses to delete them.

Audio and video streaming involve transferring a lot of data. This is why even apparently generous bandwidth allowances can vanish overnight.

### SHOPPING CARTS AND SECURE SERVERS

If you plan to sell items from your website, look for a web host that offers shopping carts and secure servers. A *secure server* is one to which the user connects using encryption to make sure that nobody can snoop the data exchanged by the browser and the server.

## QUICKFACTS

### UNDERSTANDING DOMAINS

The *Domain Naming System* or *Domain Name Service* (abbreviated to DNS in either case) is a system (or service) that maps domain names to IP addresses. A domain name is essentially a human-friendly shortcut to a particular IP address. For example, as of this writing, the domain name yahoo.com maps to the IP address 206.190.60.37.

Domains are divided into different organizational types and geographical areas. The key organizational types are .com (commercial organization), .org (organization), .edu (educational institution), .gov (government agency), .mil (U.S. military), and .net (networking organization); there are many other types, such as .biz (business), .info (information), and .name (personal name). All types are widely available except for .gov and .mil.

The most widely used geographical areas are .us (United States), .de (Germany or Deutschland), .cn (China), .jp (Japan), .uk (United Kingdom), .es (Spain or España), .in (India), .br (Brazil), and .it (Italy); there are others for most major, and many minor, countries. Some countries with memorable country codes, such as Tuvalu (.tv) and Tonga (.to), have made a good business out of selling domain names to anyone who wants them.

The .com designation is king of the domain world, which is why almost all web browsers default to the .com address when the domain type isn't specified. So if you're planning to register a domain name, .com should be your first choice—even though you may have a hard time finding a suitable name that hasn't already been taken.

## Evaluate an ISP

If you already have an Internet connection via an ISP rather than through a school, company, or organization, investigate the web hosting services that the ISP provides. Having your ISP host your website is a convenient solution, provided that the ISP provides all the web features you need (see the previous section, "Decide on Web Hosting Features," for a discussion of the features you should evaluate).

## Evaluate a Web-Hosting Service

Unless your ISP specializes in hosting websites, you will find more options and greater flexibility in a web hosting service—a service that hosts websites but does not provide Internet access. Most web hosting services offer various packages aimed at different levels of users, from basic packages (for example, 1GB disk space, 100 mailboxes, 25GB-a-month traffic, and basic scripting capabilities) to developer packages (for example, 50GB disk space, 500 mailboxes, 200GB-a-month traffic, extra FTP logins for extra users with different privileges, secure server facilities, and advanced scripting capabilities). By choosing a suitable web hosting service and an appropriate package, you can get almost exactly the space, traffic, and capabilities you need.

Evaluate the cost of paying separately for your Internet access and for your web hosting. If your website requires only the features and amount of space that your ISP includes with an Internet access account, paying for separate web hosting will be more expensive. If your site needs a significant amount of space and bandwidth, however, using a web hosting service is likely to be less expensive than getting that same amount of space and bandwidth from your ISP.

## Register a Domain Name

To make your web presence not only felt but also easy to find, you'll probably want to register your own domain name. (See the "Understanding Domains" QuickFacts for an overview of domain names and how they work.)

## TIP

Most people prefer to spend the time and effort coming up with a unique domain name for which you can get the .com extension rather than settle for one of the less usual extensions (such as .ws or .cc). Even if you prefer an extension other than .com for your site, register the .com domain as well so that you can redirect it to your site and prevent anyone else from buying it, either so they can grab your traffic or so that they can resell the domain to you at a hefty markup. For example, if your site is for a nonprofit organization, the .org domain type would more accurately reflect its nature. By securing the .com domain name and redirecting it to the .org site, however, you can avoid losing traffic to someone who subsequently registers the .com domain name. Also, because most browsers default to the .com domain type, visitors who type only the basic name of your site rather than the full address will be directed to the correct site.

## NOTE

Some domain registrars will hide your personal information from public view, which can be handy when you register a personal domain and don't want people tracking you down. For example, DreamHost (www.dreamhost.com) provides this service by default, while Go Daddy can provide it through their Domains By Proxy service.

Having a domain name (for example, www.acmevirtualindustries.com) gives your website much more impact—and makes it easier to access—than a name contained within another domain (for example, www.yourisp.com/~yourname).

Draw up a short list of domain names that would be suitable for your site. Huge numbers of domain names have already been registered, so you'll need to be creative to find a suitable name that's still available. Most registration services provide suggestions of available domain names that are similar to unavailable domain names you request. Sometimes you may strike it lucky with these automated suggestions, but usually you will do better to start with your own list and work through it in order of preference.

Domain name registration used to be centrally controlled, but nowadays there are many registration sites. You can either register a domain directly through your web host—which is often the best option—or use a specialist domain registrar. Four of the most popular domain registrars are:

- Network Solutions (www.networksolutions.com; shown in Figure 2-3) was the first domain registration site and remains the largest.
- eNom (www.enom.com) is a large domain registrar that specializes in business services and reselling domain registrations.
- Go Daddy (www.godaddy.com) manages about 30 million domain names. Go Daddy is notorious for innuendo-heavy advertising featuring celebrities such as Danica Patrick. Go Daddy has also made the headlines through having customer service problems in the past, so you may want to surf its support forums before signing on the dotted line.
- Register.com (www.register.com) is another large registration site with a good reputation.

Start your web browser and go to a domain name registration site. The procedure for registering a domain name starts by searching to see if it's available. If it is, and if you decide to proceed, you will need to provide payment (via credit card), billing information, and the name and address of an administrative contact (usually you) and a technical contact (usually the web host) for the domain name. Ideally, you will also provide the IP addresses of

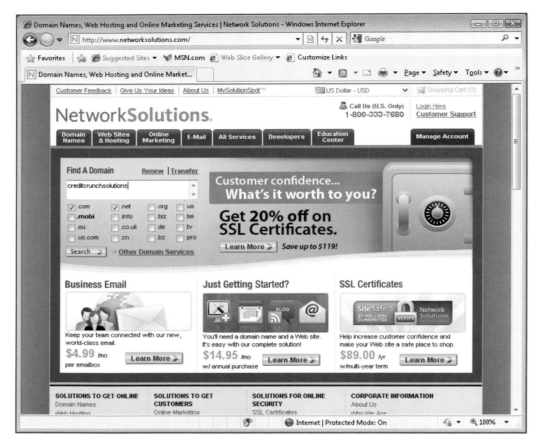

the web server that will host the domain name. If you don't know them yet, you can leave the domain name with the registration service until you find a web host, but you may then have to pay extra to transfer the domain name to the web host.

# Plan, Design, and Create Your Site

You can start a website by creating individual web pages using a text editor (as discussed in Chapter 1), an HTML editor, or a web-authoring application and linking the pages to each other using hyperlinks. Before you start creating your site, however, you should plan the site's contents and decide its basic design.

## Plan Your Site's Contents

A snappy URL may stick in a web surfer's mind, and a good design will please the eye

*Figure 2-3:* **You can register a domain name—or just find out whether a name is available—at a registration site such as Network Solutions.**

(assuming that the browser renders it correctly), but content is what makes or breaks your website. To make people come to your site and to persuade them to come back, you need strong—and preferably unique—content.

Focus on what your site's purpose is—why you're creating it in the first place. This should be obvious: You'd think few people would create a website for no reason, but a surprising number of people do start off with, at best, a hazy idea of what they're trying to achieve. While you *can* start creating pages without a firm goal and then let it grow in whichever direction your enthusiasm takes

**CAUTION**

Make sure any domain name you register doesn't infringe on any trademark. If it does, the trademark holder may be able to claim the domain name from you.

you, you're unlikely to end up with a focused, unified site that will draw interest. (If you do begin creating your website this way, be prepared to make root-and-branch changes if you realize you should have chosen a different direction.)

Establish what value you will provide to the people who visit your site. Will you provide tips, resources, or evaluations of products? Will you link to other sites? Will you sell, promote, or support products? All of the above?

Once you have decided the purpose of your website, focus on how you will deliver that purpose. In particular, decide who is going to generate content, who is going to edit it, who will create the web pages, and who will post them to the site and maintain it. On a small site, such as a personal site, you may end up doing all the tasks yourself.

## Make Your Site Effective

You must design your website so that it can be viewed successfully by everyone who accesses it. That's not as easy as it might seem, for several reasons.

- How a given page looks will depend on the browser, the screen resolution the computer is using, and the window size of the browser.

- The browsers that your site's visitors use may interpret HTML a little differently. You can minimize these problems by writing your web pages to standards and testing them in the major browsers (Internet Explorer, Firefox, and Safari), as discussed in Chapter 1.

- Even if the users are using the same browser, the operating system on their computers may cause the pages to be displayed in slightly different ways. For example, font sizes appear smaller on a Mac than on Windows, so your pages will typically look different on a Mac.

- Most browsers have highly configurable display settings that will affect how the pages look. You can change the text size, text color, background color, and even the display resolution of most browsers.

Figure 2-4 shows how even the simple page used as the example in Chapter 1 looks different using different browsers and browser settings.

Text is the key to communicating via web pages, so you must ensure that your site is navigable even if only the text is displayed. Organize it so that the most important text will catch the reader's eye and draw him or her into the page. Provide alternative text for all graphics used so that visitors using text-only

*Figure 2-4: **Even when they are not customized using all their options, different browsers can display the same page in different ways, especially with different window dimensions.***

browsers (either on personal computers or on other devices, such as handheld computers or cell phones) will be able to see all the important information on any page. The text will also benefit visitors using a browser with the graphics turned off to speed up browsing, because they'll be able to tell which placeholders they should click to navigate your site, which placeholders they should click to display relevant graphics, and which placeholders are irrelevant to their needs.

## Keep Your Web Pages Small Enough to Download Quickly

One day, the whole world will have screaming-fast broadband connections—maybe—but for the time being, all too many people are stuck with either grindingly slow dial-up connections or lesser broadband connections that barely deserve the term. To allow for such slow Internet connections, keep the file sizes of your pages as small as possible. HTML files themselves contain only text, so their file sizes remain quite compact unless you add heroic numbers of unnecessary tags and comments, but large graphics, audio files, and video files quickly increase the time it takes to download a web page.

If your site is primarily providing information, use graphics with discretion rather than as a rule, and keep their sizes small. (Chapter 4 discusses how to use graphics and how to prepare them for the Web.) On the other hand, if your site is demonstrating examples of design, you may need to use more graphics to produce the effects you need.

Where possible, reuse the same small graphics, such as those for your logo and navigation buttons. Most browsers cache graphics so that they can quickly supply them the next time the user requests the same page or another page that uses the same graphics.

Use audio and video only in moderation, as they can quickly chew through your bandwidth allowance.

**TIP**

If possible, have several other people look at your website while it is in development to make sure that they find it navigable and workable. Ask these people to note any difficulties that they have with the layout, navigation, text, or graphics. Resolve any persistent difficulties that surface. For example, you may need to add explanatory text to your home page to help visitors find parts of the site or add redundant links to simplify navigation.

**NOTE**

*Dithering* is a means of producing colors that aren't in the display color palette by mixing colors in adjacent pixels to produce a blended color that's approximately the color required. Dithering helps to make pictures that use more colors than the palette provides look better than they would if only the colors in the palette were used. For example, if you reduce a graphic from millions of colors to 256 colors to decrease its file size, the colors that aren't in the palette will have to be substituted by colors in the palette. Dithering helps to reduce the detrimental effects of this substitution.

# Check Your Website

Once you've gotten your website to a stage at which you want to make it available to your audience, check it using Internet Explorer before transferring it to your web host. If possible, check your website using browsers other than Internet Explorer, such as Firefox and Safari. (See Chapter 1 for a table of other browsers for Windows, Mac OS X, and Linux.) Verify that the site functions correctly and that all pages are readable. As discussed earlier in this chapter, it's quite normal for the pages to look different on different browsers and operating systems even if the browsers are configured with default settings.

Be sure to use different sizes of browser window as you test and, if it's practical to do so, assorted screen resolutions as well. Most modern desktop and laptop computers use at least 1024 × 768 pixel resolution, but it's a good idea to check your pages at lower resolutions, such as 800 × 600 pixels and 640 × 480 pixels, given the increasing popularity of small-screened "netbook" computers, handheld computers, and Web-capable mobile phones.

Try turning down the display to 256 colors and make sure that the pages are viewable. Graphics that use more colors will be noticeably dithered, using a mixture of colors to deliver roughly the colors you specified.

# Update and Maintain Your Website

Few websites are static; almost all sites contain information that needs updating, either every day (for example, a restaurant's menu pages) or from time to time. New content will help to bring visitors back to your site, provided that they know it is there and can easily find it, so make sure your new content is easy to access and that it is flagged from the home page.

Develop a schedule for creating and posting new content and for moving previously new content to the longer-established areas of your site or to an archive. Decide how frequently the different areas of your website will need to be updated and, if you have a team, establish whose responsibility the updates are.

**TIP**

Windows Vista also includes a command-line FTP client named ftp that you can run from a Command Prompt window (click the **Start** button, click **All Programs**, click **Accessories**, and then click **Command Prompt**). Unless you're comfortable with UNIX-style FTP commands, however, chances are that Internet Explorer or a third-party FTP client with a graphical interface will be faster and easier to use.

**NOTE**

Many web server administrators configure their servers to direct you automatically to your folder when you log in using your username and password, but you may also need to navigate to a particular subfolder within your folder.

Add this information to your site-description document (the document explaining your site, its structure, and its contents, as discussed in Chapter 1) so that it is recorded and available to those who need to know it.

# Transfer Your Site to the Web

There are three main ways of transferring your site's web pages and files to the web host.

- **Use an FTP client program**   An FTP client program lets you connect to a web server and transfer files to it, much as you would do using Explorer on Windows or the Finder on the Mac. This is the usual way of transferring files.

- **Use a web-authoring program with built-in FTP**   Web-authoring programs such as Expression Web and Dreamweaver include built-in FTP functionality, so you can upload files directly from within the program.

- **Use a custom upload mechanism**   Web hosts that provide custom website-building software often also give you a custom mechanism for uploading web pages and files. For example, you go to an upload web page, click a button, use the resulting Browse For Folder dialog box or Open dialog box to select the file, and then click a button to upload it.

This section shows you how to use an FTP client program to upload files to your web host.

## Get the Information Required for FTP

To transfer files via FTP, you must get the following information from the server's administrator (at your ISP, at the hosting service, or on your company's or organization's network):

- The web server's address (for example, ftp.acmevirtualindustries.com) and the folder in which you should put the files.

- Your username and password for the web server.

# Transfer a Site Using an FTP Client

Many different FTP client programs are available for Windows, Mac OS X, and other operating systems. For most of them, you have to pay—but here are two good free FTP clients:

- **FileZilla**   FileZilla (http://filezilla-project.org) is an FTP client program that runs on Windows, Mac, and Linux.

- **Cyberduck**   Cyberduck (http://cyberduck.ch) is an FTP client program that runs only on Mac OS X.

With a typical FTP client program (such as FileZilla), you set up a shortcut for accessing a site so that you can then connect to it quickly. For example, here's how you set up a shortcut in FileZilla and connect to the site:

1. Click the **File** menu, and then click **Site Manager**. FileZilla opens the Site Manager window (see Figure 2-5).

2. Click the **New Site** button. FileZilla adds a new site to the Select Entry box, calls it New site, and displays an edit box around the name.

3. Type the name you want to give the FTP site, and then press **ENTER** to apply the name.

4. Click in the **Host** box and then type the address for the FTP site—for example, ftp.acmevirtualindustries.com.

5. If your web host has given you a port number, type it in the Port box. Otherwise, leave this box blank to use the default port.

6. Make sure the Servertype drop-down list shows FTP – File Transfer Protocol, unless your web host has told you to use a different protocol (for example, SFTP – SSH File Transfer Protocol).

7. Open the Logontype drop-down list, and choose **Normal**.

8. Type your logon name for the FTP server in the User box.

9. Type your password in the Password box.

10. Type any comments about the FTP site in the Comments box. If you have many FTP sites, the comments can help you to distinguish them easily.

11. Click the **Connect** button. FileZilla connects to the FTP site.

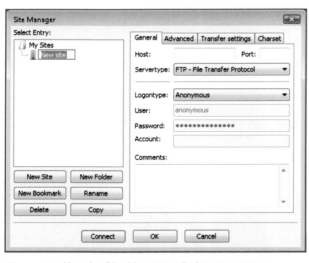

*Figure 2-5: **Use the Site Manager window to set up a shortcut to an FTP site in FileZilla.***

Once you've created a shortcut to an FTP site, you can connect to the site in moments. Figure 2-6 shows FileZilla connected to an FTP site.

Once you've connected to the site, transfer files by dragging them from the pane showing your local folders to the pane showing the folders on the FTP site, or vice versa.

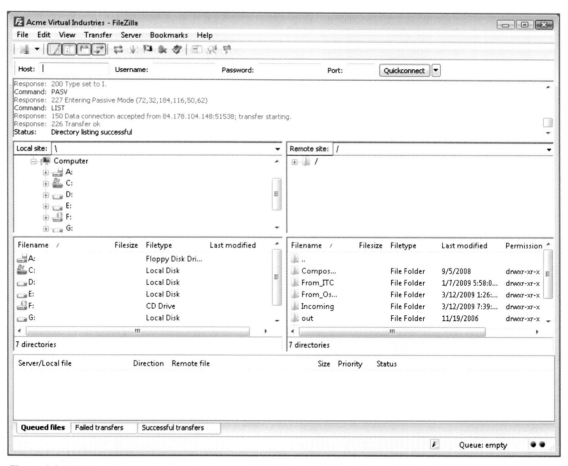

Figure 2-6: *FileZilla is a freeware FTP client that runs on Windows, Mac OS X, and Linux.*

## How to...

- *Using Proportional and Monospaced Fonts*
- *Create Paragraphs*
- *Group Paragraphs into Division*
- *Control Breaks*
- *Inserting Special Characters*
- *Keep Text Together with Nonbreaking Spaces*
- *Control Hyphenation with Optional Hyphens*
- *Create Headings, Lists, and Indents*
- *"Physical" and "Logical" Style Tags*
- *Apply Boldface*
- *Apply Italics*
- *Apply Underline*
- *Apply Strikethrough*
- *Apply Monospaced Font*
- *Apply Subscript and Superscript*
- *Understanding Other Formatting*
- *Control Font Formatting*
- *Working with Fonts*
- *Change Style Using Inline Styles*
- *Catch the Eye with Moving Text*

# Chapter 3
# Structuring Web Pages and Applying Manual Formatting

Each web page you create needs a structure that shapes its contents. For example, a typical web page needs one or more levels of headings to present its contents in a coherent order. Under each heading, you'll normally break up the text into body paragraphs, just as you would in a book or article. You may also use lists to present information.

To make a web page appear the way you want it to, you can format it in either of two ways. The old-style way is to apply manual formatting to individual elements, as described in this chapter. This type of formatting is not recommended any more, because there's a better type of formatting: Cascading Style Sheets (CSS), described in detail in Chapter 8, let you organize your formatting centrally, improving consistency and

**USING PROPORTIONAL AND MONOSPACED FONTS**

Each browser has a default proportional font and a default monospaced font.

- A *proportional* font is one in which the letters are different widths, like the body fonts used in this book. For example, an uppercase M is wider than a lowercase i or l.

- A *monospaced, constant-width,* or *fixed-width* font is one in which all the letters are all the same width (in the same font size). Courier, the font used on most typewriters, is the most widely used monospaced font, but there are plenty of others.

Proportional fonts are easier on the eye than monospaced fonts, and normal practice is to use proportional fonts for most of the text that appears on web pages, keeping monospaced font for when you need to differentiate some text or display it in a clear format. The <pre> tag and some other tags automatically use the monospaced font. While you *can* use monospaced font more widely, there's usually little to be gained from doing so.

When checking your web pages, try changing the default proportional and monospaced fonts used by your browsers. In most Windows browsers, you'll find the settings in the Options dialog box (click the **Tools** menu and then click **Internet Options** or **Options**). For example, to change the fonts on Internet Explorer:

1. If Internet Explorer isn't running, click the **Start** button and then click **Internet**.

2. Click the **Tools** menu and then click **Internet Options**. The Internet Options dialog box appears.

*Continued . . .*

saving time and effort. But because manual formatting is still widely used, and you will almost certainly need to work with pages that use it, it's important to understand how it works, even if you use CSS to format your own web pages.

# Understand Considerations for Web Formatting

When you create a document with a word processor, such as Microsoft Word or Corel WordPerfect, you can specify the exact formatting you want for each character, paragraph, and page. For example, you can make a character bold, underlined, 18-point Times New Roman font; apply one-inch indents and 1.5-line spacing for a paragraph; and set one-inch margins for the top, bottom, and sides of a page. When you print out the page, you'll get the formatting you applied.

Similarly, you can apply formatting to elements in the web pages you create: font formatting, line breaks, alignment, indentation, and more. But you can't be sure that this formatting will appear as you intended it to when your pages are displayed in a browser, for several reasons.

- Different browsers interpret even standard HTML tags differently.

- If the fonts you use in the page are installed on the browser's computer, they will be displayed; if not, the browser will substitute its default proportional font for any proportional font you use and its default monospaced (fixed-width) font for any monospaced font you use.

- The viewer can change how the browser displays particular items. For example, the viewer can increase or decrease the text size to make a page readable, or change the text color or the background color.

- Unless you use CSS (discussed in Chapter 8), you can't apply precise indents to paragraphs.

## USING PROPORTIONAL AND MONOSPACED FONTS *(Continued)*

3. On the General tab, click the **Fonts** button. The Fonts dialog box appears.

4. Choose the proportional font you want in the Webpage Font list box.

5. Choose the monospaced font you want in the Plain Text Font list box.

6. Click **OK** to close the Fonts dialog box, click **OK** again to close the Internet Options dialog box, and, if desired, close Internet Explorer.

## TIP

If you use a text editor to create all your web pages, save the basic structure of one of your pages in a file as a template so that you can reuse it quickly to save yourself typing the common elements. Alternatively, keep a text file containing boilerplate sections of web pages that you can paste into new pages as needed.

# Use Paragraphs, Divisions, Breaks, and Hyphens

As discussed in Chapter 1, each web page you create must include an HTML statement, a header section, and a body section. Normally, each page has a DOCTYPE declaration as well to tell the browser how to interpret the document type. Each page should have a title that appears in the browser's title bar (or on a tab, if it is a tabbed browser) when the page is displayed.

The basic structure of a web page typically looks like this:

```
<!DOCTYPE html PUBLIC "-//W3C//DTD XHTML 1.0 Transitional//EN"
    "http://www.w3.org/TR/xhtml1/DTD/xhtml1-transitional.dtd">
<html>
<head>
<title></title>
</head>
<body>
</body>
</html>
```

Within the body of the web page, you use *block elements*, such as headings, paragraphs, and images, to form the major parts of the page.

## Create Paragraphs

Use the `<p>` and `</p>` tags to create a body text paragraph in the default proportional font. A body text paragraph includes extra vertical space afterward to separate it from the next paragraph. For correctness, always use the opening tag (`<p>`) and the closing tag (`</p>`), even though many browsers will display pages correctly that use only the opening tag to indicate a paragraph.

You can apply formatting directly to paragraphs or to text within paragraphs.

## Group Paragraphs into Divisions

If you need to apply formatting to two or more paragraphs, you can create a *division*, or group of paragraphs, and apply the formatting to the division. By doing so, you can cut down on the number of formatting codes. You can also achieve different effects, such as applying a border around the division as a whole instead of applying a separate border around each of the paragraphs.

To create a division:

1. Type the opening `<div>` tag before the first paragraph you want to include in the division.

2. Include in the opening `<div>` tag the division identifier or any formatting instructions for the division as a whole—for example:

   ```
   <div id="services">
   ```

3. Type the closing `</div>` tag after the last paragraph you want to include in the division.

For example, here is a division that includes a heading, an image, and two paragraphs:

```
<div id="services">
<h1>Acme Virtual Industries: Services</h1>
<p>Acme Virtual Industries offers a market-leading variety of
services.</p>
<p>We offer the ultimate in document security services.</p>
<img src="shred.jpg" alt="Shredded paper" height="200"/
</div>
```

## Control Breaks

Web browsers automatically rebreak the lines within paragraphs as necessary to display all the text within the current window size so viewers will see your web page differently, depending on their screen resolution, browser window size, and the default text size they've chosen.

To force browsers to break a line at a particular point or to insert extra space between paragraphs, insert a `<br/>` tag.

| CHARACTER | NAME | CODE |
|---|---|---|
| ® | &reg; | &#174; |
| © | &copy; | &#169; |
| ™ | &trade; | &#153; |
| " | | &#147; |
| " | | &#148; |
| < | &lt; | &#60; |
| > | &gt; | &#62; |
| ¡ | &iexcl; | &#161; |
| ¿ | &iquest; | &#191; |
| ¢ | &cent; | &#162; |
| ± | &plusmn; | &#177; |
| ¼ | &frac14; | &#188; |
| ½ | &frac12; | &#189; |
| ¾ | &frac34; | &#190; |
| × | &times; | &#215; |
| ÷ | &divide; | &#247; |
| ñ | &ntilde; | &#241; |
| ← | &larr; | &#8592; |
| ↑ | &uarr; | &#8593; |
| → | &rarr; | &#8594; |
| ↓ | &darr; | &#8595; |
| € | &euro; | &#8364; |
| – (en dash) | | &#8211 |
| — (em dash) | | &#8212 |

*Table 3-1: Special Character Codes*

## Keep Text Together with Nonbreaking Spaces

To prevent two words from being broken at the end of a line, use the   code to create a nonbreaking space. For example, you might want to prevent your name or your company's name from being broken:

```
<p>To contact us at Acme Virtual Industries, write
to:</p>
```

## Control Hyphenation with Optional Hyphens

If a compound word always uses a hyphen, type a hyphen in it, just as you would in any document. You can also instruct the browser to break a long word when it is at the end of a line but not break it at other times. To do so, you place one or more *soft hyphens*, or *optional hyphens*, by typing the &shy; code at the appropriate places in the word—for example:

```
<p>Our industry-leading methods of document destruction ensure
that all data is fully non&shy;recoverable.</p>
```

# Create Headings, Lists, and Indents

To lay your web pages out logically, you'll usually need to break them up into headings. You may also need to create lists—for example, numbered lists and bulleted list—and indents.

## Create Headings

HTML offers six levels of headings, using paired tags, from Heading 1 (opening tag <h1>, closing tag </h1>) to Heading 6 (opening tag <h6>, closing tag </h6>). Each browser displays the headings in boldface, using its default proportional font and descending font sizes, from Heading 1 (the biggest) to Heading 6 (the smallest). The actual font size used depends on the browser and on the user's display settings: If the user increases the text size to make a page more readable, the font size of the headings increases as well.

**CAUTION**

Avoid using nonbreaking spaces on more than three consecutive words because doing so can create awkward breaks in lines.

**TIP**

You can also use nonbreaking spaces at the beginning of a paragraph to force indentation. Such usage is discouraged, but is nonetheless effective.

**TIP**

When structuring your documents, use as few heading levels as is practical. Start by breaking each topic into major sections: These become your Heading 1s, and typically you'll have only one of them on a web page, as this helps search engines index your pages correctly. Under the Heading 1, break up the document's content into Heading 2 sections as necessary; if those sections need subsections, use Heading 3s, and then Heading 4s if you need them. You'll seldom need to use the lower heading levels. For example, most of the chapters in this book have a chapter heading (the equivalent of Heading 1) and then three levels of headings—and your web pages should normally be much shorter than even the shortest chapter in this book. If not, consider breaking up your material into further separate pages.

For example, to create a short section of headings and text on an existing web page:

1. Position the insertion point within the body of the web page.

2. Type the opening tag for a Heading 1, the text for the heading, and then the closing tag—for example:

   `<h1>Acme Virtual Industries Services</h1>`

3. Type a text paragraph between `<p>` and `</p>` tags—for example:

   `<p>Acme Virtual Industries helps you to get the best out of your business by providing an easy way to grow.</p>`

4. Type the opening `<h2>` tag for a Heading 2, the text for the heading, and then the closing `</h2>` tag—for example:

   `<h2>Virtual Office Space</h2>`

5. Type a text paragraph after the Heading 2—for example:

   `<p>We provide virtual office space in prime locations in the US and in Europe.</p>`

6. Type the opening `<h3>` tag for a Heading 3, the text for the heading, and then the closing `</h3>` tag—for example:

   `<h3>US Locations: West Coast</h3>`

7. Enter further headings and paragraphs (or other items, such as links) as necessary.

8. Save the file, switch to your browser, and update the display. Figure 3-1 shows an example of three levels of headings.

## Create Numbered, Bulleted, and Definition Lists

HTML lets you create three different types of lists.

- **Unordered list**   A bulleted list (like this one). The browser automatically displays the bullets and indents the list items.

- **Ordered list**   A numbered list, like those used for the steps in this book. The browser automatically displays the numbers in the correct sequence.

- **Definition list**   A list that alternates paragraphs aligned with the left margin and indented paragraphs. The first of each pair of paragraphs is the term being defined, and the second is the definition of the term. (You'll see an example of this a little later in this chapter.)

*Figure 3-1: Use two or three levels of headings to break your documents into major sections.*

## CREATE A BULLETED LIST

A bulleted list is a block element that starts with a <ul> (unordered list) tag and ends with a </ul> tag. Within the list, each item starts with an <li> (list item) tag and ends with an </li> tag.

To create a bulleted list:

**1.** Type the opening and closing tags for the unordered list:

```
<ul>
</ul>
```

**2.** Within the tags, type the list items, one to a line, marking each with <li> and </li> tags—for example:

```
<ul>
<li>San Diego</li>
<li>Los Angeles</li>
<li>San Francisco</li>
</ul>
```

**3.** Save the file, switch to your browser, and update the display. Your list will be displayed with default black bullets, as in the example shown.

**4.** Try changing the bullets to squares by adding the type attribute to the <ul> tag and specifying the square parameter:

```
<ul type="square">
```

**5.** Save the file, switch to your browser, and update the display. The bullets will have turned to squares. Depending on your browser, the squares may be filled in (as in the example shown) or empty.

**6.** Change the bullets to empty circles by changing the type attribute to circle:

```
<ul type="circle">
```

## US Locations: West Coast

Choose among these West Coast locations:

- San Diego
- Los Angeles
- San Francisco

**NOTE**

Being able to manipulate the bullets like this can be handy, but you can take greater control over your lists by using CSS. For example, you can change the indentation of the bullets and the text, and you can use images as bullets.

## Our Most Popular Services

These are our most popular services today:

1. Answering live telephone queries
2. Providing customer service via phone
3. Providing customer service via e-mail
4. Providing customer service via online chat
5. Telemarketing

| TYPE | EFFECT | EXAMPLE |
|------|--------|---------|
| 1 | Standard numbering | 1, 2, 3 |
| I | Uppercase roman numerals | I, II, III |
| i | Lowercase roman numerals | i, ii, iii |
| A | Uppercase letters | A, B, C |
| a | Lowercase letters | a, b, c |

*Table 3-2: Types of Numbered Lists*

7. Save the file, switch to your browser, and update the display. The bullets will have turned to circles.

8. Change the bullets back to regular bullets by either changing the type attribute to disc or by removing the attribute altogether. disc is the default bullet type, so you don't need to specify it if you want a default bulleted list.

9. Save the file.

### CREATE A NUMBERED LIST

A numbered list is a block element that begins with an <ol> (ordered list) tag and ends with an </ol> tag. Within the list, each item starts with an <li> (list item) tag and ends with an </li> tag.

To create a numbered list:

1. Type the opening and closing tags for the ordered list:

```
<ol>
</ol>
```

2. Within the tags, type the list items, one to a line—for example:

```
<ol>
<li>Answering live telephone queries</li>
<li>Providing customer service via phone</li>
<li>Providing customer service via e-mail</li>
<li>Providing customer service via online chat</li>
<li>Telemarketing</li>
</ol>
```

3. Save the file, switch to your browser, and update the display. Your list will be numbered from 1 to 5, as in the example shown.

### CHANGE THE NUMBERING TYPE

The default type of numbered list uses standard numbers, as in the previous example. You can specify different types of numbering by adding the type attribute to the <ol> tag, as described in Table 3-2.

1. Change the numbering on the numbered list to uppercase roman numerals by changing the type attribute to I:

```
<ol type="I">
```

2. Save the file, switch to your browser, and update the display. When changed, the example list looks like this:

### Our Most Popular Services

These are our most popular services today:

   I.  Answering live telephone queries
  II.  Providing customer service via phone
 III.  Providing customer service via e-mail
 IV.  Providing customer service via online chat
  V.  Telemarketing

3. Change the numbering back to standard numbering by either changing the type attribute to 1 (<ol type="1">) or removing the type attribute altogether. Standard numbering is the default for numbered lists, so you don't need to specify the type attribute if you want a list with standard numbering.

4. Save your file again.

### CHANGE THE STARTING NUMBER

By default, HTML starts each numbered list with 1 or the equivalent in the numbering scheme used: I, i, A, or a. Sometimes, you may need to use a different starting number for a list. For example, if you break a numbered list with a graphic or a paragraph, you will need to start the second part of the list with the appropriate number rather than with 1.

To change the starting number, add the start attribute to the <ol> tag, and specify the appropriate number—for example:

```
<ol type="1" start="5">
```

### CREATE A DEFINITION LIST

A definition list is a block element that begins with a <dl> (definition list) tag and ends with a </dl> tag. Each of the terms defined begins with a <dt> tag and ends with a </dt> tag. Each of the definitions for those terms begins with a <dd> tag and ends with a </dd> tag.

**TIP**

A definition list is a great tool for presenting terms and their definitions, but if you need to make the terms appear in the outline of your document, you'll be better off using headings for the terms and paragraphs for the definitions.

To create a definition list:

**1.** Type the opening and closing tags for the definition list:

```
<dl>
</dl>
```

**2.** Within the tags, type each of the definition terms within `<dt>` and `</dt>` tags, and type the definitions for those terms within `<dd>` and `</dd>` tags:

```
<dl>
<dt>Telephone</dt>
<dd>Just call us&#8212;couldn't be easier.</dd>
<dt>Online chat</dt>
<dd>Talk to a customer service representative via text. The
representative will help you immediately or will call back if
research is required.</dd>
<dt>E-mail</dt>
<dd>Send a query to one of our customer service representatives.
You will receive an answer within 24 hours.</dd>
</dl>
```

**3.** Save the file, switch to your browser, and update the display. The example list looks like this:

> Telephone
> > Just call us—couldn't be easier.
>
> Online chat
> > Talk to a customer service representative via text. The representative will help you immediately or will call back if research is required.
>
> E-mail
> > Send a query to one of our customer service representatives. You will receive an answer within 24 hours.

## CREATE A NESTED LIST

You can *nest,* or position, any list within another list—for example, a bulleted list within a numbered list, a numbered list within a bulleted list, a definition list within a bulleted list, or a list within the same type of list as itself.

To nest a list, place the tags for the nested list within the tags for the list that will contain it. The browser then displays the nested list with more indent than the list that contains it. You can nest another list within the nested list if necessary; the second nested list receives even more indent than the first nested list.

To create a nested list:

**1.** Position the insertion point at the appropriate point within the existing list.

**2.** Close and reopen the ordered list, and add the opening and closing tags for the sublist—for example, as shown in bold font here:

```
<ol type="1">
<li>Answering live telephone queries</li>
</ol>
<ul>
</ul>
<ol>
<li>Providing customer service via phone</li>
<li>Providing customer service via e-mail</li>
<li>Providing customer service via online chat</li>
<li>Telemarketing</li>
</ol>
```

**3.** Within the bulleted list tags (<ul> and </ul>), type the items for the sublist:

```
<ul>
<li>Provide information</li>
<li>Redirect to customer service</li>
<li>Redirect to sales agents</li>
</ul>
```

**4.** Save the file, switch to your browser, and update the display. The example list looks like this:

**Our Most Popular Services**

These are our most popular services today:

1. Answering live telephone queries
   - Provide information
   - Redirect to customer service
   - Redirect to sales agents
2. Providing customer service via phone
3. Providing customer service via e-mail
4. Providing customer service via online chat
5. Telemarketing

## Apply an Indent

Indentation is a standard feature of word-processing applications, but HTML doesn't offer a direct means of creating an indent. CSS (discussed in Chapter 8) makes it easy to indent paragraphs, but if you're not using CSS, you have to use a workaround.

**NOTE**

Indenting text by using the <blockquote> tags is officially frowned upon, but it's widely used by manual coders and web-authoring programs, so it seems to be here to stay. The preferred way of indenting content is by using CSS. See Chapter 8 for details.

The workaround for indenting both margins is to use the block quote tags, <blockquote> and </blockquote>. As its name suggests, the block quote tag was originally intended for longer quotations that needed to be set off from the rest of the page, but you can also use it for other types of text that need indentation.

Here is an example of a block quote:

```
<h3>The Value of Gold</h3>
<p>Here's what &#147;The Loan Ranger&#148; has to say about gold
versus paper money:</p>
<blockquote>Paper money is the fiat currency of governments and
has no real value. If you hold paper money, you are at the mercy
of governmental attempts to manipulate money supply. But gold has
intrinsic value, even if its price in paper money rises and falls
like the tide.</blockquote>
```

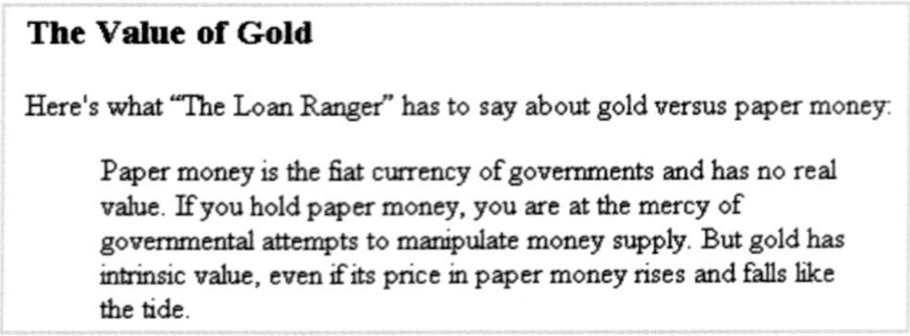
**The Value of Gold**

Here's what "The Loan Ranger" has to say about gold versus paper money:

> Paper money is the fiat currency of governments and has no real value. If you hold paper money, you are at the mercy of governmental attempts to manipulate money supply. But gold has intrinsic value, even if its price in paper money rises and falls like the tide.

# Align Elements

As in a word-processing document, you can apply left, center, and right alignment to an element such as a paragraph, heading, or image. The old way of doing so, now deprecated, is to use the align attribute in the element's tag and specify the appropriate value: left, center, or right. Left is the default alignment, so you don't need to specify it. (The new way of applying alignment is to use CSS, as discussed in Chapter 8.)

For example, the following code centers the heading, aligns the first paragraph right, and aligns the second paragraph left (see Figure 3-2):

```
<h3 align="center">Mail Fulfillment</h3>
<p align="right"><em>Everything from daily correspondence to
massive mailshots!</em></p>
<p align="left">When you let Acme Virtual Services handle your
mailing needs, you save time and money&#8212;and you get high-
quality results.</p>
```

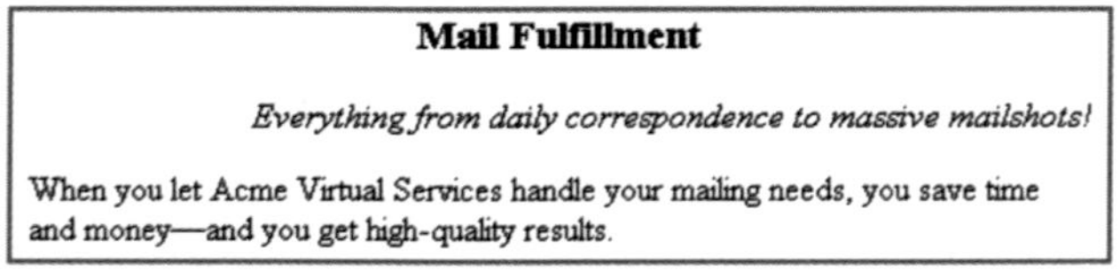
**Mail Fulfillment**

*Everything from daily correspondence to massive mailshots!*

When you let Acme Virtual Services handle your mailing needs, you save time and money—and you get high-quality results.

***Figure 3-2:** You can align elements (such as paragraphs) left, right, or center.*

# Use Preformatted Text

If you need to lay out text precisely using spaces and carriage returns, use preformatted text. To create preformatted text, which is monospaced or fixed-width text, enter the text between the opening <pre> tag and the closing </pre> tag.

The following is an example of preformatted text:

```
<h3>Prices</h3>
<pre>
Service ID    Description               Hours    Price (US$)
------------------------------------------------------------
A3892         Mail administration         1        19.99
A3893         One-time mailshot (200)     3        36.99
A3894         Customer-service template   2        49.99
------------------------------------------------------------
</pre>
```

**Prices**

```
Service ID    Description             Hours    Price (US$)
----------------------------------------------------------
A3892         Mail administration       1        19.99
A3893         One-time mailshot (200)   3        36.99
A3894         Customer-service template 2        49.99
----------------------------------------------------------
```

# Apply Formatting Tags and Attributes

After setting the basic formatting for the blocks of text in a page, you can apply specific formatting to individual words, phrases, or elements using inline styles. Inline styles are the HTML equivalent of direct formatting or character styles in a word processor.

### CAUTION

Whereas most applications use a separate font for italic text (for example, Times New Roman Italic instead of Times New Roman), browsers simulate italic by slanting the default font. The result is that the italic often doesn't look like real italics and is best used only for emphasis on small amounts of text. It's usually best not to apply italic-text or emphasis-text formatting to whole sentences or paragraphs at a time.

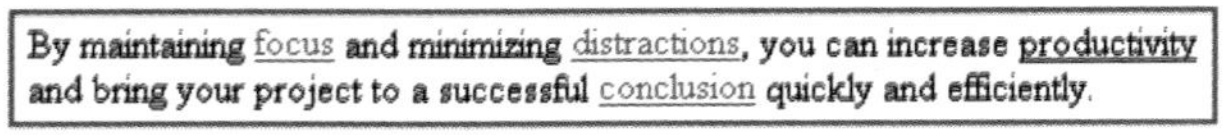

> By maintaining focus and minimizing distractions, you can increase productivity and bring your project to a successful conclusion quickly and efficiently.

*Figure 3-3: You can apply underline manually, but because most browsers use colored underline to indicate hyperlinks on text, underline can be confusing.*

## Apply Boldface

To apply boldface, enclose the text in either the bold-text tags (<b> and </b>) or the strong-text tags (<strong> and </strong>). Both pairs of tags typically have the same effect, although you can change the effect of the strong-text tags by using CSS.

Here is an example of using both bold-text tags and strong-text tags:

```
<p>This is an example of <b>boldface</b> using &lt;b&gt; and
&lt;/b&gt; tags.</p>
<p>This is an example of <strong>boldface</strong> using
&lt;strong&gt; and &lt;/strong&gt; tags.</p>
```

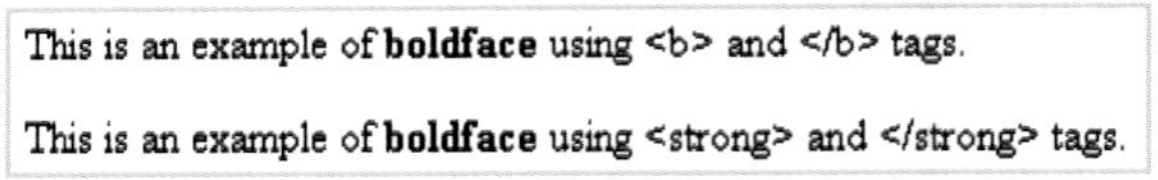

> This is an example of **boldface** using <b> and </b> tags.
>
> This is an example of **boldface** using <strong> and </strong> tags.

## Apply Italics

To apply italics, enclose the text in either the physical italic-text tags (<i> and </i>) or the logical emphasis-text tags (<em> and </em>). Both pairs of tags typically have the same effect, although you can change the effect of the emphasis-text tags by using CSS.

Here is an example of using both italic-text tags and emphasis-text tags:

```
<p><i>Today Only</i>: 15% discount on telephone services!</p>
<p><em>Special offers</em> on <b>answering</b> and <b>marketing
calls</b>.</p>
```

## Apply Underline

To apply a single underline, enclose the text in <u> and </u> tags, as in the example shown (see Figure 3-3):

```
<p>By maintaining <a href="concentration.jpg">focus</a> and
minimizing <a href="office_busy.jpg">distractions</a>, you
can increase <u>productivity</u> and bring your project to a
successful <a href="consultant.jpg">conclusion</a> quickly and
efficiently.</p>
```

## Apply Strikethrough

To apply strikethrough, enclose the text in either <strike> and </strike> tags or <s> and </s> tags:

```
<p>Special Assistance Package <strike>$349.99</strike> NOW ONLY
$299.99!</p>
```

## Apply Monospaced Font

As well as displaying whole paragraphs in monospaced font using the <pre> and </pre> tags, you can format characters as monospaced font by using the teletype inline style. To apply this style, enclose the text in the <tt> and </tt> tags, as in the example shown, which also uses the <big> and </big> tags to increase the size of the monospaced font displayed:

```
<h3>Contact Us</h3>
<p>You can contact us via e-mail at
<big><tt>info@acmevirtualindustries.com</tt></big>.</p>
```

> **Contact Us**
>
> You can contact us via e-mail at
> `info@acmevirtualindustries.com`

## Apply Subscript and Superscript

To apply subscript, enclose the text in <sub> and </sub> tags. To apply superscript, enclose the text in <sup> and </sup> tags. This example uses a superscript:

```
<p>Our one-hundred square meter (100m<sup>2</sup>) conference
room can easily accommodate full board meetings.</p>
```

> Our one-hundred square meter ($100m^2$) conference room can easily accommodate full board meetings.

## UNDERSTANDING OTHER FORMATTING

HTML supports various other types of formatting beyond those discussed in this section, including the following:

- Smaller text (<small> and </small>) appears in a smaller size than the default size set in the browser.

- Bigger text (<big> and </big>) appears in a larger size than the default size set in the browser.

- Sample text (<samp> and </samp>) appears in the browser's default monospaced font to indicate that it is a program or script example. Sample text usually looks the same as typewriter text (<tt> and </tt>), but it is a logical tag that can be interpreted by screen readers and accessibility tools.

- Variable text (<var> and </var>) appears in italicized (slanted) font.

- Keyboard text (<kbd> and </kbd>) appears in the browser's default monospaced font. Keyboard text also usually looks the same as typewriter text, but it is a logical tag that can be interpreted by screen readers and accessibility tools.

# Control Font Formatting and Styles

To make your pages look good, you may want to change the font formatting directly. Another option is to use inline styles, as discussed later in this section.

## Control Font Formatting

The <font> tag lets you control the typeface, type size, and type color displayed in the browser.

### CONTROL THE TYPEFACE

To specify the typeface the browser should use for some text, enter the opening <font> tag with the face attribute and the name of the font or fonts you want to use, then the text on which to use the font, and then the closing </font> tag. The font name can be either a specific font name (for example, Times New Roman) or one of the five generic font families (serif, sans-serif, monospace, fantasy, and cursive) that all browsers recognize. For example, you can specify the Times New Roman typeface like this:

```
<font face="Times New Roman">Terms and Conditions</font>
```

Unless you know that visitors to your website will have specific fonts installed (as you might know if you are designing an internal website for a company), it's better provide a list of alternative fonts or families to ensure that the browser doesn't substitute its default proportional font or monospaced font if it doesn't have the exact font you specify; for example:

```
<font face="Times New Roman, Times, serif">Terms and Conditions</font>
```

### CONTROL THE TYPE SIZE

To control the type size via HTML, you do not use the point size (as in most word-processing applications), but rather the type size relative to the default size set in the browser.

Browsers use the values 1 through 7 to measure type sizes, with 1 being the smallest and 7 the largest. Each size is about 20 percent bigger than the size preceding it: Size 2 is 20 percent bigger than size 1, size 3 is 20 percent bigger than size 2, and so on. Each browser assigns the value 3 to its default type size, no matter how big or small that size is. You can then control the type size by using the size attribute with either an absolute value (1 through 7) or a relative value, the amount to be added to or subtracted from the current type size. For example:

- size="4" is an absolute value that makes the type size 4, about 20 percent bigger than the default size.
- size="+2" is a relative value that makes the type size 5, about 40 percent (two 20 percent increments) bigger than the default size 3.
- size="−1" is a relative value that makes the type size 2, about 20 percent smaller than the default size 3.

## CONTROL THE TYPE COLOR

To change the font color, use the <font> tag with the color attribute. You can display many different colors by using either their names (for example, color="blue" or color="red") or the hexadecimal (base 16) code for the color (for example, color="#99FF00" for a lime-green shade). Most web-authoring tools and HTML editors make it easy to find the exact color you want. If you're working in a text editor, consult a color-codes reference, such as that found at http://webmonkey.wired.com (search for "color charts") to learn the hexadecimal codes you need.

The following example changes the formatting of the text to sans-serif (preferring Arial or Trebuchet), navy (dark blue), and two sizes larger than the default:

```
<p><font face="Arial, Trebuchet, sans-serif" size="+2"
color="navy">Support Services</font></p>
```

The next example changes the formatting of the text to sans-serif (preferring Comic Sans MS or Trebuchet) and one size smaller than the default:

```
<p><font face="Comic Sans MS, Trebuchet, sans-serif"
color="#990099" size="-1">Product Support</font> keeps your
customers satisfied with your goods they've purchased.</p>
```

## Support Services

Product Support keeps your customers satisfied with your goods they've purchased.

## WORKING WITH FONTS

While you *can* control font formatting using the <font> tag, you should usually avoid doing so. Any font you specify in a web page will be displayed correctly only if it is installed on the computer that's viewing the page. If the font isn't installed, the computer substitutes its default proportional font (for a proportional font) or its default monospaced font (for a monospaced font). This substitution can wreck the effects you carefully create.

Cascading Style Sheets (CSS) are now the preferred method for applying formatting such as font formatting; because CSS let you instantly apply a font change to a whole document, they can save you a great deal of time and effort. Chapter 8 shows you how to use CSS.

To avoid font substitutions changing the look of your pages, stick with widely used fonts as much as possible, and design your pages so that fonts can be substituted without the pages suffering. The most widely used serif fonts are Times New Roman, Times, and Georgia. The most widely used sans-serif fonts are Arial, Helvetica, Trebuchet, and Verdana. The most widely used monospaced font is Courier.

If you simply *must* ensure that a particular font is used, create a graphic containing the text, and insert the graphic at the appropriate place in the web page. Remember that anyone who has turned off the display of pictures or who is using a text-only browser will not see such graphics. See Chapter 4 for more information.

## NOTE

The style attribute is different from the <style> element, which is used for defining internal style sheets and importing style rules found in external style sheets. Chapter 8 discusses how to use CSS.

# Change Style Using Inline Styles

You can change the style of an element (such as a paragraph or a heading) by applying the style attribute to the element's tag. The style attribute takes the format style="*property1:value1; property2:value2*", where *property1* and *property2* are properties of the style attribute, and *value1* and *value2* are the values assigned to those properties.

To change the style of an element, follow these general steps. See the rest of this section for specific examples of using the style attribute.

1. Type the opening tag (except for its closing angle bracket) and enter the style attribute, an equal sign, and double quotation marks:

   ```
   <p style="
   ```

2. Type the name of the first property that you want to set for the element, a colon, and the value for that property:

   ```
   <p style="line-height:3
   ```

3. If you want to set a second property for the element, type a semicolon, a space, the name of the property, a colon, and the value for that property:

   ```
   <p style="line-height:3; text-align:center
   ```

4. If you want to set a third property for the element, repeat step 3.

5. When you've set all the properties for the element, type the closing angle bracket, the text for the element, and then the closing tag:

   ```
   <p style="line-height:3;text-align:center">Choose from our
   selection of powerful mailing lists&#8212;and customize the
   list to suit your mailing's needs.</p>
   ```

6. Save the page, switch to your browser, and view the effect.

## CREATE A FIRST-LINE INDENT

To apply a first-line indent to a paragraph, use the text-indent property and specify the indent as a number of pixels or as a percentage. For example, to apply a first-line indent of 10 percent to the paragraph:

```
<p style="text-indent:10%">This paragraph is indented 10
percent.</p>
```

Document Management

~~Filing and Assessment~~

Scanning and Shredding

## CHANGE LINE SPACING

To change the line spacing of a paragraph, use the line-height property and specify the spacing as 1 (single spacing), 1.5 (one-and-a-half line spacing), 2 (double spacing), or a higher number. For example, to apply double spacing to the paragraph:

```
<p style="line-height:2">Our one-hundred square meter
(100m<sup>2</sup>) conference room can easily accommodate full
<font>board</font> meetings.</p>
```

## CHANGE THE CAPITALIZATION OF TEXT

To change the capitalization of the text in an element, use the text-transform property and specify the case you want.

- uppercase capitalizes every letter in the text.
- lowercase lowercases every letter in the text.
- capitalize applies initial capitals to the text. HTML changes the first letter in every word to a capital but doesn't change the case of other letters in the words.

For example, to apply initial capitals to the text:

```
<h1 style="text-transform:uppercase">Return on Investment</h1>
```

## APPLY UNDERLINING, OVERLINING, OR STRIKETHROUGH

As discussed earlier in this chapter, you can apply underlining to individual words using the <u> and </u> tags, and you can apply strikethrough using either the <strike> and </strike> or <s> and </s> tags. To affect an entire paragraph, you can use the text-decoration property of the style attribute with the underline value (for an underline) or the line-through value (for strikethrough). You can also use the text-decoration property to apply *overlining*—a line above the text—by using the overline value.

For example, to apply underline to the first paragraph, strikethrough to the second paragraph, and overline to the third paragraph:

```
<p style="text-decoration: underline">Document Management</p>
<p style="text-decoration: line-through">Filing and Assessment</p>
<p style="text-decoration: overline">Scanning and Shredding</p>
```

### MAKE TEXT BLINK ON BROWSERS OTHER THAN INTERNET EXPLORER AND SAFARI

To make a text element blink on and off, use the text-decoration property of the style attribute with the blink value—for example:

```
<h2 style="text-decoration:blink">Don't Miss This Offer!</h2>
```

### CHANGE FONT FORMATTING

To set font formatting on an element, you can use the style attribute's properties shown in Table 3-3.

For example, to apply bold, blue, extra-large Comic Sans MS font to the text:

```
<p style="font-family:Comic Sans MS; font-size:x-large; font-weight:bold; color:blue">Modular and Functional Services</p>
```

### APPLY A BACKGROUND COLOR TO AN ELEMENT

To apply a background color to an element, use the background-color property of the style attribute, and specify the color either by name or its hex code.

| PROPERTY | CONTROLS | VALUES |
|---|---|---|
| font-family | The font displayed | A specific font name—for example, Arial |
| font-size | The font size | Either an absolute size (xx-small, x-small, small, medium, large, x-large, or xx-large) or a relative size (smaller or larger) |
| font-style | The font style—normal, italic, or oblique | normal, italic, or oblique. oblique works only if the font includes oblique characters; otherwise, oblique produces slanted text that gives an italic effect |
| font-variant | Whether the font is normal or small caps | normal or small-caps |
| font-weight | How bold the font is | normal, lighter, bold, bolder, 100, 200, 300, 400, 500, 600, 700, 800, or 900 |
| color | The color of the font | A specific color name or hex code |

*Table 3-3: Font Properties for the style Attribute*

## CATCH THE EYE WITH MOVING TEXT

Here's a feature that's popular even though it works only on some browsers and is officially frowned upon: moving text. Internet Explorer and Safari support this feature, but Firefox does not.

To add moving text to a web page, use the <marquee> tag. Moving text can help draw the viewer's eye to important information, such as an advertisement or the latest headline. Quite apart from not working in every browser, moving text can be distracting to viewers, so use it with care.

The <marquee> tag uses the following attributes:

- behavior can be scroll, alternate, or slide. scroll is the default and makes the text scroll in the direction specified by direction. alternate makes the text scroll in alternating directions. slide makes the text appear from the direction specified by direction and stop when it reaches the opposite margin.

- direction can be left (the default), right, up, or down. Scrolling left is the most common usage. Scrolling up or down can be effective but takes up more space.

- bgcolor specifies the background color for the marquee. bgcolor can be any valid color—either a color name (such as red) or a hexadecimal code (such as #FFFF00).

- loop specifies how many times the marquee repeats the scrolling. The default setting is to loop endlessly, which you can also specify explicitly using the value infinite.

*Continued . . .*

---

### Save Time by Outsourcing the Effort

We provide a full set of services to meet every business need.

*Figure 3-4: **To make text stand out, you can apply a background color that contrasts with the text color.***

For example, the following code applies a different background color to a division to make the heading and paragraph text stand out (see Figure 3-4):

```
<div style="background-color:turquoise">
<br/>
<h1 style="color:blue" align="center">Save Time by Outsourcing
the Effort</h1>
<p align="center" style="color:navy; font-family:serif; font-
weight:bold; font-size:large">We provide a full set of services
to meet every business need.</p>
<br/>
</div>
```

### APPLY BORDERS

To apply borders to an element, you can use the style properties shown in Table 3-4.

For example, to use most of the border settings and many of the other properties of the style attribute discussed in this section to create the box shown in the illustration:

```
<p style="border-style:solid; border-color:black; border-width:
thick; width:200px; height:100px; padding-top:10px; padding-
left:10px; padding-right:10px; background-color:gray; color:
white; padding-left:30px; padding-right:20px; padding-top: 20px;
font-weight:bold">Use our personalized services to slash costs
and turbo-charge your business performance.</p>
```

Use our personalized services to slash costs and turbo-charge your business performance.

## CATCH THE EYE WITH MOVING TEXT (Continued)

For example, to create a marquee with a cyan (light blue) background:

1. Type the opening <marquee> tag:

   ```
   <marquee>
   ```

2. Before the closing angle bracket, type the behavior attribute and specify scroll, alternate, or slide, as appropriate—for example:

   ```
   <marquee behavior="scroll">
   ```

3. Type the direction attribute and specify left, right, up, or down, as appropriate—for example:

   ```
   <marquee behavior="scroll"
   direction="left">
   ```

4. Type the bgcolor attribute and specify the color you want to use—for example:

   ```
   <marquee behavior="scroll"
   direction="left" bgcolor="cyan">
   ```

5. Type the loop attribute and specify either the number of loops or the value infinite—for example:

   ```
   <marquee behavior="scroll"
   direction="left" bgcolor="cyan"
   loop="2">
   ```

6. On the next line, type the text you want the marquee to display—for example:

   ```
   April Special: Get an extra week of
   service free!
   ```

7. Type the closing </marquee> tag:

   ```
   </marquee>
   ```

8. Save the file, switch to your web browser, and refresh the page to see the effect.

| PROPERTY | CONTROLS | VALUES |
|---|---|---|
| border-style | Whether the border is hidden or appears as a single line or a double line | none (for no border), solid, dotted, dashed, or double |
| border-color | The border color | A specific color name or hex code |
| border-width | The border width | undefined, a number of pixels (for example, 10px), thin, or thick |
| border-top-width | The width of the top border | medium, a number of pixels, thin, or thick |
| border-bottom-width | The width of the bottom border | medium, a number of pixels, thin, or thick |
| border-left-width | The width of the left border | medium, a number of pixels, thin, or thick |
| border-right-width | The width of the right border | medium, a number of pixels, thin, or thick |
| margin-top | The width of the top margin (from the border to the element above it) | A number of pixels |
| margin-bottom | The width of the bottom margin | A number of pixels |
| margin-left | The width of the left margin | A number of pixels |
| margin-right | The width of the right margin | A number of pixels |
| padding-top | The amount of padding from the top edge to the top of the contents | A number of pixels |
| padding-bottom | The amount of padding from the bottom edge | A number of pixels |
| padding-left | The amount of padding from the left edge | A number of pixels |
| padding-right | The amount of padding from the right edge | A number of pixels |

Table 3-4: Border Properties for the style Attribute

### HIDE AN ELEMENT

To hide an element, set the visibility property of the style attribute to hidden; to display the element, set the visibility property to visible (or remove the visibility property).

## How to...

- *Creating or Acquiring Graphics Files*
- *Insert a Graphic*
- *Use Suitable Alternative Text*
- *Choose Where to Locate the Graphics File*
- *Add a Long Description URL*
- *Align a Graphic*
- *Change the Size of a Graphic*
- *Using Graphics to Control How Text Appears*
- *Apply Borders to a Graphic*
- *Add a Title to a Graphic*
- *Position a Graphic with Spacers*
- *Understanding GIF, JPEG, and PNG*
- *Laying Out Your Web Pages*
- *Create an HTML Signature File*
- *Use an HTML Signature File in Windows Mail*
- *Keeping Down Graphic Size to Make Pages Load Faster*

# Chapter 4

# Adding Graphics to Your Web Pages

Much of the Web's popularity is due to its ability to present graphical content rather than only text, and even a few well-placed graphics can make a huge difference in the look of a web page. Graphics of any size increase the time it takes to download a page, however, so you should use them with care to avoid making your pages awkward to access.

This chapter shows you how to insert graphics in your web pages and control how they appear. You can place graphics either with the text and other elements in the foreground of a web page or in the background behind the text and other elements. You'll also learn to add horizontal rules to your pages, and how to create and use an e-mail signature containing a graphic.

## CREATING OR ACQUIRING GRAPHICS FILES

Before you can add graphics to your web pages, you'll need to create or acquire the files. If you're creating the web pages for a company, the company may supply suitable files. Otherwise, the following are the main ways of creating and acquiring graphics:

- **Create graphics from scratch on your computer** Windows includes the Paint applet (choose Start I All Programs I Accessories I Paint), but it is painfully limited, and you will normally do better with a more powerful tool. Start by looking at The Gnu Image Manipulation Program, known as GIMP, which you can download for free from www. gimp.org. For a paid program, consider Paint Shop Pro (Windows), Photoshop Elements (Windows and Mac), or Photoshop (Windows and Mac).

- **Create graphics from scratch online** If you need to create only a few graphics, try an online image editor such as pixlr (www.pixlr.com).

- **Download pictures from your digital camera** A digital camera is great for getting photos of your products or other items you're selling. Connect your digital camera or its memory card to your computer via Universal Serial Bus (USB). On Windows, import your digital photos into Windows Photo Gallery; on Mac OS X, import them into iPhoto.

- **Scan graphics from documents or pictures** Use a scanner to create graphics of hard-copy documents or pictures of flat objects that are difficult to photograph with a camera, such as slides or jewelry. If your scanner did not include custom software, use Windows Fax and Scan (on Windows Vista) or Image Capture (on Mac OS X) to perform the scan.

*Continued . . .*

# Add an Inline Graphic

An *inline* graphic is one that appears in the same layer of a web page as the text—in other words, not in the background. You can control the size of graphics, specify alignment and alternative text, and apply borders, as needed.

## Insert a Graphic

To insert a graphic, you use an <img/> tag. This is a self-closing tag, so it requires the forward slash (/) before the closing angle bracket.

You must always use the src attribute to specify the source of the graphic and the alt attribute to specify alternative text—for example:

```
<img src="brainstorm.jpg" alt="Brainstorming session"/>
```

The alternative text explains what the graphic is for any browser that has graphics turned off (as shown on the left in Figure 4-1), for a text-only browser, or for someone using a screen reader. Under normal circumstances, the graphic appears and the alternative text does not (as shown on the right in Figure 4-1).

## Use Suitable Alternative Text

Because the alternative text is used not only by humans but also by screen readers, it's important to make it suitable. Follow these guidelines to try to balance the needs of screen readers with the needs of humans who have turned off the display of graphics:

- **Illustrative picture** Type a short description so that visitors will know what they're missing. There's no hard-and-fast length limit, but if you need to use more than 150 characters to describe the picture, use the longdesc attribute to provide the URL of a page that gives a detailed description.

- **Decorative picture** Use alt="" (an empty string in double quotation marks). This tells the screen reader to ignore the picture. If you use text that describes the picture, the screen reader will speak the text.

- **Bullet picture** Use alt="*" so that the visitor sees an asterisk.

- **Horizontal-line picture** Use alt="------" so that the visitor sees a horizontal line of dashes.

## CREATING OR ACQUIRING GRAPHICS FILES *(Continued)*

- **Find clip-art graphics that are free to use** Office suites such as Microsoft Office include clip art graphics that you can use freely. You can also find free clip art online. For specific needs, you may be able to get permission to reuse other people's copyrighted graphics on your website.

- **Buy the rights to use professional stock photos** Stock photography agencies license photos for use, acting for the photographer. For low-cost images, start your search at "microstock" photography sites—sites that offer stock photos for modest fees—such as Shutterstock (www.shutterstock.com) or iStockphoto (www.istockphoto.com).

## CAUTION

Never use someone else's copyrighted content—be it text, image, audio, or video—without specific permission. Unless an item is in the public domain, either because its copyright term has expired or because the copyright holder has specifically put the item in the public domain, unauthorized reuse is a violation of copyright law. For example, it's seldom legal to scan a picture and use it on your website, borrow a graphic from another website, or rip a song from a CD and use it as background audio on your website. Always verify that an item is in the public domain or get permission (and pay if necessary) before using it.

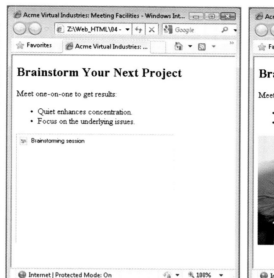
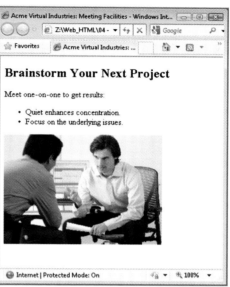

*Figure 4-1: Alternative text appears in placeholders when graphics are turned off.*

# Choose Where to Locate the Graphics File

The graphics file you add can be located either on the same computer as the web page or on another computer.

- **Graphics file on the same computer** Use either an absolute path (one that shows each folder from the web root—for example, src="/site/images/thoughtshower.jpg") or a relative path (one that shows only the folders needed to reach the file from the current file—for example, src="webimages/brainstorm.jpg"). If the graphics file is in the same folder as the web page, you need supply only the filename.

- **Graphics file on another computer** Specify the full URL of the graphics file—for example, http://www.acmevirtualindustries.com/graphics/brainstorm.jpg. Bear in mind that the file will have to be transferred from the server you specify and that this server may respond more slowly than the main server you're using. If this happens, the visitor won't see the graphic on the web page at first, although they may see a placeholder.

Top-class brainstorming facilities

**Figure 4-2: Use the** *align* **attribute to specify the horizontal or vertical alignment of a graphic.**

| ALIGN VALUE | ALIGNS THE GRAPHIC |
|---|---|
| top | With the top of the object |
| middle | With the vertical middle of the object |
| bottom | With the bottom of the object |
| left | To the left of the object |
| right | To the right of the object |

**Table 4-1: Values for the** *align* **Attribute**

## Add a Long Description URL

When you need to provide a detailed description of a graphic, put that description on a separate web page (preferably with the picture there as well) and add the longdesc attribute to the <img/> tag pointing to that page's URL. Here's an example:

```
<img src="brainstorm.jpg" alt="Brainstorming session"
longdesc="photo_details.html"/>
```

## Align a Graphic

By default, most browsers align a graphic vertically with the baseline of any text or object on the same line. Figure 4-2 shows an example. The bottom of the graphic is aligned with the base of the text.

The quick-and-dirty way to control horizontal and vertical alignment is by using the align attribute (see Table 4-1). This approach still works as of this writing, but it has been deprecated in favor of using CSS (see Chapter 8).

The following example aligns the graphic to the left of the text. To ensure that this works, place the <img> tag before the text to whose left it should appear:

```
<img src="brainstorm.jpg" alt="Brainstorming session" align="left"/>
```

## Change the Size of a Graphic

When you use an <img/> tag without specifying the height or width of the graphic, the browser displays the graphic at its full size. This size might be too large or too small in the browser window, depending on the window's size and the screen resolution.

To control the size at which the browser displays the graphic, use the height attribute and the width attribute of the <img/> tag. Usually, you'll want to specify the exact number of pixels for these attributes, but you can also specify the percentage of the browser window that the graphic should occupy. The problem with specifying the percentage is that the graphic may be distorted, depending on the proportions of the browser window—and if the user resizes the window, the graphic's proportions may change, too.

The following example sets the height of the graphic to 220 pixels and its width to 325 pixels:

```
<img src="brainstorm.jpg" alt="Brainstorming session"
height="220" width="325">
```

The next example displays the graphic at 40 percent of the height of the browser window and 90 percent of its width. Figure 4-3 shows how the graphic becomes distorted when the Safari window is resized: In the left image, the graphic's proportions are correct, while in the right image, it is stretched horizontally. Some browsers (including Internet Explorer and Firefox) detect the problem and resize the graphic proportionally, ignoring the measurement that is out of kilter.

```
<img src="brainstorm.jpg" alt="Brainstorming session"
height="40%" width="90%">
```

*Figure 4-3: Using percentages to specify the height and width of a graphic can cause it to become distorted.*

**Figure 4-4: Apply borders to your graphics when you want to separate them further from the rest of the page.**

## Apply Borders to a Graphic

To apply borders to a graphic, add the border attribute to the `<img/>` tag, and specify the appropriate properties. (See Chapter 3 for a list of border properties.) The following example uses an inline style to apply a thin black border to the picture, as shown in Figure 4-4:

```
<img src="brainstorm.jpg" alt="Brainstorming session"
height="300px" style="border-style:solid; border-color:black;
border-width:thin"/>
```

## Add a Title to a Graphic

In addition to alternative text (which you supply with the alt attribute), you can add a title to a graphic by using the title attribute. The title is text that appears as a ScreenTip when a visitor hovers the mouse pointer over the graphic for a couple of seconds. Bear in mind that most visitors will not hover the mouse pointer over a graphic like this unless you encourage them to do so, so they may well not see the title.

Figure 4-5 shows an example of a title added to a graphic by the following HTML:

```
<img src="checklist.jpg" alt="Check list with one box checked"
title="Track your progress by making a list of commitments and
marking each one completed." width="400" style="border-style:
solid; border-color:black; border-width:thin"/>
```

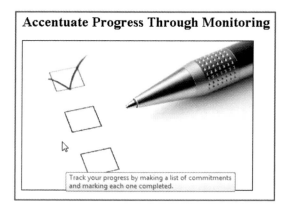

**Figure 4-5: You can use the title attribute to display a ScreenTip for any visitor who hovers the mouse pointer over a graphic.**

## Position a Graphic with Spacers

As discussed in Chapter 3, HTML enables you to specify the relative alignment of paragraphs and other items. If you need to align items precisely, however, you must either use styles (as discussed in Chapter 8) or work around the problem. One rough-and-ready but widely used solution is to use *spacer images*—images that take up a certain amount of space, but that don't display their physical presence on the web page because they're either transparent or the same color as the background.

To use a spacer image:

**1.** Use a graphics program such as Paint or GIMP to create a small graphic—just a few pixels (or even one pixel) in each direction.

**2.** Type an <img src= /> tag that specifies the location of the graphic you want to use as a spacer and a blank alt attribute to tell screen readers to ignore it. Here's an example:

```
<img src="images/spacer1.jpg" alt="" />
```

**3.** Use the width attribute and the height attribute to specify the size at which you want the spacer graphic to be displayed—for example:

```
width="50" height="80"
```

**4.** If the spacer graphic isn't transparent, use the border attribute to set the border to a zero width:

```
border="0"
```

**5.** Place the graphic you want to indent after the spacer graphic by using the <img> tag as usual—for example:

```
<img src="checklist.jpg" alt="Check list with one box checked"
width="400" style="border-style:solid; border-color:black;
border-width:thin"/>
```

**6.** Save the web page, switch to your browser, and refresh the display so that you can see the effect of using the spacer graphic.

Figure 4-6 shows an indent produced by using the spacer graphic specified in the following code:

```
<h2>Accentuate Your Progress Through Monitoring</h2>
<img src="spacer1.jpg" width="50" height="80" alt="" />
<img src="checklist.jpg" alt="Check list with one box checked"
width="400" style="border-style:solid; border-color:black; border-
width:thin"/>
<p>Marking down each completed task helps you focus on your remaining
tasks and gain confidence from what you have achieved.</p>
```

> **NOTE**
>
> The spacer graphic can be a much smaller size than the amount of space that you need it to occupy because you can use the width attribute and height attribute of the <img> tag to make it occupy more space.

**Accentuate Your Progress Through Monitoring**

Marking down each completed task helps you focus on your remaining tasks and gain confidence from what you have achieved.

*Figure 4-6: You can use an invisible graphic to indent an element, such as a graphic, as in the example here.*

## UNDERSTANDING GIF, JPEG, AND PNG

Most images used in web pages are in one of the three main graphics formats that the majority of browsers support: PNG, JPEG, or GIF.

### LOSSY AND LOSSLESS COMPRESSION

All three formats use compression to reduce the size of the image file so that it will download faster. There are two main types of compression.

- *Lossless compression* doesn't discard any of the information required to display the graphic, so graphics compressed with lossless compression are as high in quality as the original, uncompressed file.

- Lossy *compression* discards some of the information required to display the graphic, so graphics compressed with lossy compression are lower in quality than the original file.

### PNG

PNG (Portable Network Graphics) is a graphics format developed for Internet usage. It uses lossless compression to create a high-quality picture with as small a file size as possible. PNG doesn't offer different compression levels, but it lets you make parts of the graphic transparent so that the background shows through.

PNG is a good choice for web graphics and is supported by all current browsers. Some older versions of browsers don't support PNG, but most people have now stopped using these versions.

*Continued . . .*

**Figure 4-7: You can use a JPEG, GIF, or PNG file as a background graphic for a web page. Choose a contrasting text color to make sure that the text is legible.**

# Add a Background Graphic

Instead of placing a graphic inline with the text, you may want to use it to form the background of a web page. A background graphic can make your web pages much more colorful and dramatic, but you must make sure that the graphic neither obscures the text of the page nor clashes with any graphics you place inline. In practice, this means that the background image should provide a considerable contrast with the content of the page. For example, you might use a subtle, light-toned image in your background that does not obscure black text.

To add a background image, add the background attribute to the <body> tag, and specify the filename (and, if needed, the path) in double quotation marks. The following example (shown in Figure 4-7) uses the file named fieldwork.jpg in the images folder:

```
<body background="images/fieldwork.jpg">
```

## UNDERSTANDING GIF, JPEG, AND PNG (Continued)

**JPEG**

JPEG (Joint Photographic Experts Group) is a graphics format widely used on the Web. JPEG uses lossy compression and is supported by all browsers. It offers different levels of compression, allowing you to choose a suitable quality of picture. JPEG does not let you make parts of the graphic transparent.

Use JPEG when you want to make sure that all browsers can view the graphics on your web pages. (If a visitor has turned off the display of graphics in the browser, however, he or she will not see the graphics.)

For best performance, use *progressive* JPEGs; JPEG files created so that they can display a rough version of the graphic while downloading the rest of it. When a browser requests a progressive JPEG, the web server first supplies every eighth line of the JPEG so that a rough version can be displayed and then fills in the missing lines gradually. The result is that the visitor can get an idea of what the graphic looks like without waiting for the whole graphic to download.

**GIF**

GIF (Graphics Interchange Format) is a standard graphics format that has been widely used on the Web for many years. GIF uses lossless compression and maps the colors in a graphic to 256 colors and uses dithering to represent colors not included in those 256. It also lets you make parts of the graphic transparent. *Interlaced GIFs* work in the same way as progressive JPEGs, enabling the visitor to see a rough version of the graphic while the rest is being downloaded.

For line art, GIF provides a good balance of picture quality with file size. Avoid using GIF for photos, however, because they'll suffer.

# Add a Horizontal Rule

To divide a web page into different horizontal areas, add one or more horizontal rules by using the <hr /> tag. Used on its own, this tag creates a horizontal rule of the default color (black) and default width that is left-aligned and that spans the whole browser window.

The preferred way of formatting a horizontal rule is by using CSS (see Chapter 8), but you can also format a horizontal rule by setting the four attributes listed in Table 4-2.

The following example includes a plain horizontal rule (shown at the top of Figure 4-8) and a thicker, centered horizontal rule with the noshade attribute applied (shown at the bottom of the figure):

```
<p>Virtual office space can save you time, effort, and hard
cash.</p>
<hr/>
<h2>Industry-Leading Physical Office Space</h2>
<p>When you do need to meet your clients in person, take
advantage of our spacious meeting rooms.</p>
<img src="conference_room.jpg" alt="Berlin office" width="550" />
<p><em>Berlin, Germany</em></p>
<hr align="center" width="350" size="5px" noshade/>
<img src="office_view.jpg" alt="Paris office" width="550" />
```

| ATTRIBUTE | VALUE |
|-----------|-------|
| align | left, center, right |
| size | The thickness of the rule in pixels |
| width | The length of the rule in pixels; if you omit width, the rule runs all the way across the window |
| noshade | No value; if included, it prevents the rule from having a 3-D effect |

*Table 4-2: Attributes for the <hr> Tag*

Virtual office space can save you time, effort, and hard cash.

## Industry-Leading Physical Office Space

When you do need to meet your clients in person, take advantage of our spacious meeting rooms.

*Berlin, Germany*

**Figure 4-8: Use horizontal rules to break up a page into different areas. You can specify the alignment, length, and thickness of the rule for effect.**

**TIP**

Normally, when you put a background graphic in a web page, that image moves when the user scrolls through the web page. If you want the image to stay in place when the user scrolls so that it is always in the same position in the browser window and the text and other content scrolls over it, add bgproperties="fixed" to the <body> tag. This effect can be useful, but you must make sure that the page's content will be visible no matter which part of the background image it is displayed over.

**TIP**

HTML doesn't have a tag for a vertical line, but you can apply vertical lines by using a table. See Chapter 6.

# Create an E-mail Signature Containing a Graphic

A *signature* is an item that most e-mail applications can automatically insert at the end of each outgoing message, if you choose to include it. A signature normally consists of text that identifies the sender—for example, by supplying the sender's full name, position and company (if applicable), physical address, phone numbers, and other relevant information, such as the URL of the sender's website. Many signatures also include a short quote for the recipient's enjoyment, edification, or annoyance.

## LAYING OUT YOUR WEB PAGES

As discussed in Chapter 2, people trying to view your web pages may be using any of a variety of browsers and operating systems, page sizes, and connections.

Keep your web pages small so that they can be viewed in small windows if necessary. Even so, the only area of a page that you can be certain will be visible is the upper-left corner—so this is where you should put all the vital information on the page. This crucial area is sometimes called "above the fold," a term taken from newspaper publishing—when the newspaper is folded, the most important information must be visible.

On most pages, the most important information is the site's name (and perhaps logo) and description, and primary means of navigation (perhaps including a Search tool), the page's name or description, and contact information. If your site carries advertising, above the fold is prime screen real estate, and you should charge accordingly.

You should probably also put a brief version of the site's name and the page's content in the page's title (using the <title> tag).

You can also add a graphic to your signature by creating a suitable page using HTML. This example shows you how to create a graphical signature and then apply it in Windows Mail, the e-mail application included with Windows Vista and Windows 7. Windows Mail is the successor to Outlook Express, which came with Windows XP and earlier versions, and works in much the same way—so you can use this technique with Outlook Express as well.

# Create an HTML Signature File

To create an HTML signature file:

1. In your text editor (for example, Notepad), create an HTML file that contains the information you want. An example including a graphic follows.

```
<?xml version="1.0" encoding="utf-8"?>
<!DOCTYPE html PUBLIC "-//W3C//DTD XHTML 1.0 Transitional//EN"
        "http://www.w3.org/TR/xhtml1/DTD/xhtml1-transitional.
dtd">
<html xmlns="http://www.w3.org/1999/xhtml" xml:lang="en"
lang="en">
<head>
    <meta http-equiv="content-type" content="text/html;
charset=utf-8" />
    <title></title>
</head>
<body>
<p>Anna Connor<br/>Account Executive</p>
<br/>
<img src="http://www.acmevirtualindustries.com/webimages/acme.
png" alt="Acme logo" height="180" align="left"/>
<h3> Acme Virtual Industries</h3>
<p> Website: <a href="http://www.acmevirtualindustries.com">
<tt>http://www.acmevirtualindustries.com</tt></a></p>
<p> E-mail: <a href="mailto:anna_connor@acmevirtualindustries.
com">
<tt>anna_connor@acmevirtualindustries.com</tt></a></p>
<p> Office: 510-555-1298<br/>
Mobile: 408-555-9823</p>
</body>
</html>
```

2. Make sure the file is correctly formed, with the DOCTYPE, a starting <html> tag, a header section, a body section, and a closing </html> tag.

3. Create an <img/> tag, add the src attribute, and specify the full path and filename of the graphics file. Add the alt attribute and alternative text. If necessary, use the height and width attributes to size the graphic.

4. Save the file and view it in your browser to make sure it looks the way you want. Figure 4-9 shows the example signature. Make any necessary adjustments and save the file again.

*Figure 4-9: You can add graphics to an e-mail signature.*

## Use an HTML Signature File in Windows Mail

To use an HTML signature file in Windows Mail:

1. If Windows Mail isn't already running, start it: Click the **Start** button, click **All Programs**, and then click **Windows Mail**.

2. Click the **Tools** menu and then click **Options**. The Options dialog box appears. Click the **Signatures** tab (shown in Figure 4-10 with a signature applied).

3. Click **New**, click the **File** option button, and then click **Browse**. The Open dialog box appears. Select **HTML Files** in the Files Of Type drop-down list, select the signature file, and then click **Open**. Windows Mail closes the Open dialog box and enters the path and filename on the Signatures tab.

## KEEPING DOWN GRAPHIC SIZE TO MAKE PAGES LOAD FASTER

Unless you know that all visitors to your website will be accessing it across a high-speed connection (for example, a corporate intranet), you should keep the size of your web pages small so that they load quickly across even a slow connection. In many cases, the key factor determining how quickly a page loads is how many graphics it contains and how large the file size of those graphics is.

To make your pages load faster:

- Reduce the number of graphics you use in your pages. Look at the web pages you visit most frequently, and analyze their use of graphics. Some major sites, such as Google (www.google.com), use very few graphics indeed—and so load quickly even over dial-up connections.

- Reduce each graphic to the size at which it will be displayed, rather than using a larger graphic and displaying it at a smaller size.

- Reduce the number of colors used in your graphics. (If you use GIFs, you're automatically reducing the number of colors to 256 or fewer.)

- Compress each graphic by using a compressed file format (GIF, JPEG, or PNG). If you use JPEG, choose a degree of compression that provides adequate image quality with as small a file size as possible.

- Reuse graphics where possible so that the browser needs to download them only once. For example, use the same logo on each page rather than using variations of the logo.

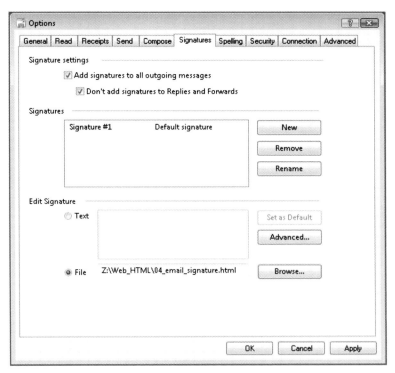

Figure 4-10: *Define a signature on the Signatures tab of the Options dialog box in Windows Mail.*

4. Select the **Add Signatures To All Outgoing Messages** check box if you want Windows Mail to add your signature automatically to all messages you send. Ensure that the **Don't Add Signatures To Replies And Forwards** check box is selected so that replies and forwarded messages you send do not receive a signature.

5. Click **OK**.

When you create a new message, Windows Mail automatically inserts the signature if you selected the **Add Signatures To All Outgoing Messages** check box. Otherwise, you can insert the signature manually when needed by clicking the **Insert** menu and then clicking **Signature**.

## How to...

- *Understanding Absolute and Relative Links*
- *Link to Another Web Page*
- *Link Within a Web Page*
- *Link to a Particular Point on a Web Page*
- *Making Your Site Navigable*
- *Open a Link in a New Window*
- *Create a Link to Download a File*
- *Display a ScreenTip for a Link*
- *Create Links to Send E-mail*
- *Making Your Imagemaps Useful and Intelligible*
- *Create Two or More Links in a Graphic*
- *Understand Audio and Video Formats*
- *Understand Audio and Video Delivery Methods*
- *Create a Link for Downloading an Audio or Video File*
- *Create a Link to Play an Audio or Video File*
- *Embedding a Video File in a Web Page*

# Chapter 5

# Adding Links

*Hyperlinks*—links that connect one web page to other pages—are the key to the Web. This chapter shows you how to create links to other web pages and links to different locations on the same web page. You'll also learn how to create links that start e-mail messages for a specified address, links that use graphics rather than text, and links that download or play audio or video files.

## Create Links

Most links on the Web go to other web pages, but others go to a different point on the same web page. You can also create links that take whoever clicks them directly to a specific point on another web page.

## UNDERSTANDING ABSOLUTE AND RELATIVE LINKS

You can use either absolute links or relative links in your web pages.

### ABSOLUTE LINKS

An *absolute link* is a link that includes the full address of the destination to which it links. The full address can be either a complete URL (for example, http://www. acmevirtualindustries.com/services/index.html) for a page on the Web or a complete file path (for example, \\acmeserver44\services\index.html) on a web server on your local network.

Complete URLs to websites must always include the appropriate prefix, which tells the browser which protocol to use. When linking to a website, you'll almost always use http:// to designate the HTTP protocol. Most browsers automatically supply this prefix if you omit the prefix when browsing, but you must include it in your absolute links. That way, the browser knows that it shouldn't try the HTTPS protocol (for secure sites) or the FTP protocol (for file transfer) instead.

### RELATIVE LINKS

A *relative link* is a link that supplies just that part of the address needed to access the destination from the current page. For example, if the destination page is in the same folder as the current page, only the name of the destination page is needed—for example, href="index.html" to access the page named index.html in the current folder.

If the destination file is in a subfolder of the folder that contains the current page, specify the folder name, a forward slash, and the filename. For example, href="products/index.html" refers to the page named index.html in the subfolder named products contained in the same folder as the current page.

*Continued . . .*

# Link to Another Web Page

A link consists of an anchor element that controls how the link appears on its web page and the URL of the destination to which the link leads. The anchor element can be text, a graphic, or a graphical element. For example, many links appear as underlined text so that when the visitor clicks the text, the browser displays the page specified by the URL in the link. Other links appear as graphics that the visitor can click, or as buttons.

## CREATE A TEXT LINK

To create a text link:

1. Position the insertion point in the element in which you want to create the link. For example, if you want to create the text link in a paragraph, create the paragraph and type any preliminary text.

2. Type the beginning of the anchor tag for the link:

   ```
   <a
   ```

3. Type the href attribute, an equal sign, the destination URL (within double quotation marks), and the closing angle bracket—for example:

   ```
   href="http://www.acmevirtualindustries.com/contact_us.html">
   ```

4. Type the text that you want to have displayed as the anchor for the hyperlink—for example:

   ```
   click here to contact us
   ```

5. Type the closing </a> tag for the anchor:

   ```
   </a>
   ```

The next example contains the entire link in a paragraph:

```
<p>If you have any questions about our services, <a href="http://
www.acmevirtualindustries.com/contact_us.html">click here to
contact us</a>.</p>
```

## CREATE A GRAPHIC LINK

To create a graphic link:

1. Position the insertion point where you want to place the graphic between other HTML elements.

## UNDERSTANDING ABSOLUTE AND RELATIVE LINKS (Continued)

If the destination file is in a different part of the folder structure, enter two periods and a forward slash before the filename to instruct the browser to move up one level before traversing to the folder you specify. For example, href="../webs/content/index.html" causes the browser to move up one level, switch to the folder called webs, switch to the subfolder called content, and then open the file named index.html. To go up more than one level, use ../ as many times as necessary. For example, to go up two levels, use ../../.

When creating the pages on your local computer, make sure that you don't include any drive letters (for example, C: or D:) or any backslashes (\) in your relative links. Neither will work after you transfer your website to the web host.

### WHEN TO USE ABSOLUTE AND RELATIVE LINKS

Relative links continue to work even if you move your entire website from one location to another. For example, if you create your website on your local computer and then transfer it to your web host, the links will continue to work. By contrast, if you use absolute links on your local computer, you will need to change all of the links to the correct URLs when you transfer your site to your web host.

Typically, you'll want to use relative links when linking to pages within your own website. When linking to other websites, use absolute URLs.

### NOTE

The anchor element (<a>) is an inline element that should always appear within a block element such as a paragraph. Many browsers can handle anchor elements that appear outside block elements, but other browsers have problems displaying them properly.

2. Type the opening anchor tag, including the href attribute and the target address—for example:

```
<a href="http://www.acmevirtualindustries.com/services/
meetings.html">
```

3. Type the <img/> tag, including the src attribute and the graphic name (and, if needed, the file path)—for example:

```
<img src="conference_room.jpg"/>
```

4. Type the closing anchor tag:

```
</a>
```

The complete tag looks like this:

```
<p><a href="http://www.acmevirtualindustries.com/services/
meetings.html"><img src="conference_room.jpg" alt="Conference
room" width="500"/></a></p>
```

When the user hovers the mouse pointer over the graphic, the pointer changes to a hand with a pointing finger to indicate the hyperlink and the status bar displays the destination of the link (see Figure 5-1).

http://www.acmevirtualindustries.com/services/meetings.html

*Figure 5-1: **By default, HTML displays a blue border around a linked graphic to indicate that it is a hyperlink. Specify a zero-width border if you want to remove the blue border.***

HTML displays a blue border around a linked graphic to draw the viewer's attention to the hyperlink. To prevent this border from being displayed, include the border attribute in the <img/> tag and set it to zero:

```
<p><a href="http://www.acmevirtualindustries.com/services/
meetings.html"><img src="conference_room.jpg" alt="Conference
room" width="500" style="border: none"/></a></p>
```

## Link Within a Web Page

Instead of linking to a different web page, you can link to a different place on the same page by placing a named anchor at that point. This technique is useful for long pages that might otherwise be awkward for visitors to navigate, such as FAQ pages. By providing at the top of the page a table of contents whose entries are linked to the relevant parts of the page, you can enable visitors to access those parts quickly. By also providing links from all regions of the page back to the top of the page, you can enable visitors to return to the table of contents easily.

To create a link within a web page:

1. Insert an anchor at the point within the page to which you want to be able to link. Type an anchor tag (<a>) and use the name attribute to specify the name for the anchor—for example:

   ```
   <a name="Question_01"></a>
   ```

2. Create a link to the anchor you just inserted. Type an anchor tag (<a>) and use the href attribute to refer to the anchor, putting a hash symbol (#) before the name—for example:

   ```
   <a href="#Question_01">What are the benefits of virtual office
   space?</a>
   ```

3. Save the file, switch to your browser, and test the link.

4. Add further anchors and links to the page as necessary. For example, insert an anchor named Top at the top of the page, and then insert links farther down the page to this anchor so that visitors can quickly return to the top of the page:

   ```
   <p>Return to the <a href="#Top">top</a> of the page.</p>
   ```

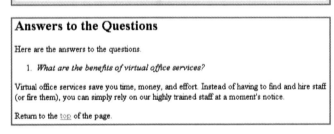

**Figure 5-2:** *Create links within long web pages to enable the user to move easily about the page. Include links back to the top of the page.*

The following code shows the beginning of a page that uses internal links for navigation between a list of questions at the top and answers to the questions farther down the page (see Figure 5-2). Note the anchor named Top in the first-level heading at the top of the page and the links to the anchors (#Question_01 through Question_08) farther down the page.

```
<body>
<a href="index.html" target="_blank" accesskey="H">Home Page</a>
<h1><a name="Top"></a>Frequently Answered Questions (FAQ)</h1>
<p>Customers often ask us similar questions about how our
services meet their needs. Please read this list of questions
before contacting us to see if we've already answered your
question.</p>
<h2>List of Questions</h2>
<ol>
<li><a href="#Question_01" accesskey="b" tabindex="1">What are
the benefits of virtual office space?</a></li>
<li><a href="#Question_02" accesskey="s" tabindex="2">Which
services do you offer?</a></li>
<li><a href="#Question_03" accesskey="p" tabindex="3">What is
your pricing structure?</a></li>
<li><a href="#Question_04">Where are your offices?</a></li>
<li><a href="#Question_05">How many people can your meeting rooms
hold?</a></li>
<li><a href="#Question_06">How do you answer my virtual
telephone?</a></li>
<li><a href="#Question_07">How do I organize a mailshot?</a></li>
<li><a href="#Question_08">Do you provide real staff for
tradeshows?</a></li>
```

# Link to a Particular Point on a Web Page

You can use the anchor technique to create a link to a particular anchor on another web page. To do so:

1. Insert an anchor at the point on the destination page to which you want to be able to link. Type an anchor tag (<a>) and use the name attribute to specify the name for the anchor—for example:

   ```
   <a name="mailshots"></a>
   ```

2. Save the destination page.

## MAKING YOUR SITE NAVIGABLE

To make your site easy for visitors to get around, you should provide effective navigation. You may also need to assign keyboard shortcuts to links so that they can be "clicked" using the keyboard and change the tab order of links.

### PROVIDE EFFECTIVE NAVIGATION

To provide effective navigation in your site:

- Include plenty of links on each page, including redundant links in different areas of long pages.

- Explain in text, in title-attribute ScreenTips, or in both where the visitor will be taken if he or she clicks a link.

- Consider implementing a standard means of navigation across your entire site. For example, you might use a series of links across the top of each page to allow visitors to access the main areas of your site quickly.

### ASSIGN A KEYBOARD SHORTCUT TO A LINK

To enable users without a mouse to click links, you can assign a keyboard shortcut to a link by adding the accesskey attribute and specifying the key. For example, add accesskey="h" to specify *h* as the access key for a hyperlink.

Most browsers display no indication of the access key, so you need to mark it to make it explicit. For example, you might use bold font on the access key letter in the text to indicate the access key.

### CHANGE THE TAB ORDER OF LINKS

You can move from one hyperlink in a web page to the next hyperlink by pressing **TAB**; to move to the previous hyperlink, press **SHIFT+TAB**. Most browsers display a selection box or a highlight around the current link. To click the current link, press **ENTER**.

*Continued . . .*

3. Switch to the page that will contain the link. Type the start of an anchor tag (<a>), type the href attribute, an equal sign, the absolute or relative address, a hash symbol (#), the anchor name, and the closing angle bracket—for example:

```
<a href="http://www.acmevirtualindustries.com/services
.html#mailshots">
```

4. Type the text (or insert the graphic) that you want to use as the visible manifestation of the anchor and then the closing </a> tag—for example:

```
Mailshots</a>
```

5. Save the file, switch to your browser, and click the link. Make sure it takes you to the right point on the other web page.

## Open a Link in a New Window

When you click a link, most browsers open the linked page in the same tab or window so that you can no longer see the page that contained the link. (You can configure some browsers to open linked pages in a new window or on a new tab.) To keep the previous page visible, you can create a link that opens in a new window by default. This technique is especially useful when your pages contain links to external websites (as opposed to other pages in your site)—you can enable visitors to access other sites without entirely leaving your site.

To make a link open a new window, include the target attribute with the value _blank in the link—for example:

```
<a href="http://www.acmevirtualindustries.com/services.html"
target="_blank">Services</a>
```

## Create a Link to Download a File

Depending on the content of your site, you may choose to provide files that visitors can download. For example, if you sell items, you might want to provide product manuals in a downloadable format rather than putting all the information on your web pages. If you sell computer hardware, you might need to provide updated drivers for your products.

## MAKING YOUR SITE NAVIGABLE

*(Continued)*

The default order of the links is from the first to the last, top to bottom, and left to right. If you need to change this order, add the tabindex attribute to the links, using numbering to specify the desired order: Add tabindex="1" to the link you want to be first, tabindex="2" to the second link, and so on.

For example, here are accesskey and tabindex implemented with the list of questions described earlier in this chapter:

```
<h2>List of Questions</h2>
<ol>
<li><a href="#Question_01" accesskey="b"
tabindex="1">What are the benefits of
virtual office space?</a></li>
<li><a href="#Question_02" accesskey="s"
tabindex="2">Which services do you
offer?</a></li>
<li><a href="#Question_03" accesskey="p"
tabindex="3">What is your pricing
structure?</a></li>
```

## CAUTION

Even when you create a link that opens a page in a separate window, a visitor can override the instruction. For example, the visitor can right-click and select Open from the shortcut menu to open the linked page in the same browser window.

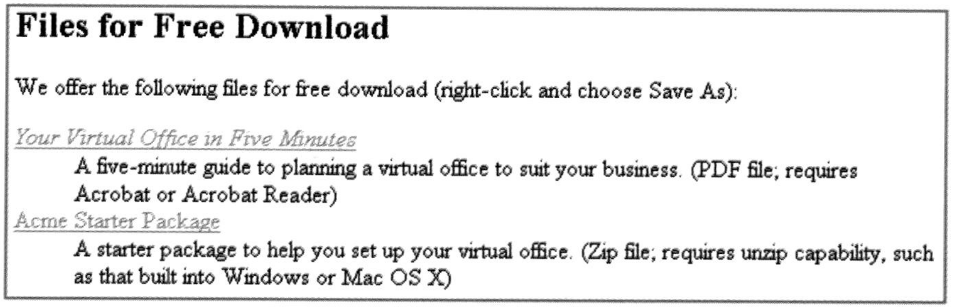

---

### Files for Free Download

We offer the following files for free download (right-click and choose Save As):

*Your Virtual Office in Five Minutes*
    A five-minute guide to planning a virtual office to suit your business. (PDF file; requires Acrobat or Acrobat Reader)
Acme Starter Package
    A starter package to help you set up your virtual office. (Zip file; requires unzip capability, such as that built into Windows or Mac OS X)

**Figure 5-3:** *When you provide files for download, it's a good idea to make sure the user knows how to download them rather than open them in the browser.*

To create a link that downloads a file, enter the absolute address or relative address of the desired file for the href attribute. For example, this code contains links to download two files (see Figure 5-3):

```
<h2>Files for Free Download</h2>
<p>We offer the following files for free download
(right-click and choose Save As):</p>
<dl>
<dt><a href="files/five_minute_virtual_office.pdf">
    <i>Your Virtual Office in Five Minutese</i></a></dt>
    <dd>A five-minute guide to planning a virtual office
    to suit your business.
    (PDF file; requires Acrobat or Acrobat Reader)</dd>
<dt><a href="files/seven_steps.zip">
    <i>Starter Package</i></a></dt>
    <dd>A starter package to help you set up your
    virtual office. (Zip file; requires Zip capability, such
    as that built into Windows or Mac OS X)</dd>
</dl>
```

## Display a ScreenTip for a Link

For some of your links, you may want to display extra information in a ScreenTip when the visitor hovers the mouse pointer over the link. To do so,

We offer the following files for free download (right-click and choose Save As):

*Your Virtual Office in Five Minutes*

A five-minute guide to planning a virtual office to suit your business. (PDF file;
Right-click here and choose Save As to save this file to your computer. Click here to
open this file in your browser (if your browser supports PDFs).

Acme Starter Package

A starter package to help you set up your virtual office. (Zip file; requires unzip capability, such as that built into Windows or Mac OS X)

**Figure 5-4: Use the title attribute to display a ScreenTip of extra information when the visitor hovers the mouse pointer over a link.**

add the title attribute to the link and specify the text string that you want to display, as in the example shown here and in Figure 5-4:

```
<dt><a href="files/five_minute_virtual_office.pdf" title="Right-
click here and choose Save As to save this file to your computer.
Click here to open this file in your browser (if your browser
supports PDFs).">
     <i>Your Virtual Office in Five Minutes</i></a></dt>
     <dd>A five-minute guide to planning a virtual office
     to suit your business.
     (PDF file; requires Acrobat or Acrobat Reader)</dd>
```

## Create Links to Send E-mail

To get feedback from visitors to your website, you can simply list your e-mail address on your site (for example, on the Contact Us page, if you have one) and allow people to start messages manually using their e-mail clients as usual.

Often, however, you can get better results by adding a link that automatically starts an e-mail message to the e-mail address you specify. This helps to ensure that the visitor gets the e-mail address right, eliminating the risk that he or she might mistype it. You can also include a subject line in the link. Provided that the user doesn't change the subject line in the e-mail client, you can then implement e-mail filters to pick out mail related to your website.

### Send Us a Customer Query

Click the e-mail icon to send us a customer query.

If you can't see the envelope icon, <u>click here</u>

*Figure 5-5: When you use a graphic as a mailto hyperlink, it's a good idea to provide an alternate hyperlink in case the visitor is unable to see the graphic.*

## USE TEXT OR A GRAPHIC TO SEND E-MAIL

A text link, such as that shown in the previous section, is the most straightforward means of enabling visitors to send you an e-mail. Another widely used option is to use a miniature JavaScript and add the onClick instruction to text or to a graphic. (See Chapter 10 for more information about JavaScript and how to add it to your web pages.) This example creates both a graphic e-mail link and a text link.

1. Enter some explanatory text for the graphic link so that the viewer knows he or she should click the link in order to start an e-mail message—for example:

```
<h3>Send Us a Customer Query</h3>
<p>Click the e-mail icon to send us a customer query.</p>
```

2. Type an <img/> tag that uses the src attribute to specify the graphic and the alt attribute to specify alternative text as usual, and specify style="border:none" to prevent the browser from displaying a blue border around the graphic to indicate the link—for example:

```
<img src="mail.png" alt="Contact Us icon" style="border:none"/>
```

3. Before the forward slash and closing angle bracket of the <img/> tag, add the onClick property with the details of the e-mail address and the subject (if desired)—for example:

```
onClick="location.href='mailto:customers@acmevirtualindustries
.com?subject=Customer Query'">
```

4. Add any explanatory text needed for the text link that will send e-mail, followed by the text hyperlink—for example:

```
<p>If you can't see the envelope icon,
<a href="mailto:customers@acmevirtualindustries
.com?subject=Customer Query">click here</a></p>
```

The complete code used in the example is as follows:

```
<h3>Send Us a Customer Query</h3>
<p>Click the e-mail icon to send us a customer query.</p>
<img src="mail.png" alt="Contact Us icon" style="border:none"
onClick="location.href='mailto:customers@acmevirtualindustries.com?
subject=Customer Query'">/>
<p>If you can't see the envelope icon,
<a href="mailto:customers@acmevirtualindustries.com?subject=Customer
 Query">click here</a></p>
```

Figure 5-5 shows the icon and link created by the code.

## CREATE AN E-MAIL BUTTON

To create an e-mail button, use the <button> tag. You then set the onClick attribute's location.href property to send e-mail to the appropriate address. For example:

1. In the body of the web page, enter the opening tag for a button, but leave off the closing angle bracket:

   `<button`

2. With the insertion point still placed after <button, type the onClick attribute with the location.href property:

   `onClick="location.href=`

3. Type a single quote, the mailto command, a colon, and the destination e-mail address:

   `'mailto:webs@acmevirtualindustries.com`

4. To add a subject line to the message, type a question mark, the word <u>subject</u>, an equal sign, and the text for the subject, as in the example here. (If you don't want to add a subject line to the message, skip this step—but a subject line helps prevent visitors sending subjectless messages that look like spam.)

   `?subject=Address Change`

5. Type a single quote, a double quotation mark, and the closing angle bracket:

   `'">`

6. Type the text you want to appear on the button—for example:

   `Send an Address Change`

7. Type the closing tag for the button:

   `</button>`

8. Save the page, switch to your browser, and refresh the display so that the button appears. The example button looks like this:

   | Send an Address Change |

9. Click the button to start a message in your default e-mail program (for example, Microsoft Outlook Express or Microsoft Outlook). Check that the address and subject are correct, and then close the message without sending or saving it.

The full code for the sample button is as follows:

```
<button onClick="location.href='mailto:webs@acmevirtualindustries
.com?subject=Address Change'">Send an Address Change</button>
```

When this code is used and someone clicks it in a browser, the e-mail program will generate an e-mail message with the To and the Subject line (if appropriate) filled in and the body blank.

# Create Two or More Links in a Graphic

Instead of linking a graphic to a single destination (such as another page or a mailto link), you can link different areas of the graphic to different destinations. A graphic with two or more different links is called an *imagemap*.

To create an imagemap, you place an image using the <img/> tag as usual, and then use the usemap attribute to specify which imagemap to use. You then use <map> and </map> tags to define a map that consists of different areas, each of which is linked to a different page or to a different anchor on the same page. The areas are defined by their coordinates from the upper-left corner of the image, which has coordinate 0,0. Each area can be a rectangle (rect), a circle (circle), or a free-form polygon (poly).

This example uses the graphic shown in Figure 5-6, which is 640 pixels wide by 480 pixels high. The graphic contains four distinct rectangular areas that are roughly the same size.

To create the imagemap:

1. Open the graphic in your graphics program, and use the program's selection tools to work out the coordinates of the areas you will need to define within the image. For example, the coordinates "0,0,320,240" define the upper-left quarter of the sample graphic.

2. Type the <img/> tag with the src attribute specifying the graphic file, the alt attribute specifying the alternative text, and the usemap attribute specifying the name of the map you'll create—for example:

```
<img src="map1.jpg"
    alt="picture showing Acme Virtual Industries' main service
areas"
    usemap="#map1_map">
```

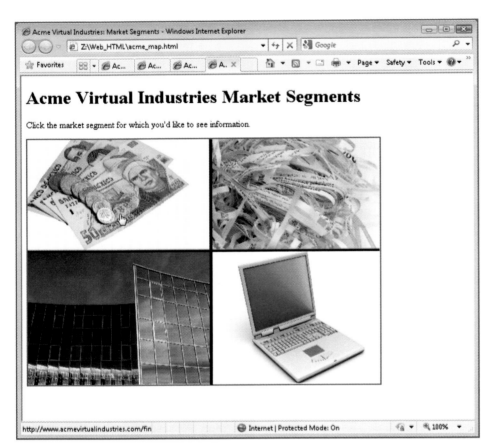

Figure 5-6: *You can use a graphic with two or more distinct areas to create an imagemap with links to different pages from different parts of the graphic.*

3. Type the opening <map> tag, and set the name attribute to the name you used for the usemap attribute of the <img/> tag—for example:

```
<map name="map1_map">
```

4. Type an <area> tag with the href attribute specifying the destination page for the hyperlink, the alt attribute specifying the alternative text for the hyperlink (if desired), the shape attribute specifying the type of area (rect, circle, or poly), and the coords attribute specifying the coordinates of the area. For example, this code defines a rectangular area 320 pixels wide by 240 pixels high, starting at the upper-left corner of the graphic:

```
<area href="finance.html"
    alt="Financial Services"
    shape="rect"
    coords="0,0,320,240">
```

Enter <area> tags for the other areas in the graphic—for example:

```
<area href="offices.html"
    alt="Office Services"
    shape="rect"
    coords="0,240,320,240">
<area href="security.html"
    alt="Security Services"
    shape="rect"
    coords="320,0,640,240">
<area href="computing.html"
    alt="Computing Services"
    shape="rect"
    coords="320,240,640,480">
```

Type the closing </map> tag:

```
</map>
```

Save the page, switch to your browser, and then refresh the display so that you can see the change.

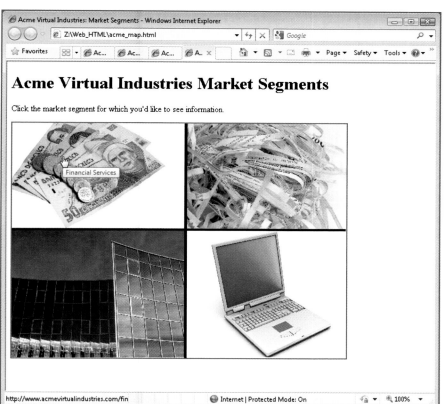

**Figure 5-7:** *Using title text with your imagemaps gives visitors an idea of what they'll see if they click a particular part of the imagemap.*

Figure 5-7 shows the page and imagemap produced by the sample code shown here:

```
<h1>Acme Virtual Industries Market Segments</h1>
<p>Click the market segment for which you'd like
to see information.</p>
<img src="map1.jpg"
    alt="picture showing Acme Virtual
Industries' main service areas"
    usemap="#map1_map">
<map name="map1_map">
<area href="http://www.acmevirtualindustries.com/
finance.html"
    alt="Financial Services"
    title="Financial Services"
    shape="rect"
    coords="0,0,320,240">
<area href="offices.html"
    alt="Office Services"
    title="Office Services"
    shape="rect"
    coords="0,240,320,480">
<area href="security.html"
    alt="Security Services"
    title="Security Services"
    shape="rect"
    coords="320,0,640,240">
<area href="computing.html"
    alt="Computing Services"
    title="Computing Services"
    shape="rect"
    coords="320,240,640,480">
</map>
```

## TIP

Creating an imagemap manually takes some time and patience, not to mention some accurate typing of coordinates. Many graphics programs include tools for creating imagemaps automatically, so check to see if your graphics program has this feature. This automation is particularly valuable for creating complex imagemaps, such as those that use polygons.

# Add Audio and Video to Your Web Pages

Now that broadband is widely available, more and more people can enjoy audio and video via the Web. If you have audio or video content to share, you can put it on your website. You can create links that allow users to download audio or video files, play audio or video files in a separate player, or play audio or video files within your web page.

## Understand Audio and Video Formats

Computers use various audio and video formats, some of which are much more widely used than others. To make sure that as many visitors to your website as possible can enjoy its audio or video, you need to choose a suitable format. You must also ensure that the file size of the audio or video is small enough that the file can be downloaded over even a dial-up connection.

Use compressed audio formats for all but the shortest audio files. Most computers can play MP3 files (which are compressed) and WAV files (which are not compressed). Also, consider reducing the complexity of the audio file—for example, by reducing it from a 16-bit sound to an 8-bit sound, or by using mono instead of stereo. The file will not sound as good, but visitors to your website will be able to get it that much more quickly.

Video contains far more data than audio, so always use compressed formats for video—even for the shortest files. Most computers can play AVI (audio-video interleave) files, which offer modest compression, and MPEG files, which offer better compression. Most Windows computers can play Windows Media Video (WMV) files, which also use a compressed format. Any PC or Mac with iTunes installed can also play files in the QuickTime movie formats.

Most digital video camcorders export video at VGA resolution ($640 \times 480$ pixels) or a high-definition resolution. VGA gives good video quality, but produces large files; high-definition gives great quality, but produces huge files. Reduce the resolution for video files you put on the Web to $320 \times 240$ pixels for reasonable quality, $240 \times 160$ pixels for acceptable quality, or $160 \times 120$ pixels for low quality.

## Understand Audio and Video Delivery Methods

The easiest way to provide audio or video to visitors of your website is to allow them to download entire files to their computers and play them when they want to. This approach has two advantages.

- People who download the files can listen to the audio or watch the video as many times as they like.

- Downloads work even over a slow or patchy connection (for example, a modem connection or a congested broadband connection), provided the downloader has enough time and patience to download the whole file. By contrast, streaming high-quality audio or any quality of video usually requires a broadband connection that's working properly. (Some streaming technologies allow the client to download the entire stream before attempting to play it, while other technologies do not.)

Allowing downloads works well if you have full distribution rights for the audio or video files—for example, if they're original works you've created. If, however, you have only rights to play the files from your server or to stream them, you will not be able to allow downloads.

## Create a Link for Downloading an Audio or Video File

If you have audio or video files that you can legally offer for download (for example, music or movies that you have created yourself), create a link to the file, and instruct visitors to right-click the link and choose Save As (or the equivalent command, depending on the browser) from the shortcut menu to download the file. (If a visitor simply clicks the link, the audio or video file will probably play rather than be downloaded, although this depends on how the computer is configured.)

This example tells visitors how to download an MP3 file:

```
<p>To download the interview on virtual offices,
    right-click <a href="media/interview01.mp3"
    title="Right-click this link and choose Save As to download
the file.">here</a>.</p>
```

## Create a Link to Play an Audio or Video File

To enable visitors to play an audio or video file, create a link to the file. This example links to the AVI video file named virtual_office_tour.avi in the media folder:

```
<p>Click <a href="media/virtual_office_tour.avi">here</a> to
watch our Virtual Office Tour video (AVI format, 12.4MB).</p>
```

**CAUTION**

Playing an audio or video file in Windows Media Player works seamlessly with Internet Explorer as the browser and Windows Media Player installed and set up. If the visitor is using another browser on Windows, such as Firefox, the browser may prompt them to choose how to open the file (see Figure 5-8); they can usually select an option such as the Do This Automatically For Files Like This From Now On check box in the figure to have the browser play the files automatically. On Mac OS X or another operating system, the visitor will normally have to choose the program in which to play the file.

## QUICK**FACTS**

### EMBEDDING A VIDEO FILE IN A WEB PAGE

Instead of linking a video file, you can embed it in the web page by using an `<object>` tag. The `<object>` tag enables you to control precisely how the video file appears and how the visitor can play it—for example, whether the video starts playing automatically when the web browser loads the page (seldom a good idea) and whether the video player displays controls that allow the visitor to control it (almost always a good idea).

The `<object>` tag is powerful but complex, as the information you must use to make it work correctly depends not only on the type of video file but also on the browser the visitor is using. If you need to use the `<object>` tag, consult a larger HTML reference work than this book.

If you work with older web pages, you may also see the `<embed>` tag used to embed a video player in a web page. This is an older HTML technique that worked in only some browsers, never became a standard, and has now been superseded by the `<object>` tag—so don't use this tag unless it's in pages that you're maintaining and that already work as they're supposed to.

Figure 5-8: *Firefox prompts the visitor to decide how to handle a multimedia file.*

When a visitor clicks the link, the default media player on his or her computer opens and plays the file. On a default configuration of Windows, the default media player for audio and video files is Windows Media Player.

## How to...

- *Plan a Table*
- *Create the Table's Structure*
- *Add Rows and Columns to a Table*
- *Add Table Borders*
- *Group Cells by Rows and Columns*
- *Set Table and Cell Width*
- *Setting Table and Cell Height*
- *Add Padding and Spacing*
- *Align a Table, Row, or Cell*
- *Make a Cell Span Two Columns or Rows*
- *Apply a Background Color or Picture*
- *Create a Nested Table*
- *Create a Vertical Line*

# Chapter 6

# Creating Tables

Many technical books (including this one) use tables to lay out information in a clear and easily understandable format. You can use tables in this way in your web pages as well, but you can also use tables with invisible gridlines and borders for arranging the layout of the elements that make up pages. This chapter explains first how to create simple tables and then shows you how to use tables to create more complex page layouts.

## Understand How Tables Work and When to Use Them

A table consists of cells made up of the intersections of rows and columns (see Figure 6-1).

- A *cell* is the basic unit of a table. It is formed by the intersection of a row and a column.
- A *row* is a line of cells running from left to right.
- A *column* is a stack of cells running up and down.
- The *border* is the rectangle that defines each cell and the outside of the table.

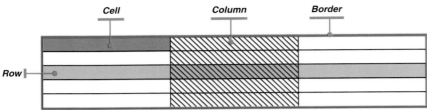

Figure 6-1: *Each table has an outside border and rows and columns that create cells.*

In a standard table, each row contains the same number of cells, and each column contains the same number of cells. Figure 6-2 shows an example of a standard table.

You can, however, change the layout of a table by *spanning*, or merging, cells together so that a single cell spans two or more columns, two or more rows, or both. Figure 6-3 shows an example of using a table for layout. The screen on the left, in which the table's borders are hidden, is how the page would normally be viewed. The screen on the right displays the borders so that you can see how the table is divided into cells.

## Plan a Table

If you want to experiment with tables, you can start by entering table tags (discussed in the next section) in your HTML editor and placing content within the cells. It's better, however, to start by planning how you want your table to look. Use any tool you find convenient—for example:

- Draw a rough sketch of the table on a sheet of paper.
- Use a graphical tool, such as Microsoft Paint (click the **Start** button, click **All Programs**, click **Accessories**, and then click **Paint**) or The GNU Image Manipulation Program (GIMP), to create a mock-up of how the table will look.
- Use an HTML-capable word processor, such as Microsoft Word or OpenOffice.org, to create a table; open the resulting file in a browser; and then copy the source code to your HTML editor for fine-tuning.

**NOTE**

Technically, you should use only *data tables*—tables that present tabular data. But many people also create *layout tables*—tables used to lay out web pages as they want them to appear. Because this practice is so widespread, it's important that you know how to work with layout tables—even if you're clear that usually CSS (discussed in Chapter 8) is a better tool for creating such web pages.

## Create the Table's Structure

To create a table, you use the following tags:

- The <table> tag marks the start of the table, and the </table> tag marks the end of the table. All the table's contents go between these tags.

| Service Code | Service Description | Service Type | Service Details | Service Cost |
|---|---|---|---|---|
| AV101 | Virtual Phone | Telecoms | 1 day | $34.99 |
| AV102 | Virtual Assistant | Staffing | 1 day | $49.99 |
| AV103 | Virtual Manager | Staffing | 1 day | $199.99 |
| AC104 | Mailshot (one-off) | Mailings | 50 pieces | $99.99 |

Figure 6-2: *You can use a table to lay out information in a grid for easy reference.*

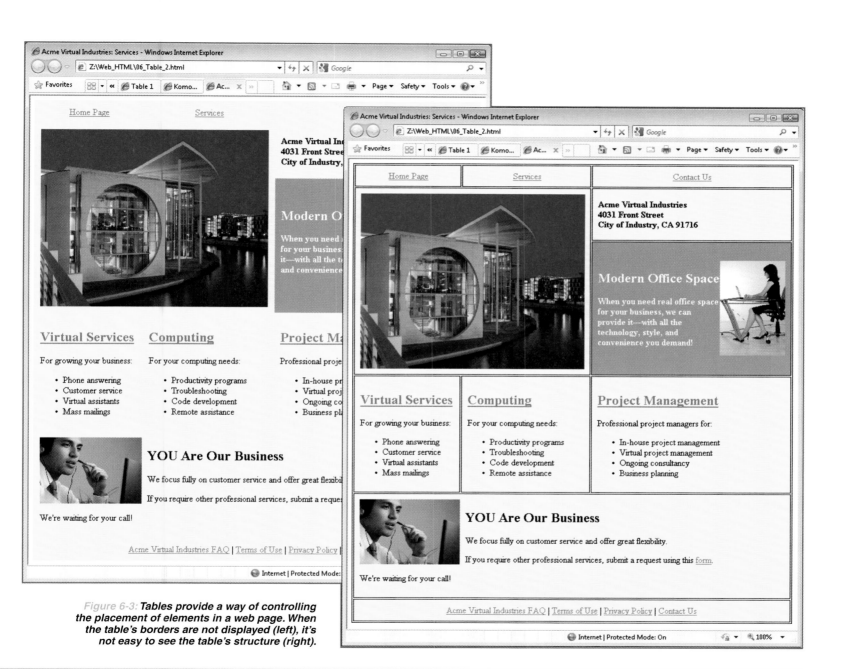

Figure 6-3: **Tables provide a way of controlling the placement of elements in a web page. When the table's borders are not displayed (left), it's not easy to see the table's structure (right).**

- The `<tr>` (table row) tag marks the start of each row, and the `</tr>` tag marks the end of each row. The number of pairs of `<tr>` and `</tr>` tags you use controls the number of rows in the table.

- The `<td>` (table data) tag marks the start of each cell within a row, and then the `</td>` tag marks the end of each cell. The number of pairs of `<td>` and `</td>` tags controls the number of cells in the row, and thus controls the number of columns.

To create a table, follow these general steps:

1. Open Notepad (or your HTML editor), and start a new web page. For example, if you have created a template file containing the basic structure of a web page, open that file and then click the **File** menu, click **Save As**, and use the Save As dialog box to save the file under a different name. Otherwise, paste in or create the basic structure of a web page manually:

```
<?xml version="1.0" encoding="utf-8"?>
<!DOCTYPE html PUBLIC "-//W3C//DTD XHTML 1.0 Transitional//EN"
        "http://www.w3.org/TR/xhtml1/DTD/xhtml1-transitional.dtd">
<html xmlns="http://www.w3.org/1999/xhtml" xml:lang="en"
lang="en"><html>
<head>
<title></title>
</head>
<body>
</body>
</html>
```

2. Position the insertion point within the body section, and then type a starting `<table>` tag and a closing `</table>` tag:

```
<table>
</table>
```

3. Within the `<table>` and `</table>` tags, type the starting `<tr>` tag and a closing `</tr>` tag for each row. For example, to create two rows:

```
<table>
    <tr>
    </tr>
    <tr>
    </tr>
</table>
```

## TIP

Tables that contain more than a few rows and cells quickly become difficult to read in a text editor. You can make your tables easier to grasp—and to edit—by indenting the contents of the table to different levels. For example, you might indent each `<tr>` and `</tr>` tag pair four spaces, indent each `<td>` and `</td>` pair a further four spaces (eight spaces total), and indent the cell contents even further.

**NOTE**

If you do not specify the width of the border for a table, most browsers use a default width of 0, making the border invisible. To ensure consistent display of your pages, however, you should always specify the border width you want. For example, to make sure that borders are not displayed, use border="0".

**CAUTION**

Using the style attribute is not recommended as your main means of formatting a table because it mixes the table's content with the table's formatting; the new and approved way of formatting the table is by using CSS (see Chapter 8). But you may need to use the style attribute in this way to override the style applied by CSS. This example uses blue borders to make the table more visible.

**NOTE**

Empty rows and cells appear as only a minute amount of white space in a table. Once you add content, the cells increase in size so that they can display the content.

**4.** To create a cell, place the insertion point between the appropriate <tr> and </tr> tags, and then type a starting <td> (table data) tag, the contents of the cell, and a closing </td> tag. For example, to create three cells in the first row of the table:

```
<table>
    <tr>
        <td>Service Code</td>
        <td>Service Description</td>
        <td>Service Type</td>
    </tr>
    <tr>
    </tr>
</table>
```

**5.** Save the page, switch to (or start) your browser, and display the page. So far, you will see only the text of the table, as in this example.

Service Code Service Description Service Type Service Details Service Cost

**6.** Position the insertion point immediately before the closing angle bracket in the <table> tag, and then add the border attribute with the value 1 and the style attribute with the value "border-color:blue":

```
<table border="1" style="border-color:blue">
```

**7.** Save the page, switch to your browser, and refresh the display. The cell borders are displayed, as shown in this example.

Service Code Service Description Service Type Service Details Service Cost

**8.** Using the technique described in step 3, create the cells in the remaining rows of the table. The following example shows the whole table with two further rows of cells added:

```
<table border="1" style="border-color:blue" >
    <tr>
        <td>Service Code</td>
        <td>Service Description</td>
        <td>Service Type</td>
        <td>Service Details</td>
        <td>Service Cost</td>
    </tr>
    <tr>
```

```
    <td>AV101</td>
    <td>Virtual Phone</td>
    <td>Telecoms</td>
    <td>1 day</td>
    <td align="right">$34.99</td>
</tr>
<tr>
    <td>AV102</td>
    <td>Virtual Assistant</td>
    <td>Staffing</td>
    <td>1 day</td>
    <td align="right">$49.99</td>      </tr>
<tr>
    <td>AV103</td>
    <td>Virtual Manager</td>
    <td>Staffing</td>
    <td>1 day</td>
    <td align="right">$199.99</td>
</tr>
<tr>
    <td>AC104</td>
    <td>Mailshot (one-off)</td>
    <td>Mailings</td>
    <td>50 pieces</td>
    <td align="right">$99.99</td>
</tr>
</table>
```

| Service Code | Service Description | Service Type | Service Details | Service Cost |
|---|---|---|---|---|
| AV101 | Virtual Phone | Telecoms | 1 day | $34.99 |
| AV102 | Virtual Assistant | Staffing | 1 day | $49.99 |
| AV103 | Virtual Manager | Staffing | 1 day | $199.99 |
| AC104 | Mailshot (one-off) | Mailings | 50 pieces | $99.99 |

9. Apply formatting to the cells, rows, and table, as discussed in the following sections, so that it looks the way you want it to.

10. Optionally, add a table caption between an opening <caption> tag and a closing </caption> tag after the <table> tag. The caption appears above the table.

```
<table border="1" style="border-color:blue" >
<caption><b>Acme Virtual Industries: Service Codes and
Descriptions</b></caption>>
```

| Acme Virtual Industries: Service Codes and Descriptions | | | | |
|---|---|---|---|---|
| Service Code | Service Description | Service Type | Service Details | Service Cost |
| AV101 | Virtual Phone | Telecoms | 1 day | $34.99 |
| AV102 | Virtual Assistant | Staffing | 1 day | $49.99 |
| AV103 | Virtual Manager | Staffing | 1 day | $199.99 |
| AC104 | Mailshot (one-off) | Mailings | 50 pieces | $99.99 |

## Add Rows and Columns to a Table

You can easily change the number of rows and columns in a table.

- To add another row, position the insertion point at the appropriate place (before, between, or after existing rows), and type another pair of <tr> and </tr> tags. Within these tags, type an opening <td> tag, the cell contents, and then the closing </td> tag for each cell you want to create.

- To add a column to a table, position the insertion point at the appropriate place (before, between, or after existing cells), and then type another pair of <td> and </td> tags with any content for the cell between them.

By default, each table has a grid pattern of rows and columns so that each row has the same number of cells. For example, if you create two cells in the first row of a table, three cells in the second row, and one cell in the third row, as in the following example, the table will have three columns:

```
<table border="1" style="border-color:blue">
    <tr>
        <td>Cell 1</td>
        <td>Cell 2</td>
    </tr>
    <tr>
        <td>Cell 1</td>
        <td>Cell 2</td>
        <td>Cell 3</td>
    </tr>
    <tr>
        <td>Cell 1</td>
    </tr>
</table>
```

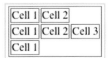

To change the grid, you make cells span two or more columns or rows. See "Make a Cell Span Two Columns or Rows," later in this chapter, for details.

## Add Table Borders

Each table has a border around its outside, and each cell has a border around it. You can set the border color for the table as a whole, and then set a different border color on particular rows or cells as necessary.

Use border="0" inside the opening <table> tag if you need to ensure that a table does not display a border—for example, when you are using a table to implement a precise layout in a web page. If you don't specify a zero-width border, some browsers may use an invisible two-pixel border, which can spoil the layout of your pages.

## SET THE BORDER WIDTH

To set the border width for the outside border of a table, add the border attribute to the opening <table> tag, and specify the number of pixels for the width of the border. For example, to create a border five pixels wide around the table:

```
<table border="5px">
```

## SPECIFY THE BORDER COLOR VIA THE STYLE ATTRIBUTE

Specifying a border width without a border color makes the browser display the border in its default color, which is usually gray. The best way to set border color is to use CSS, but you can also use the older, now deprecated method of using the style attribute. For example, to create a black border:

```
<table border="5px" style="border-color:black">
```

## CONTROL WHICH OUTSIDE BORDERS OF THE TABLE ARE DISPLAYED

To control which outside borders are displayed for a table, add the frame attribute to the opening <table> tag, and specify one of the values explained in Table 6-1.

For example, to display only the top and bottom borders of a table:

```
<table border="10px" frame="hsides" style="border-color:green">
```

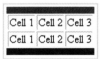

To display only the outside border of a table:

```
<table border="10px" frame="box" style="border-color:green">
```

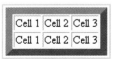

| VALUE | EFFECT |
|-------|--------|
| box | Displays the outside borders (same as border) |
| border | Displays the outside borders (same as box) |
| void | Hides all the outside borders |
| above | Displays the top border |
| below | Displays the bottom border |
| hsides | Displays the top and bottom borders |
| lhs | Displays the left border |
| rhs | Displays the right border |
| vsides | Displays both left and right borders |

*Table 6-1: **Values for the frame Attribute***

| VALUE | EFFECT |
|-------|--------|
| all | Displays rules around all cells |
| none | Displays no rules |
| groups | Displays rules around the horizontal or vertical groups that are defined. See "Group Cells by Rows and Columns" later in this chapter for details |
| rows | Displays all horizontal rules |
| cols | Displays all vertical rules |

*Table 6-2:* **Values for the** *rules* **Attribute**

To control which inside borders of a table are displayed, add the rules attribute to the opening <table> tag, and specify one of the values explained in Table 6-2. *Rules* are the lines or borders around the individual cells.

For example, to display only the horizontal borders within a table:

```
<table border="5px" frame="box" rules="rows" style="border-color:
blue">
```

To display all the inside borders of a table, but not the outside border:

```
<table border="0px" frame="void" rules="all" style="border-color:
black">
```

# Group Cells by Rows and Columns

The frame and rules attributes of the <table> tag enable you to create many arrangements of borders in your tables. But if you need more flexibility, you can use rules="groups" to put borders only on specific groups of rows and columns.

**CREATE GROUPS OF ROWS**

To create groups of rows, you split your table into a section of header rows, a body section, and a section of footer rows.

1. To create the header section, put an opening <thead> tag before the header rows and an ending </thead> tag after them.

**CAUTION**

To make your web page correct, you must put the <tfoot> section *before* the <tbody> section, not after it (as logic and sense would suggest). The browser will display it after the <tbody> section. One word of warning, though: Not all browsers support the <tfoot> tag, so use it only if you really need it, and test your pages with the browsers you expect most visitors to use.

2. Within the header section, you can use either <th> and </th> tags to create a table header (which is boldface and centered) or <td> and </td> tags to create standard table cells.

3. To create the footer section, put an opening <tfoot> tag before the footer rows and an ending </tfoot> tag after them.

4. To create the body section, put an opening <tbody> tag before the body rows and an ending </tbody> tag after them.

The next example shows a short table divided into header, body, and footer sections:

```
<table rules="groups"
    width="180"
    border="4px"
    style="border-color:blue">
    <thead>
        <tr>
            <td>Member #</td>
            <td align="right">First</td>
            <td>Last</td>
        </tr>
    </thead>
    <tfoot>
        <tr>
            <td align="right">Member</td>
            <td>count:</td>
            <td>2</td>
        </tr>
    </tfoot>
    <tbody>
        <tr>
            <td>1007</td>
            <td align="right">Jack</td>
            <td>Hobbs</td>
        </tr>
        <tr>
            <td>1008</td>
            <td align="right">Katja</td>
            <td>Reina</td>
        </tr>
    </tbody>
</table>
```

| Member # | First Last |
|----------|------------|
| 1007 | Jack Hobbs |
| 1008 | Katja Reina |
| Member count: 2 | |

This HTML code produces the table shown here, with the rules="groups" statement producing borders across the rows in the groups defined.

### CREATE GROUPS OF COLUMNS

To create groups of columns, you split your table by using the <colgroup> tag with the span attribute to specify which columns belong in each group. The following example shows a short table divided into two column groups, each of which contains two columns:

```
<table rules="groups"
    width="240"
    border="4px"
    style="border-color:blue">
    <colgroup span="2"></colgroup>
    <colgroup span="2"></colgroup>
    <tr>
        <td>Employee</td>
        <td>Item</td>
        <td>Quantity</td>
        <td>Total $</td>
    </tr>
    <tr>
        <td>Johns</td>
        <td>A384</td>
        <td align="right">48</td>
        <td align="right"> 480.00</td>
    </tr>
    <tr>
        <td>Bills</td>
        <td>C839</td>
        <td align="right">11</td>
        <td align="right">4492.00</td>
    </tr>
    <tr>
        <td>Acinth</td>
        <td>X420</td>
        <td align="right">88</td>
        <td align="right">6295.00</td>
    </tr>
</table>
```

## TIP

You can also affect the size of the table by adding padding and spacing to it. See "Add Padding and Spacing," later in this chapter, for more information.

## CAUTION

You can use tables to fix the width of a page, but before you do so, consider that some visitors to your site may be using a screen resolution or window size that will prevent them from seeing the entire page.

## CAUTION

One method of preventing the text in a cell from wrapping is to add the nowrap attribute to the <td> tag or the <th> tag—for example, <td nowrap="nowrap">Don't wrap this text!</td>. You should use nowrap with care for three reasons: First, it doesn't work with all browsers (though it does work with Internet Explorer and Firefox); second, it may cause your tables to be too wide for narrow browser windows; and third, CSS provides better alternatives.

## NOTE

If the browser window isn't wide enough to accommodate the measurements specified, most browsers override them so as to be able to display the table within the space available. If the table becomes too squashed to display usefully, the browser displays only part of it and adds a horizontal scroll bar so that you can reach the rest.

This HTML code produces the table shown here, with the rules="groups" statement producing a vertical border between the groups of columns and no border between the columns that make up each group.

| Employee | Item | Quantity | Total $ |
|----------|------|----------|---------|
| Johns | A384 | 48 | 480.00 |
| Bills | C839 | 11 | 4492.00 |
| Acinth | X420 | 88 | 6295.00 |

## Set Table and Cell Width

If you don't specify the width of a table or the width of the cells in the table, browsers automatically fit the width of the cells to their contents (as in most of the examples shown so far in this chapter). The result is economical on space, but can produce crowded layouts, so it's often better to specify the table width or the width of particular cells within the table manually.

### SPECIFY TABLE WIDTH

To specify the width of a table, add the width attribute to the opening <table> tag, and specify either the number of pixels (without a designation for pixels) or the percentage of the window width (with a percentage sign).

For example, to create a table 600 pixels wide:

```
<table width="600" border="1">
```

To create a table that is 90 percent of the width of the browser window and that varies in width if the browser window's width is changed:

```
<table width="90%" border="1">
```

### SPECIFY CELL WIDTH

To specify the width of a cell, add the width attribute to the opening <td> tag, and specify either the number of pixels (without a designation for pixels) or the percentage of the window width (with a percentage sign).

The next example uses the width attribute of the <table> tag to set the width of the entire table to 90 percent of the width of the browser window. It then uses the width attribute of the <td> tags to set the width of the first cell to 200 pixels and the width of the second cell to 140 pixels. The width attribute is

## SETTING TABLE AND CELL HEIGHT

In addition to being able to set the width of a table or of the cells that constitute it, you may be able to set the height of the table or of its cells instead of letting the browser set the height automatically to accommodate the contents of the table or cells.

Most browsers (including Internet Explorer, Firefox, and Safari) support setting the height of tables, but table height is not a part of the HTML standard, so you may find that some browsers do not support it. For this reason, it is best not to set the height of a table unless the design of a page absolutely requires a fixed height. Cell height *is* a part of the HTML standard and should work in all browsers, but setting it directly instead of using Cascading Style Sheets (CSS) is not recommended.

To set the height of a table, add the height attribute to the opening <table> tag, and specify the number of pixels. For example, to set the table height to 400 pixels:

```
<table width="300" height="400"
border="0">
```

To set the height of a cell, add the height attribute to the opening <td> tag, and specify the number of pixels. For example, to set the height to 100 pixels:

```
<td height="100">Tall cell</td>
```

You can also set the height of tables and cells by using CSS, which are discussed in Chapter 8.

**NOTE**

If you specify two width measurements for cells in the same column, the browser uses the larger measurement.

not specified for the third <td> tag, so the browser sets the width of this cell automatically to the remaining space (90 percent of the window width minus the space allocated to the first and second cells).

```
<table width="90%" border="1" style="border-color:blue">
    <tr>
        <td width="200">This cell is 200 pixels wide.</td>
        <td width="140">This cell is 140 pixels wide.</td>
        <td>This cell's width is set automatically.</td>
    </tr>
</table>
```

| This cell is 200 pixels wide. | This cell is 140 pixels wide. | This cell's width is set automatically. |
|---|---|---|

## Add Padding and Spacing

Most of the example tables shown so far in this chapter have been tightly packed. This is because they haven't added any extra blank space between the contents of each cell.

In HTML, you can add extra space between cells in two different ways.

- You can use the cellpadding attribute to add padding between the walls of each cell and the cell's content. The default setting is 1 pixel. (You can also use a setting of 0 to remove all cell padding.)
- You can use the cellspacing attribute to change the width of the space between cells. Typically, you use cellspacing to increase the amount of space from its default setting, which is 2 pixels; you can also reduce the amount of cell spacing to 1 pixel or 0 pixels if you wish.

For example, to create a table that uses 10 pixels of cell spacing and 10 pixels of cell padding:

```
<table border="1" cellspacing="10" cellpadding="10">
```

Figure 6-4 shows the effect of changing cell spacing and padding on a table.

## TIP

Cell padding and cell spacing have visibly different effects when used on a table with visible borders. When used on a table with hidden borders, however, the effects of cell padding and cell spacing can be hard to distinguish from each other.

**cellspacing="2" cellpadding="1" (default)**

| Service Code | Service Description | Service Type | Service Details |
|---|---|---|---|
| AV101 | Virtual Phone | Telecoms | 1 day |
| AV102 | Virtual Assistant | Staffing | 1 day |
| AV103 | Virtual Manager | Staffing | 1 day |
| AC104 | Mailshot (one-off) | Mailings | 50 pieces |

**cellspacing="5" cellpadding="5"**

| Service Code | Service Description | Service Type | Service Details |
|---|---|---|---|
| AV101 | Virtual Phone | Telecoms | 1 day |
| AV102 | Virtual Assistant | Staffing | 1 day |
| AV103 | Virtual Manager | Staffing | 1 day |
| AC104 | Mailshot (one-off) | Mailings | 50 pieces |

**cellspacing="10" cellpadding="10"**

| Service Code | Service Description | Service Type | Service Details |
|---|---|---|---|
| AV101 | Virtual Phone | Telecoms | 1 day |
| AV102 | Virtual Assistant | Staffing | 1 day |
| AV103 | Virtual Manager | Staffing | 1 day |
| AC104 | Mailshot (one-off) | Mailings | 50 pieces |

*Figure 6-4:* **Cell spacing controls how far apart the cells are from each other. Cell padding controls how much blank space there is between the cell contents and the cell walls.**

## Align a Table, Row, or Cell

To achieve the placement you want, you can align a whole table, a whole row, or the contents of individual cells.

### ALIGN A TABLE HORIZONTALLY

You can align a table horizontally within a web page by adding the align attribute to the opening <table> tag and specifying left, right, or center,

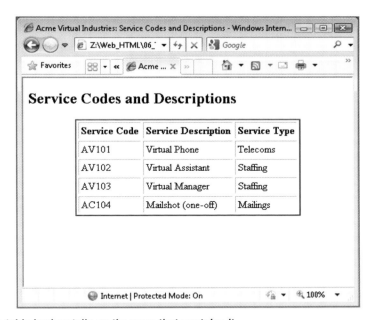

Figure 6-5: *Instead of using the default left alignment, you can align a table horizontally on the page that contains it.*

as needed. For example, to center a table on the web page that contains it (see Figure 6-5):

```
<table align="center" border="2" cellspacing="5">
```

### ALIGN A ROW HORIZONTALLY

You can align the contents of a row within their cells by adding the align attribute to the opening <tr> tag and specifying left, right, center, or justify, as needed. For example, to apply justified alignment (where both the left and right edges of text are aligned) to a row:

```
<tr align="justify">
```

### ALIGN A CELL'S CONTENTS HORIZONTALLY

You can align a cell's contents horizontally by adding the align attribute to the opening <td> tag and specifying left, right, center, or justify, as needed.

**NOTE**

Horizontal alignment applied to a cell overrides horizontal alignment applied to the row that contains the cell.

For example, the following code uses centered alignment in the third column and right alignment in the first and fifth columns:

```
<table border="2" cellpadding="4" cellspacing="3" style="border-
color:blue" summary="This table provides the codes, details, and
prices of services offered by Acme Virtual Industries." >

<caption><b>Acme Virtual Industries: Service Codes and
Descriptions</b></caption>
    <tr>
        <th>Service Code</th>
        <th>Service Description</th>
        <th>Service Type</th>
        <th>Service Details</th>
        <th>Service Cost</th>
    </tr>
    <tr>
        <td align="right">AV101</td>
        <td>Virtual Phone</td>
        <td align="center">Telecoms</td>
        <td>1 day</td>
        <td align="right">$34.99</td>
    </tr>
    <tr>
        <td align="right">AV102</td>
        <td>Virtual Assistant</td>
        <td align="center">Staffing</td>
        <td>1 day</td>
        <td align="right">$49.99</td>
    </tr>
    <tr>
        <td align="right">AV103</td>
        <td>Virtual Manager</td>
        <td align="center">Staffing</td>
        <td>1 day</td>
        <td align="right">$199.99</td>
    </tr>
    <tr>
        <td align="right">AC104</td>
        <td>Mailshot (one-off)</td>
        <td align="center">Mailings</td>
        <td>50 pieces</td>
        <td align="right">$99.99</td>
    </tr>
</table>
```

| Acme Virtual Industries: Service Codes and Descriptions | | | | |
| --- | --- | --- | --- | --- |
| Service Code | Service Description | Service Type | Service Details | Service Cost |
| AV101 | Virtual Phone | Telecoms | 1 day | $34.99 |
| AV102 | Virtual Assistant | Staffing | 1 day | $49.99 |
| AV103 | Virtual Manager | Staffing | 1 day | $199.99 |
| AC104 | Mailshot (one-off) | Mailings | 50 pieces | $99.99 |

**NOTE**

The baseline value aligns the contents of the cells along the baseline, the imaginary line on which the bottom of a letter that does not have a descender rests.

**NOTE**

Vertical alignment applied to a cell overrides vertical alignment applied to the row that contains the cell.

### ALIGN A ROW VERTICALLY

You can align a row's contents by adding the valign attribute to the opening `<tr>` tag and specifying top, middle, bottom, or baseline, as needed. For example, to apply top alignment to a row:

```
<tr align="top">
```

### ALIGN A CELL'S CONTENTS VERTICALLY

Instead of applying the same vertical alignment to an entire row, you may need to apply different vertical alignment to the individual cells in a row. To do so, add the valign attribute to the opening `<td>` tag, and specify top, middle, bottom, or baseline, as needed.

The following example produces the table shown in Figure 6-6:

```
<?xml version="1.0" encoding="utf-8"?>
<!DOCTYPE html PUBLIC "-//W3C//DTD XHTML 1.0 Transitional//EN"
        "http://www.w3.org/TR/xhtml1/DTD/xhtml1-transitional.dtd">
<html xmlns="http://www.w3.org/1999/xhtml" xml:lang="en" lang="en">
<head>
        <meta http-equiv="content-type" content="text/html;
charset=utf-8" />
        <title>Baseline alignment</title>
</head>
<body>
<h2>Table Showing Vertical Alignment</h2>
<table border="6" style="border-color:purple" cellspacing="2"
cellpadding="2">
    <tr>
        <td height="100" valign="top">Top alignment.</td>
        <td valign="middle">Middle alignment</td>
        <td valign="bottom">Bottom alignment</td>
    </tr>
    <tr>
        <td height="75" valign="bottom">Bottom alignment</td>
        <td valign="baseline"><font size="+3">Baseline alignment</
font></td>
        <td valign="baseline">Baseline alignment</td>
    </tr>
</table>
</body>
</html>
```

**Table Showing Vertical Alignment**

| Top alignment. | | |
| | Middle alignment | |
| | | Bottom alignment |
| Bottom alignment | Baseline alignment | Baseline alignment |

*Figure 6-6:* **Use vertical alignment to control the vertical placement of text in a cell. Note how the two "Baseline alignment" examples are aligned on the baseline of the letters rather than on the bottom of the descender on the letter g.**

# Make a Cell Span Two Columns or Rows

Tables that use a regular grid are useful for presenting data in a tabular format, but to lay out a page with tables, you'll often need to remove some of the borders between rows and columns. To do so, you make a cell *span* two or more rows or columns—in other words, you merge the cells in two or more rows, or in two or more columns, into a single larger cell.

## MAKE A CELL SPAN TWO COLUMNS

To make a cell span two or more columns, add the colspan attribute to the opening <td> tag of the cell in the leftmost of the columns involved, and specify the number of columns to span. If there are cells in the columns that will be spanned, delete them (if you don't, they will create extra columns in the table).

For example, to make a cell span three columns:

```
<table border="1" style="border-color:purple" cellspacing="2"
cellpadding="4">
    <tr>
        <td colspan="3">This cell spans all three columns.</td>
    </tr>
    <tr>
        <td>Column 1</td>
        <td>Column 2</td>
        <td>Column 3</td>
    </tr>
</table>
```

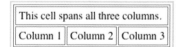

## MAKE A CELL SPAN TWO ROWS

To make a cell span two or more rows, add the rowspan attribute to the opening <td> tag of the cell in the topmost of the rows involved, and specify the number of rows to span. If there are cells in the rows that will be spanned, delete them.

`<td colspan="2" rowspan="2">`

`<td colspan="3">`

Figure 6-7: **You can span columns, rows, or both to create larger cells in order to produce the layout effects your web pages require.**

For example, to produce the cell containing the larger image in Figure 6-7 (shown with borders displayed), spanning two columns and two rows:

```
<td colspan="2" rowspan="2">
     <img src="images/logo_03.jpg" width="420"
align="center">
</td>
```

## Apply a Background Color or Picture

To make a table more colorful or distinctive, you can apply a background color or a background picture.

### APPLY A BACKGROUND COLOR TO A TABLE, ROW, OR CELL

To apply a background color to a table, add the bgcolor attribute to the opening <table> tag, and specify the color either by name or by hexadecimal code. For example, to apply yellow as the background color:

```
<table bgcolor="yellow">
```

To apply a background color to all cells in a row, add the bgcolor attribute to the opening <tr> tag. For example:

```
<tr bgcolor="black">
```

To apply a background color to an individual cell, add the bgcolor attribute to the opening <td> tag. For example:

```
<td bgcolor="blue">
```

## Create a Nested Table

Spanning columns, spanning rows, or spanning both columns and rows gives you decent flexibility in laying out your tables; however, if you must create a truly intricate table design, you may need to nest one table within another.

To nest a table, enter the complete structure of the nested table within the `<td>` and `</td>` tags for the cell in which you want the nested table to appear. The next example creates the simple nested table shown here.

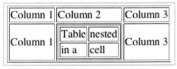

```
<?xml version="1.0" encoding="utf-8"?>
<!DOCTYPE html PUBLIC "-//W3C//DTD XHTML 1.0 Transitional//EN"
        "http://www.w3.org/TR/xhtml1/DTD/xhtml1-transitional.dtd">
<html xmlns="http://www.w3.org/1999/xhtml" xml:lang="en" lang="en">
<head>
    <meta http-equiv="content-type" content="text/html;
charset=utf-8" />
    <title>Demo of Nesting a Table in a Cell</title>
</head>
<body>
<h1>Example Table Within a Table</h1>
<table border="1">
    <tr>
        <td>Column 1</td>
        <td>Column 2</td>
        <td>Column 3</td>
    </tr>
    <tr>
        <td>Column 1</td>
    <td>
        <table border="1">
            <tr>
                <td>Table</td>
                <td>nested</td>
            </tr>
            <tr>
                <td>in a</td>
                <td>cell</td>
            </tr>
        </table>
    </td>
        <td>Column 3</td>
    </tr>
</table>
</body>
</html>
```

## Create a Vertical Line

The <hr> tag (discussed in Chapter 4) lets you easily insert a horizontal line in a web page. To insert a vertical line, create a two-column table and specify frame="void" and rules="cols", as shown in this example:

```
<table width="500" border="3"
    style="border-color:black"
    frame="void" rules="cols"
    cellspacing="0"
    cellpadding="10">
    <tr>
        <th valign="top" align="left">
            Business Terminology</th>
        <th valign="top" align="left">
            Plain English</th>
    </tr>
    <tr>
        <td><i>top-of-the-mind, back-of-the-envelope</i></td>
        <td>seat-of-the-pants</td>
    </tr>
    <tr>
        <td><i>leverage the paradigm</i></td>
        <td>[untranslatable: this is gibberish]</td>
    </tr>
        <tr>
        <td><i>target profile psychodemographics</i></td>
        <td>our customers</td>
    </tr>
</table>
```

**TIP**

You can see that creating HTML tables can be laborious, especially when you nest tables within tables—but you retain total control of what you're creating. Many programs, including Microsoft Web Expression and Macromedia Dreamweaver, allow you to create web tables directly in a What You See Is What You Get (WYSIWYG) environment, which is much easier.

| Business Terminology | Plain English |
|---|---|
| *top-of-the-mind, back-of-the-envelope* | seat-of-the-pants |
| *leverage the paradigm* | [untranslatable: this is gibberish] |
| *target profile psychodemographics* | our customers |

## How to...

- **Understanding Frames and Their Alternatives**
- Plan a Web Page That Uses Frames
- Define Frame Height and Width
- Create the Component Documents
- Create the Frameset Document
- Lay Out the Frames
- Add the Component Documents to the Frameset
- **Adding Alternative Text for a Frames Page**
- Change a Frame's Borders and Margins
- Control Whether a Frame Scrolls
- Prevent Visitors from Resizing the Frame
- Nest One Frameset Inside Another
- Create Inline Frames
- Create a Link That Changes the Contents of a Frame

# Chapter 7
## Creating Frames

Frames are one of HTML's ways of dividing the browser window into two or more separate rectangular areas whose contents you can supply separately. For example, you might create a frame in the left third of the window that contains navigation links, while the right two-thirds of the window display the content associated with the navigation link that the viewer clicks. By setting up the right frame's content to scroll independently of the left frame, you could enable the viewer to keep the links available on the screen all the time, even while scrolling down to the depths of the right frame.

Frames can make a powerful addition to your web tools, but they're not suitable for every page—or indeed for every browser. In this chapter, you'll learn when to use frames (and when to avoid using them), how frames work, and how to create and use them in your web pages.

## UNDERSTANDING FRAMES AND THEIR ALTERNATIVES

As of this writing (Summer 2009), frames are still in widespread use in web pages, so if you maintain or update existing pages, you'll need to know how frames work and how to create them. Overall, though, frames seem to be on their way out, so you may need to create new frame documents only seldom.

Frames are especially useful when you need to keep a particular element on a web page visible while the rest of the web page scrolls. For example, you can keep a navigation bar fixed to the left side of the web page so that it's always available even after the visitor has scrolled way down on the text part of the page. You can also use an inline frame to keep most of a page fixed, but display one element in a scrolling container.

Instead of using frames to create separate areas of web pages, you can use floating layouts in CSS, as discussed in the next chapter.

Some devices that have smaller screens, such as mobile phones and other handheld devices, may not be able to display frames. To cover these cases, you can provide alternative text to be displayed in any browser that cannot handle the frames. See the QuickFacts "Adding Alternative Text for a Frames Page," later in this chapter, for details.

Frames also have several other things going against them.

- In general, search engines have a hard time ranking frameset pages and typically give them lower page rankings overall. This can make a website appear less popular than it is.

- Framed pages may not print correctly.

*Continued . . .*

# Understand How Frames Work

In the web pages shown so far in this book, the browser window contains a single rectangular frame, or area, that displays a single document. Frames enable you to divide the browser window to display different content in different areas of the browser window (see Figure 7-1), each of which displays a different document. Each frame can be either fixed in place or able to scroll independently of the other frames. Together, the frames used in a web page make up a *frameset*, a set of frames that are laid out so that they fit together.

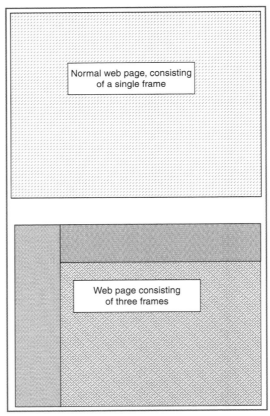

*Figure 7-1:* **You can use frames within the browser window instead of displaying a single area.**

## NOTE

The frameset document isn't displayed in the browser. It simply tells the browser which pages to display and how to lay them out. The title of the frameset document, however, is displayed in the browser's title bar, as usual.

# Plan a Web Page That Uses Frames

A web page that uses frames consists of:

- A *frameset document* that specifies the frames involved in the frameset, how the frames are laid out and how they behave, and which document to display in each frame

- An HTML document for each frame in the web page

Begin the process of creating a web page that uses frames by planning how you will lay the page out.

- Decide how many frames you will use (for example, two frames, three, or more).

- Decide how to position the frames relative to each other. For example, a two-frame layout might have a shallow row at the top of the window with a deeper row below it, or a narrow column at the left side of the window and a wider column occupying the remaining space. A three-frame layout might have a shallow row at the top, a narrow column at one side, and a larger rectangle occupying the remaining space (look back to Figure 7-1 for an example).

- Make a rough diagram, either on your computer (for example, in a graphics application, such as Paint or GIMP, or a word processor, such as Word) or on paper, of your chosen layout. Include the dimensions that you will use for the frames (see the following discussion).

# Define Frame Height and Width

You can define the height of a row and the width of a column. For either height or width, you can use either an *absolute* (fixed) dimension or a *relative* (variable) dimension. You can specify a dimension in three ways.

- Use an exact number of pixels—for example, create a column 200 pixels wide or a row 100 pixels high.

- Use a percentage of the width or height of the browser window.

- Use wildcards to allocate any remaining space left after you've specified an exact width or height.

### USE RELATIVE DIMENSIONS FOR MOST PAGES

For most pages, your best choice is to use relative dimensions for your frames by specifying the percentage of space you want to devote to each row or column. For example, to create a two-column layout, you might allocate 25 percent of the space to the first column and the remaining 75 percent to the second column. If a visitor resizes the browser window, the columns resize so that they retain their proportions.

### ALLOCATE EXACT HEIGHT OR WIDTH TO ONE FRAME AND SHARE THE REMAINING SPACE

For some pages, you may want to allocate an exact amount of space to a particular frame and tell the browser to share the rest of the available space among the other frames. This technique is useful when you have content that requires a certain amount of space and will suffer from being resized. For example, if you put an image in a frame on the left of a page, set that frame's width. The other frames then get the remaining space and can be resized as necessary.

To allocate exact height or width, specify the relevant dimension in pixels, and then use the * wildcard to allocate the remaining space. Use the * wildcard on its own to mean "one share of the remaining amount," use 2* to mean two shares, 3* for three shares, and so on.

The following example makes the first column in the frameset 200 pixels wide and then allocates all the remaining space to the second column:

```
<frameset cols="200,*">
```

The next example makes the first row 150 pixels high and then allocates three-quarters of the remaining space to the second row and one-quarter to the third row:

```
<frameset rows="150,3*,*">
```

Figure 7-2 shows three examples using pixel measurements, percentages, and wildcards, respectively, to specify the width of columns.

| 200 (pixels) | 200 (pixels) | 400 (pixels) |
|---|---|---|
| Columns Using Fixed Widths in Pixels | | |
| 25% (of the available space) | 25% (of the available space) | 50% (of the available space) |
| Columns Using Variable Widths in Percentages | | |
| 200 (pixels) | * (1 share of the remaining space) | 2* (2 shares of the remaining space) |
| Columns Using Fixed Widths in Wildcards | | |

Figure 7-2: *Using percentages (as in the middle example) or wildcards (as in the bottom example) gives greater flexibility to your frames than using absolute pixel dimensions (as in the top example).*

# Create the Component Documents

Create the component documents of the web page by using the techniques described in the other chapters of this book. Keep the following points in mind:

- Each component document should be a complete HTML page, starting with a DOCTYPE declaration and <html> tag, ending with an </html> tag, and containing a header section (within <head> and </head> tags) and a body section (within <body> and </body> tags).

- Design each component page to occupy the appropriate amount of space. For example, a column that will occupy only a narrow column in the window should not contain any wide elements. Similarly, a row with a small height should not contain any tall elements.

- If the frame is resizable, specify the size of any graphic as a percentage of the available space rather than using a fixed pixel size that may cause part of the graphic to be obscured when the size of the browser window changes.

- Although the titles of the component documents will not be displayed, you may want to add the <title> information anyway for the benefit of any search engines that visit your site.

# Create the Frameset Document

To create a frameset document:

1. Open Notepad (or your HTML editor), and start a new web page using the XHTML 1.0 Frameset DOCTYPE:

```
<?xml version="1.0" encoding="utf-8"?>
<!DOCTYPE html PUBLIC "-//W3C//DTD XHTML 1.0 Frameset//EN"
        "http://www.w3.org/TR/xhtml1/DTD/xhtml1-frameset.dtd">
<html xmlns="http://www.w3.org/1999/xhtml" xml:lang="en"
lang="en">
<head>
<title></title>
</head>
</html>
```

2. Position the insertion point between the opening <title> tag and the closing </title> tag, and then type the text you want to use as the title for the web page.

**3.** Instead of the opening <body> tag and closing </body> tag you would use for a standard web page, type an opening <frameset> tag right after the closing </head> tag and a closing </frameset> tag before the closing </html> tag:

```
<?xml version="1.0" encoding="utf-8"?>
<!DOCTYPE html PUBLIC "-//W3C//DTD XHTML 1.0 Frameset//EN"
        "http://www.w3.org/TR/xhtml1/DTD/xhtml1-frameset.dtd">
<html xmlns="http://www.w3.org/1999/xhtml" xml:lang="en"
lang="en">
<head>
<title></title>
</head>
<frameset>
</frameset>
</html>
```

**4.** Position the insertion point before the closing angle bracket of the opening <frameset> tag, and then type the details of the frameset. (See the next section for instructions on specifying the frameset.)

**5.** Position the insertion point between the <frameset> and </frameset> tags, and type a <frame/> tag for each frame in the frameset, including the appropriate attributes for each frame. See the next section for instructions on specifying the frames.

## Lay Out the Frames

You can create frame layouts that use rows, columns, or both.

### CREATE FRAMES USING ROWS

To create frames using rows:

**1.** Create the skeleton of the frameset document as described in the previous section.

**2.** Position the insertion point before the closing angle bracket of the <frameset> tag.

**3.** Type the rows attribute; an equal sign; double quotation marks; the height of each row, separated by commas; and another set of double quotation marks.

For example, to create two frames, the first with a height of 200 pixels and the second occupying the remainder of the height of the browser window:

```
<frameset rows="200,*">
```

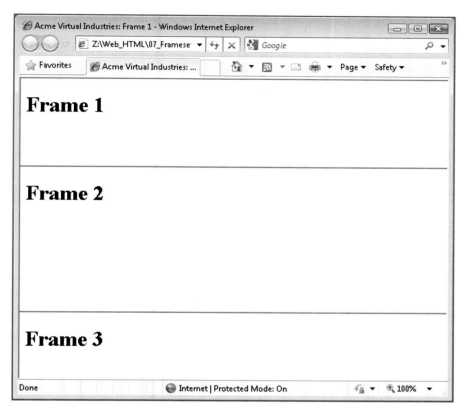

Figure 7-3: *In a multirow frame layout, the component documents are arranged from top to bottom.*

To create two frames, the first occupying one-quarter of the height of the browser window and the second occupying the remaining three-quarters:

```
<frameset rows="25%,75%">
```

To create three frames, the first with a height of 130 pixels, the third with a height of 100 pixels, and the second occupying the remainder of the height of the browser window (shown in Figure 7-3 with documents in the frames):

```
<frameset rows="130,*,100">
```

### CREATE FRAMES USING COLUMNS

To create frames using columns:

1. Create the skeleton of the frameset document as described in "Create the Frameset Document," earlier in this chapter.

2. Position the insertion point before the closing angle bracket of the <frameset> tag.

3. Type the cols attribute; an equal sign; double quotation marks; the width of each column, separated by commas; and another set of double quotation marks.

For example, to create two frames, the first with a width of 175 pixels and the second occupying the remainder of the width of the browser window:

```
<frameset cols="175,*">
```

To create two frames, the first occupying approximately one-third of the width of the browser window and the second occupying the remaining two-thirds:

```
<frameset cols="33%,67%">
```

To create three frames, the first and third with a width of 125 pixels each and the second occupying the remainder of the width of the browser window (shown in Figure 7-4 with easy-to-identify documents in the frames):

```
<frameset cols="125,*,125">
```

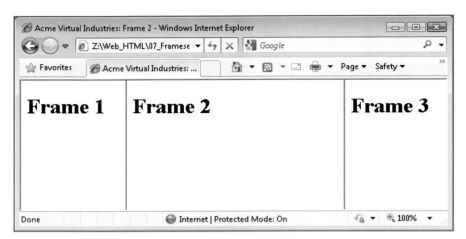

*Figure 7-4: **In a multicolumn frame layout, the component documents are arranged from left to right.***

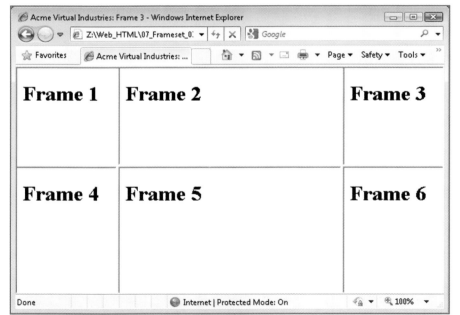

*Figure 7-5: **In a frame layout that uses multiple columns and multiple rows, the component documents are arranged from left to right and from top to bottom.***

## CREATE FRAMES USING BOTH ROWS AND COLUMNS

To create frames using both rows and columns, thus producing four (2 × 2), six (3 × 2 or 2 × 3), eight (4 × 2 or 2 × 4), nine (3 × 3), or more frames:

1. Create the skeleton of the frameset document as described in "Create the Frameset Document," earlier in this chapter.

2. Position the insertion point before the closing angle bracket of the <frameset> tag.

3. Type the rows attribute; an equal sign; double quotation marks: the height of each row, separated by commas; and another double quotation mark.

4. Type a space; the cols attribute; an equal sign; double quotation marks; the width of each column, separated by commas; and another set of double quotation marks.

For example, to create six frames in the arrangement shown in Figure 7-5:

```
<frameset rows="200,*" cols="150,*,150">
```

# Add the Component Documents to the Frameset

To add the component documents to the frameset:

1. Position the insertion point after the end of the <frameset> tag, and press **ENTER** to start a new line. Type the beginning of the opening <frame/> tag for the first frame:

   ```
   <frame
   ```

2. Type a space, the name attribute, an equal sign, opening double quotation marks, the name for the frame, and closing double quotation marks. For example:

   ```
   <frame name="page1"
   ```

3. Type a space, the src attribute, an equal sign, opening double quotation marks, the path (if necessary) and name of the web page to display in the frame, and closing double quotation marks. For example, to display the web page named page_1.html:

```
<frame name="page1" src="page_1.html"
```

4. Type the slash and closing angle bracket to complete the <frame/> tag:

```
<frame name="page1" src="page_1.html"/>
```

5. Press **ENTER** to start a new line, and then repeat steps 1 through 4 for each of the remaining frames.

## Change a Frame's Borders and Margins

To make frames appear exactly as you want them, you can control whether they display borders and the width of their margins.

### CHANGE A FRAME'S BORDERS

By default, a browser displays a border on each frame you create, as in Figure 7-5. Borders are convenient for when you want users to be aware that a web page consists of different frames—for example, when you use a frame to implement a navigation area that remains static while the contents of the other parts of the web page can move.

To remove borders from a frame, add the frameborder attribute to the appropriate <frame/> tag, and set its value to 0. For example:

```
<frame name="mission" src="mission.html" frameborder="0"/>
```

Figure 7-6 shows the sample page with all its frame borders hidden.

To ensure that borders are displayed on a frame, add the frameborder attribute to the appropriate <frame/> tag, and set its value to 1; however, because this is the default setting, there is no benefit to adding this to your code unless you want to make the code completely clear to anyone who needs to review or edit it.

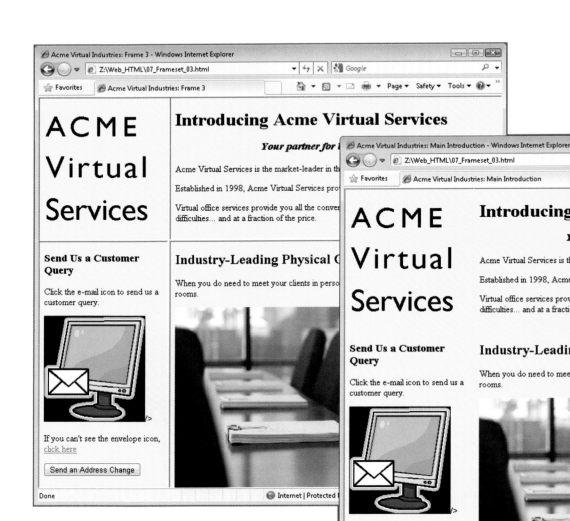

NOTE

The name attribute enables you to link other web pages directly to the frame rather than to the frameset document that contains it. If you will not need to link directly to the frame, you can omit the name attribute.

Figure 7-6: *Hiding frame borders makes the layout of a frameset page less obvious.*

**NOTE**

The alternative text does not appear when the web page is displayed in a browser that can handle frames, but a visitor can view the alternative text by displaying the source code for the web page.

**NOTE**

A visitor can resize a frame, even if its border is hidden, unless you specify the noresize attribute for the frame. See the discussion of this attribute later in this chapter.

**TIP**

When you use a frame to display a graphic, you'll often want to remove all the white space around the graphic. To do so, specify 0 for both the marginheight attribute and the marginwidth attribute.

**CAUTION**

How much space a frame's contents occupy will vary, depending on the settings that visitors have chosen in their browsers. If you prevent a frame from scrolling, the visitor will be able to view more of its contents by increasing the size of the frame—unless you prevent resizing as well (as described next).

CHANGE A FRAME'S MARGINS

To control the amount of space between a frame's contents and its margins, add the marginheight attribute and the marginwidth attribute to the <frame/> tag, and specify a value in pixels for each attribute. For example:

- To set a margin of 10 pixels at the left and right sides of the frame:

  ```
  marginwidth="10"
  ```

- To set a margin of 15 pixels at the top and bottom of the frame:

  ```
  marginheight="15"
  ```

The following is a complete tag using marginheight and marginwidth:

```
<frame name="mission" src="mission.html" frameborder="0"
marginheight="10" marginwidth="10"/>
```

## Control Whether a Frame Scrolls

By default, each frame displays scroll bars if its contents are too large to fit in the frame at its current size; if, however, the contents will fit in the frame, the scroll bars are not displayed.

To control the scroll bars, add the scrolling attribute to the appropriate <frame/> tag, and specify yes (to make the scroll bars always appear), no (to prevent the scroll bars from appearing), or auto (to apply automatic scrolling behavior). Given that there is little point in displaying scroll bars when they are not needed, you'll usually want to include the scrolling attribute only with a value of no; otherwise, the default setting (auto) is preferable.

## Prevent Visitors from Resizing the Frame

By default, visitors can resize the frames on your web pages by moving the mouse pointer over the frame border. In most cases, leaving frames resizable is a good idea because it enables visitors to adjust any frames whose contents don't fit in the frame because of the settings on the visitors' web browsers. For precise layouts, however, you may want to prevent visitors from resizing one or more frames. To do so, add the noresize attribute to the <frame/> tag with either the value "noresize" or the value "true" (either works)—for example:

```
<frame name="logo" src="logo.html" noresize="noresize"/>
```

## Nest One Frameset Inside Another

To create more complex frame layouts, you can nest one frameset inside another. Figure 7-7 shows a nested frameset used to produce a three-row frameset in which only the second row is divided into columns.

The following example shows the code for the nested frameset that produces the layout shown in Figure 7-7. For conciseness, this example does not include the <noframes> information included in the previous examples; however, you would normally include <noframes> information in a frameset page:

```
<frameset rows="15%,*,15%">
    <frame name="contacts" src="offices
.html"/>
    <frameset cols="150,*">
        <frame name = "nav1"
src="navigation1.html"/>
        <frame name="content"
src="european_offices.html"/>
    </frameset>
    <frame name="mission" src="mission
.html"/>
</frameset>
```

**Figure 7-7:** *Nesting one frameset inside another enables you to produce frame layouts with varying numbers of rows and columns.*

## Create Inline Frames

If you need to display a single frame within another web page, you can use an *inline frame*—one that appears as part of the page that contains it, without any other frames being involved. The advantage of the inline frame is that it enables you to place scrolling content within an otherwise static web page. For example, you might place a scrollable description in an inline frame alongside a product so that a visitor could scroll through the description without its occupying

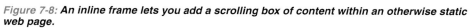

*Figure 7-8:* **An inline frame lets you add a scrolling box of content within an otherwise static web page.**

## CAUTION

Inline frames are suitable only for some purposes. One widespread use for which inline frames are *not* well suited is displaying an end user license agreement for software: Because the visitor can see only a small portion of the entire text at a time, the agreement becomes even harder to read than the smallest print of a tough contract.

much space on the page. Similarly, you might place a series of graphics in an inline frame so as to let each visitor choose the service area he or she wants, as in Figure 7-8.

To create an inline frame:

1. Position the insertion point where you want to place the inline frame.

2. Type the beginning of the `<iframe>` tag:

```
<iframe
```

3. Type the src attribute, an equal sign, double quotation marks, the URL of the web page that you want to display within the frame, and another pair of double quotation marks. For example:

```
<iframe src="service_list.html"
```

4. To specify the position of the inline frame relative to the next element in the page, type a space, the align attribute, and the appropriate value (see Table 7-1). For example, to align the inline frame to the left of the element in the page:

```
<iframe src="service_list.html" align="left"
```

5. To specify the height and width of the inline frame (rather than accepting default values which may not suit your page), add the height attribute and a suitable value, and the width attribute and a suitable value. Each value can be either a number of pixels or a percentage of the browser window's height or width. For example, to make the inline frame 150 pixels wide by 450 pixels high:

```
<iframe src="service_list.html" align="left" width="150"
height="540"
```

6. To change the size of the inline frame's internal margins instead of accepting the default settings, add the marginheight attribute and a suitable value in pixels for the vertical margins and add the marginwidth attribute and a suitable value in pixels for the horizontal margins. For example, to set horizontal and vertical margins of 5 pixels in the inline frame:

```
<iframe src="service_list.html" align="left" width="175"
    height="600" marginheight="5" marginwidth="5"
```

7. If you need to be able to refer to the inline frame using a hyperlink, add the name attribute and specify the name within double quotation marks—for example:

```
<iframe src="service_list.html" align="left" width="175"
    height="600" marginheight="5" marginwidth="5" name="selector"
```

| VALUE | ALIGNS THE INLINE FRAME |
|---|---|
| left | With the left margin, allowing subsequent elements to flow to its right |
| right | With the right margin, allowing subsequent elements to flow to its left |
| top | With the top of the surrounding content |
| middle | With its center aligned vertically with the baseline of the surrounding content |
| bottom | With the bottom of the surrounding content |

Table 7-1: *Values for the align Attribute*

8. By default, each inline frame automatically displays scroll bars if its contents are too large to fit in the frame. If you want to suppress the scroll bars, add the scrolling attribute with the value no.

9. Type the closing angle bracket for the opening <iframe> tag and the closing </iframe> tag. The following example shows the complete code for the inline frame:

```
<iframe src="service_list.html" align="left" width="175"
    height="600" marginheight="5" marginwidth="5"
name="selector"></iframe>
```

## Create a Link That Changes the Contents of a Frame

To create a link that changes the content of a frame:

1. Open the frameset document that defines the frame, and then verify that the <frame/> tag includes the name attribute. If it does not, add the name attribute—for example:

```
<frame name="mainframe" src="products.html">
```

2. If you made changes to the frameset document, save the changes. Then close the frameset document.

3. Open the component document that includes the link.

4. Add the target attribute and the name of the target frame to each link that should be opened within that frame. For example:

```
<h3><a href="services.html"
    target="mainframe">Services</a></h3>
<p>  <a href="offices.html"
    target="mainframe">Offices</a></p>
<p>  <a href="staff.html"
    target="mainframe">Staff</a></p>
```

5. Save the component document, switch to your browser, and test the links that you have just created.

## How to...

- Understanding the Style Cascade
- Create a Style Rule
- Understanding Other Ways of Creating Style Rules
- Create an Embedded Style Sheet
- Understanding CSS Versions
- Create and Apply an External Style Sheet
- Use Special Selectors
- Apply a Style to Part of an Element
- Override Style Sheets
- Control Font Formatting
- Set Alignment, Indents, Margins, and Line Height
- Prevent a Background Graphic from Being Tiled or Scrolling
- Create a Floating Layout with CSS
- Creating a Three-Column Floating Layout
- Overriding Style Sheets in Your Browser

# Chapter 8
# Applying Formatting Using Cascading Style Sheets

Style sheets—known formally as Cascading Style Sheets, or CSS—are the preferred means of applying formatting consistently to your web pages. Unlike the HTML codes for direct formatting discussed so far in this book, which can be overridden by browser settings, CSS enable you to lay out web pages exactly as you want them: You can specify margins, indents, line spacing, font sizes, and more.

This chapter starts by discussing the basics of how CSS work and how you apply them. You will then learn how to write style rules, how to create style sheets, and how to use style sheets to implement widely useful effects.

# Understand CSS Essentials

As discussed earlier in this book, much of the formatting that you can apply directly with HTML is either imprecise or can be overridden by the settings a visitor has chosen in his or her browser. For example, you can specify that a word or phrase be displayed in a font size two sizes larger than the default, but you do not usually know which size is being used as the default on a visitor's browser. Similarly, you can specify that a particular font be used, but it may not be installed on the visitor's computer—in which case, the browser will substitute a default font.

Styles enable you to apply consistent formatting to elements in your web pages. For example, by entering text between an opening <h1> tag and a closing </h1> tag, you apply the h1 style (or first-level heading style) to it. The browser displays all the instances of the h1 style using the same formatting. By defining different formatting for the h1 style in the style sheet, you can change all the instances of the h1 style in a web page.

Style sheets also enable you to apply some types of formatting—such as indents, line spacing, and precise positioning—that are either difficult or impossible to implement via direct formatting. Figure 8-1 shows a web page that uses a style sheet to implement indents and line spacing.

Style sheets enable you to specify exact formatting that overrides a browser's setting, unless the visitor has turned off style sheets or applied a style sheet of his or her own, as discussed at the end of this chapter.

You can create a style sheet either as a part of a web page or as an external file that contains instructions.

- **External style sheet** Using an external style sheet has the advantages of keeping the layout instructions separate from the content and enabling you to quickly apply style changes to all the web pages that use that style sheet. This is the best method to use for most purposes.

- **Internal style sheet** Using an internal (or *embedded*) style sheet enables you to implement style effects only on that page, which can be useful in some circumstances. You can also use an internal style sheet to override the styles in the external style sheet.

## QUICKFACTS

### UNDERSTANDING THE STYLE CASCADE

CSS are described as "cascading" because styles are applied at up to four different levels, with the properties flowing down from the top level and masking any duplicate properties in the lower levels. At the bottom of the cascade, the prevailing properties are applied to the web page.

1. The top level of the cascade is any style that is applied using the style attribute for a tag (see Chapter 3 for more information on the style attribute).

2. The second level is any style defined in a <style> element within the web page itself (considered an internal style sheet).

3. The third level is any style defined in the external style sheet (or style sheets) linked to the web page.

4. The fourth level is the settings that the visitor chooses in his or her browser.

These four levels give the following results:

- Formatting in an external style sheet overrides the visitor's browser settings.

- Formatting defined in an internal style sheet (a <style> element) overrides formatting in an external style sheet. However, if the <link> tag appears after the <style> element in the header, the external style sheet overrides the internal style sheet. (This breaks the cascade of style sheets.)

- Formatting applied to an element using the style attribute overrides formatting in both internal and external style sheets.

- Non-style attributes (such as the deprecated align attribute) override style formatting.

Figure 8-1: *Style sheets not only simplify the layout and maintenance of your pages, but also enable you to create effects you cannot create via direct formatting.*

**TIP**

If you want an external style sheet to take effect and have the controlling influence, you cannot have internal style sheets (the <style> element) or use the style attribute in tags that conflict with those in the external style sheet.

**NOTE**

The *selector* is the part of a style rule that declares which markup element the style rule affects. For example, in a style rule that specifies that the h1 style have the color blue, h1 is the selector. The next part of the style rule—in this case, the color—is the *property* affected. The final part of the style rule is the *value* assigned to the property—in this case, blue.

**NOTE**

If the value includes spaces, you must put double quotation marks around it—for example, font-family: "Arial Black". If the value does not include spaces, you do not need to put double quotation marks around it—for example, font-family: Arial.

**TIP**

You can place a semicolon at the end of the final value in a style declaration if you find doing so helpful for consistency. For example, the declaration h2 { font-size: 20pt } can also be written h2 { font-size: 20pt; } (with the final semicolon).

---

Even when you use an embedded style sheet, you save time on formatting; instead of needing to change every instance of a type of formatting throughout the page, you need change only the definition of the style, which appears at the beginning of the document.

## Create a Style Rule

Each internal or external style sheet consists of *style rules,* items that specify which markup element they affect and how that element should appear or behave. For example, a style rule might specify that the h1 (heading 1) style have the color blue and the font size 24 points.

To create a style rule:

1. Open the document in which you want to create the style rule.
   - For an internal style sheet, open the web page that contains it. Position the insertion point in the header area but not within a tag (see "Create an Embedded Style Sheet," later in this chapter, for more information).
   - For an external style sheet, open the style sheet, or create a new style sheet. (See "Create and Apply an External Style Sheet," later in this chapter.)

2. Type the selector:

   h1

3. Type a space, an opening brace, the name of the property you want to affect, and a colon:

   h1 { size:

4. Type a space and the value you want to assign to the property. For example, to make the font size 24 points:

   h1 { size: 24pt

5. If you want to specify another property for the same selector, type a semicolon, a space, the property, a colon, a space, and the value. For example, to make the font color blue:

   h1 { size: 24pt; color: blue

## UNDERSTANDING OTHER WAYS OF CREATING STYLE RULES

The section "Create a Style Rule" shows you what's usually the easiest way to create a style rule: specifying a single selector and then specifying each property you want to set for that selector and the value for the property, separating the property declarations with semicolons. But you can also create style rules in two other ways.

### SET ONE PROPERTY AT A TIME

If you choose, you can set a single property at a time. For example, to set the paragraph font's color to black and 10 points:

```
p { color: black }
p { font-size: 10pt }
```

The properties you set for a style are cumulative, so the style ends up with all the properties defined. Setting properties like this makes your code easier to read even though it occupies more lines than if you had separated the properties with semicolons.

### SET PROPERTIES FOR MULTIPLE SELECTORS AT ONCE

A technique you may sometimes want to use is to set properties for multiple styles in a single statement. To do so, separate each style from the previous one with a comma and a space. For example:

```
h1, h2 { color: blue ; font-family: Arial }
```

This technique is most useful when you want to give two or more styles several of the same properties, but you can also use it to set a single property. Normally, you'll set only some of the properties for each selector this way; you can then set other properties separately. For example, if you make the h1 and h2 styles blue Arial like this, you can then set different font sizes or font weights separately to distinguish them.

---

6. Repeat step 5 to add additional properties to the style rule. For example, to make the font Garamond:

```
h1 { size: 24pt; color: blue; font-family: Garamond
```

7. End the style rule by typing a space and a closing brace:

```
h1 { size: 24pt; color: blue; font-family: Garamond }
```

You can also break the style rule across multiple lines to make it easier to read—for example:

```
h1 { size: 24pt;
     color: blue;
     font-family: Garamond }
```

## Create an Embedded Style Sheet

To create an embedded style sheet, you place the style declarations in the header of the web page.

1. In your text editor, open the web page to which you want to add the style.

2. Place the insertion point in the header section. Anywhere in the header section is acceptable, provided that it is not within another element (such as the <title> and </title> tags), but your pages will be easier to edit if you use a consistent location—for example, on the line directly after the closing </title> tag or immediately before the closing </head> tag.

3. Type the opening <style> tag. Include the type attribute and set its value to text/css:

```
<style type="text/css">
```

4. Press ENTER to start a new line, and then type the definition for the style. For example:

```
h1 { font-family: Garamond }
```

5. Repeat step 4 for each additional style rule you want to create. For example:

```
<style type="text/css">
   h1 { font-family: Garamond }
   h2 { color: blue }
   h3 { color: magenta }
```

6. Press ENTER to start a new line, and then type the closing </style> tag:

```
</style>
```

### UNDERSTANDING CSS VERSIONS

As of this writing (Summer 2009), the current version of the CSS specification is CSS 2.1. CSS 3 is under development, but the due date keeps being pushed out.

Here is a brief summary of the differences in CSS versions:

- CSS 1 enables you to control major elements, such as the font (size, color, and type), how lists are displayed, margins and borders, alignment, line spacing, and background graphics and background colors.

- CSS 2 improves font support, provides more control over positioning objects, and enables you to control tables. It also includes text-to-speech capabilities.

- CSS 3 is in development as of this writing. It consists of different modules that can be implemented separately. For example, the Template Layout module gives a new method of positioning elements, while the Aural Style Sheets module provides multimedia capabilities.

Current browsers—Internet Explorer 8, Firefox 3, and Safari 4—implement CSS 2 with a high degree of accuracy, though there are still some bugs.

You do not need to specify the CSS version that you are using in your web pages, but you should be aware that elements added more recently to CSS may not work properly in all browsers.

The easiest way to identify problems is to test your web pages in several browsers and make sure that they are displayed correctly. At a minimum, test every page using Internet Explorer, Firefox, and Safari, because these three browsers between them have more than 90 percent of the browser market.

## Create and Apply an External Style Sheet

To use an external style sheet, you create it as a separate file in your text editor or HTML editor, and then link to it each web page for which you want to use the style sheet.

### CREATE AN EXTERNAL STYLE SHEET

To create an external style sheet:

1. Open Notepad (or your HTML editor), and start a new document.

2. Optionally, on the first line of the style sheet, type a comment explaining what the style sheet is and what it is for. To create a comment in a style sheet, type a forward slash, an asterisk, a space, the text of the comment, another space, another asterisk, and another forward slash. For example:

   ```
   /* Acme Virtual Industries standard style sheet, acme_standard
   .css */
   ```

3. Type the definition for each style you want to include in the style sheet. For example:

   ```
   h1 { color: green; font-size: 24pt; font-weight: bold }
   h2 { color: olive; font-size: 18pt; font-weight: bold }
   h3 { color: #339900; font-size: 14pt; font-weight: bold }
   p {font-size:14pt ; color: black }
   ```

4. Click the **File** menu, click **Save**, and then save the style sheet with the .css extension. (You can also use other extensions, but using .css is clearest.)

5. Click the **File** menu and then click **Exit** to exit Notepad.

### LINK A WEB PAGE TO AN EXTERNAL STYLE SHEET

After creating the external style sheet you want to use, link your web pages to it.

1. Open the web page that you want to link to the style sheet.

2. Position the insertion point within the header section of the web page. Anywhere in the header section will work, but your pages will be easier to edit if you use a consistent location—for example, on the line immediately before the closing </head> tag.

3. Type the start of a <link> tag, specifying the rel attribute (which specifies the relationship of the link) with the value stylesheet and the type attribute with the value text/css:

   ```
   <link rel="stylesheet" type="text/css"
   ```

# CAUTION

If you use both an external style sheet and an internal style sheet, put the `<link>` tag for the external style sheet before the `<style>` tag for the internal style sheet. Otherwise, you may break the style cascade and get unexpected results.

# NOTE

You can use two or more pairs of `<style>` and `</style>` tags if you prefer, but in most cases, it's easier and clearer to use only a single pair.

4. Type the href attribute and assign to it the path (if required) and filename of the external style sheet. For example:

```
href="styles/acme_standard.css"
```

5. Finish the link by typing a space, a forward slash, and the closing angle bracket:

```
href="styles/acme_standard.css" />
```

The following example shows the entire link in the header section of a web page:

```
<head>
    <meta http-equiv="content-type" content="text/html;
charset=utf-8" />
    <title>Acme Virtual Industries: Strategy Meeting</title>
    <link rel="stylesheet" type="text/css" href="acme_standard
.css" />
</head>
```

Figure 8-2 provides a quick demonstration of the changes you can make in moments by linking a style sheet to a web page.

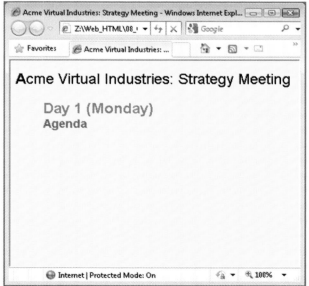

Figure 8-2: *By changing the style sheet attached to a web page, you can quickly change the look of every style defined in the style sheet. The left screen uses default styles for h1, h2, and h3, while the right screen uses a style sheet that defines custom styles for these headings.*

**NOTE**

When saving a file for the first time with Notepad, remember to choose All Files in the Files Of Type drop-down list to prevent Notepad from adding its default .txt extension to the name. You can also enclose the filename and extension within double quotation marks (for example, "standard.css").

**NOTE**

When applying an external style sheet to a frameset document, you must apply it to the component documents that make up the frameset document, not to the frameset document itself. If you want the component documents to have different looks, you can use different external style sheets for the component documents.

**NOTE**

This example assumes that the style sheet is on the same web server as the web page that is being linked to it. (The style sheet is in the /styles/ folder.) You can also link to a style sheet on another server, if necessary; to do so, assign the full URL of the style sheet to the href attribute of the <link> tag. Bear in mind that keeping the style sheet on the same server as your web pages may help to avoid performance issues.

## LINK TWO OR MORE STYLE SHEETS TO A WEB PAGE

Instead of linking a single style sheet to a web page, you can link two or more style sheets to the same page. Two common reasons for doing this are:

- The web page uses some styles that are contained in one of the style sheets and some styles that are contained in the other style sheet. Instead of integrating all the styles into a third comprehensive style sheet, you can apply both the style sheets to achieve full coverage of the styles.

- The second style sheet redefines some of the styles used in the first style sheet to produce web pages with a similar yet slightly different appearance. For example, an organization or company may use a global style sheet that produces the general look for all web pages. Each office or department then may apply a second style sheet to adapt the global style sheet to meet their needs, producing a different look for each office's or department's pages.

The following example shows two style sheets applied to a document. The second style sheet (acme_marketing.css) overrides the first style sheet (acme_standard.css) because it is listed after the first style sheet.

```
<head>
<title>Acme Virtual Industries: About Us</title>
<link rel="stylesheet" type="text/css"
    href="styles/acme_standard.css" />
<link rel="stylesheet" type="text/css"
    href="styles/acme_marketing.css" />
</head>
```

## Use Special Selectors

Up to this point, this chapter has used HTML tags as the selectors for style rules—for example, to create a style rule that applies to h1 elements. For flexibility, however, HTML also enables you to use other items—such as the id attribute, the class attribute, and the <div> and <span> types—as the selectors for style rules.

### USE THE ID ATTRIBUTE AS A SELECTOR

If you need to pick out a single instance of an element from all the other instances, add the id attribute to that element in the web page, and assign it a unique identifying value that starts with a letter. This example assigns the value breaking to the heading:

```
<h2 id="breaking">Breaking News</h2>
```

Once the item is marked with the id attribute, you can specify in the style sheet how to format the item. To do so, type a hash mark (#) followed by the ID value, a space, and the style information within braces. For example, to apply red formatting and 28-point font size to the breaking item created previously:

```
#breaking { font-size: 28pt; color: red }
```

### USE THE CLASS ATTRIBUTE AS A SELECTOR

Sometimes, it can be useful to distinguish different types of items that are formatted as the same element. For example, your web pages may include various types of content formatted as paragraphs (entered between <p> and </p> tags) and various types of content formatted as second-level headings (entered between <h2> and </h2> tags).

To distinguish between different types of content formatted as the same element, you can use the class attribute to assign a particular description to the desired instances of the element. For example, you might create a class named "new_services" so that you could apply different formatting to only the items in that class.

To create the class, on a new line in your style sheet, type a period, the name you want to assign to the class, and the style information for the class. For example, to make the new_services class large and a purple font:

```
.new_services {color: #3333ff; font-size: large }
```

To apply the class to an element in a web page, add the class attribute to the element's opening tag, and specify the name of the class. For example:

```
<h2 class="new_services">Latest Services</h2>
<p class="new_services">Here are our latest services.</p>
<ol>
<li class="new_services">Virtual Manager</li>
<li class="new_services">Virtual Mailbox</li>
<li class="new_services">Reminder Hotline</li>
</ol>
```

## USE A SPAN AS A SELECTOR

A *span* is a flexible unit that you can use to select text within an element so that you can apply formatting to it. To create a span:

1. In your style sheet, create the class, if it does not already exist. For example:

```
.new_services {color: #3333ff; font-size: large;
    font-weight: bold }
```

2. In Notepad or your HTML editor, open the web page in which you want to create the span.

3. Position the insertion point before the desired text.

4. Type the opening <span> tag, including the class attribute and specifying the name of the class you want to apply to the span. For example, to apply the class named special_offers:

```
<span class="new_services">New Services
```

5. Position the insertion point at the end of the desired text, and then type the closing </span> tag:

```
</span>
```

The following example shows the complete paragraph containing the span:

```
<p>For information about more of our
    <span class="new_services">New Services</span>,
    click <a href="new_services.html">here</a>.</p>
```

## USE A DIVISION AS A SELECTOR

As discussed in Chapter 3, you can use the <div> and </div> tags to group paragraphs (or other elements) into a division so that you can manipulate them all together. You can apply styles to a division directly (by adding the style information to the opening <div> tag) or via either an internal style sheet or an external style sheet. Using an external style sheet gives the greatest flexibility because you can change the formatting of all the divisions in your web pages by simply changing the relevant style rules in your style sheets.

**TIP**

You can use a span to apply font formatting to individual words or phrases in your documents without using the <font> tag. The advantage of using spans is that you can change them all centrally from your style sheet instead of having to change each instance of the formatting in the individual web pages.

Instead of applying the class attribute to each of the elements to which you want to apply the new_services formatting, you could create a division around the elements and apply the class attribute to the division. The following example shows how to do this:

```
<div class="new_services">
<h2>Latest Services</h2>
<p>Here are our latest services.</p>
<ol>
<li>Virtual Manager</li>
<li>Virtual Mailbox</li>
<li>Reminder Hotline</li>
</ol>
</div>
```

## Apply a Style to Part of an Element

You can apply a style to only part of an element rather than to a full element by using *pseudo-elements*: logically defined parts of elements. You don't need to tag the pseudo-element in your code—the browser identifies them on its own.

### FORMAT THE FIRST LETTER OF AN ELEMENT

Sometimes you may find it useful to apply different formatting to the first letter in an element. To do so, define a style rule for the first-letter pseudo-element of the desired element.

1. In your style sheet, type the style name, a colon, and then <u>first-letter</u>. For example:

   ```
   h1:first-letter
   ```

2. Type a space and then the details of the style rule for the first letter. For example:

   ```
   h1:first-letter { font-weight: bold }
   h1:first-letter { color: #990000 }
   h1:first-letter { font-size: 24pt }
   ```

You can see how easy and effective this is—you don't have to make any change on the web page itself, only in your style sheet. The following illustration shows an example of the effect produced.

Acme Virtual Industries: Strategy Meeting

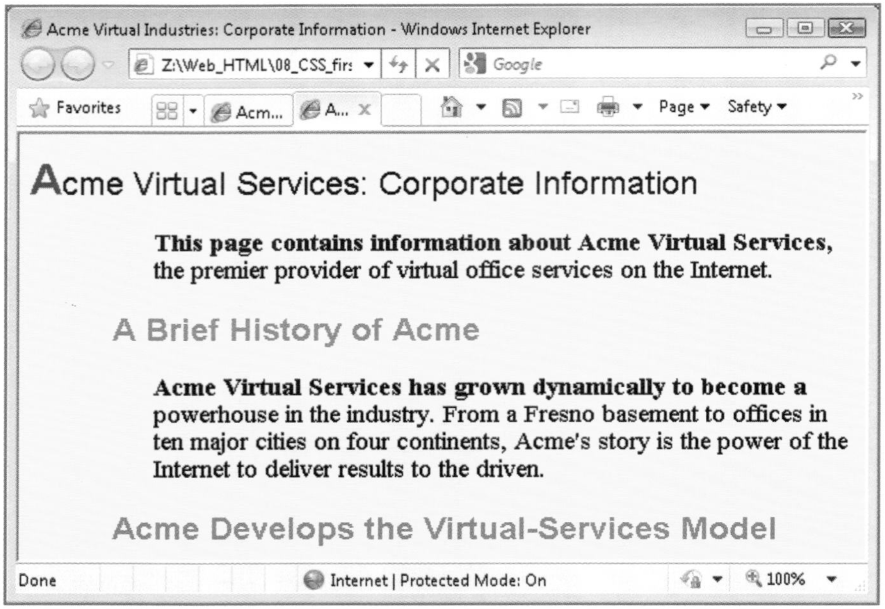

Figure 8-3: *You can use the :first-line pseudo-element to make the first line of each instance of an element pop out. The formatting applies to the first line no matter what size of browser window the page is displayed in.*

**CAUTION**

The blink value does not work in Internet Explorer and can quickly become irritating to visitors using those browsers that do support it. For this reason, it is best not to use blink.

**FORMAT THE FIRST LINE OF AN ELEMENT**

You can apply different formatting to the first line of an element by adding the :first-line pseudo-element to a style sheet. The following example, which you would place in either an internal style sheet or an external style sheet, makes the first line of each paragraph (p) bold. Figure 8-3 shows the effect.

```
p {font-size:14pt ; color: black;}
p:first-line { font-weight: bold }
```

## Override Style Sheets

If you're creating a website and want to implement a consistent look across it, use external style sheets rather than internal style sheets. External style sheets will save you considerable time and effort in keeping your web pages up-to-date with your latest styles.

Sometimes, however, you may want to override an external style sheet by using an internal style sheet to apply one or more styles to a web page. You can use the external style sheet to implement the general look of your website, and then use an internal style sheet to change one or more specific elements on a particular web page.

Beyond overriding the external style sheet by using an internal style sheet, you may sometimes need to override the internal style sheet as well. As discussed in Chapter 3, you can use the style attribute to apply formatting to an element. Any formatting you apply this way overrides any formatting applied using an internal style sheet, which in turn overrides any formatting applied using an external style sheet.

## Control Font Formatting

In style sheets, you can control font formatting by using either the individual properties explained in Table 8-1 or the all-encompassing font property.

| PROPERTY | EXPLANATION | VALUES OR EXAMPLES |
|---|---|---|
| background-color | The background color to apply | navy, magenta, #CCFFFF |
| color | The font color to apply | red, blue, #993333 |
| font-family | The name of the font family | Georgia, "Times New Roman" |
| font-size | A font size measured in points or another measurement unit (pixels, em, centimeters) or specified by keyword (for example, x-large) | 12pt, 18pt, x-large |
| font-style | The style: normal, italic, or oblique (slanted) | normal, italic, oblique |
| font-variant | Whether to use normal letters or small caps | normal, small-caps |
| font-weight | How bold the font is | lighter, normal, bold, bolder |
| letter-spacing | Whether the letters are normally spaced, closer together (a negative value), or farther apart (a positive value) | -2px, 12px, 10% |
| text-decoration | Whether to apply decoration to the text | none, blink, underline, overline, line-through |
| text-transform | Whether to apply consistent capitalization to the text | none, capitalize (initial capitals), lowercase, uppercase |
| word-spacing | Whether the words are normally spaced, closer together (a negative value), or farther apart (a positive value) | -3px, 10 px, 10% |

Table 8-1: *Individual Font Properties for Formatting Text*

**NOTE**

When using the font property, you must specify the values in the correct order; however, you do not have to use every value, as HTML figures out which values you've omitted.

For example, the following style, entered in a style sheet (internal or external), produces Heading 3 paragraphs in 36-point boldface using small caps:

```
h3 { font-weight: bold}
h3 { font-variant: small-caps }
h3 { font-size: 36pt }
h3 { color: blue }
```

The following style, entered in a style sheet, makes ordered (numbered) lists appear in maroon, italic uppercase:

```
ol { color: maroon; font-style: italic;
    text-transform: uppercase }
```

The font property has a fixed syntax that enables you to specify each of the values you want to set within a single property. The syntax, shown with vertical bars indicating the divisions between values, is as follows (the vertical bars are not used in the actual code):

```
font: style | weight | variant | size or line-height | font-family
```

The following style rule, entered in a style sheet, makes h3 elements appear in bold, italic, 24-point small capitals in the Times New Roman font:

```
h3 { font: italic bold small-caps 24pt "Times New Roman" }
```

## Set Alignment, Indents, Margins, and Line Height

As discussed in Chapter 3, you can apply basic alignment to individual items by using the align attribute, but you have little control over indents, margins, and line height via direct formatting. Style sheets offer far more control over these settings.

### ALIGN, CENTER, OR JUSTIFY TEXT

Use the text-align property to left-align, right-align, center, or justify text. (Justified text is aligned with both margins.) Table 8-2 lists the values for the text-align property.

For example, to align an element with the right margin, you can create a class with a name such as alignright in the style sheet:

```
.alignright {text-align: right }
```

Then apply the class to each item you want to align with the right margin:

```
<p class="alignright">This paragraph is aligned with the right margin.</p>
```

### SET INDENTS

Use the text-indent property to specify the indent you want to apply to the first line of a paragraph. Normally, the best option is to specify a fixed indent using a unit of measurement—for example, 0.5 inch. Your other option is to specify that the indent be a percentage of the width of the element that contains the line or paragraph. A percentage setting like this allows the indent to vary as the line width changes when the browser window is resized.

The following example creates a CSS style that sets a half-inch indent on the paragraph style (<p>):

```
p { text-indent: 0.5in }
```

| VALUE | EXPLANATION |
|-------|-------------|
| left | Aligns the text with the left margin |
| right | Aligns the text with the right margin |
| center | Centers the text between the margins |
| justify | Aligns the text with both margins |

Table 8-2: **Values for the** text-align **Property**

**TIP**

If you need to prevent browsers from adding space between elements, set the margin-bottom property of the first element and the margin-top property of the second element to 0. This technique is especially handy when you need to make a heading and a paragraph appear without extra space between them.

**TIP**

If an element needs one border measurement for both the top and the bottom margins and one border measurement for both the left and right margins, you can specify only two values for the margin property. The browser uses the first value for the top and bottom borders and the second value for the left and right borders. For example, { margin: 10px 20px } creates 10-pixel borders at the top and bottom and 20-pixel borders at each side.

**NOTE**

If you don't specify line height using the line-height property, the browser automatically adjusts the line height so that it is large enough for the font size or for the object the element contains.

**NOTE**

You can also specify the line height as a percentage. For example, a setting of 150% makes the line height one-and-a-half times as large as usual; a setting of 25% makes the line height one-quarter of the normal height.

## SET MARGINS

To control where an element appears on a web page, you can adjust the element's margins—the amount of space that appears between the element and the next element on the specified side.

To set a margin width, you use the margin-left property, the margin-right property, the margin-top property, or the margin-bottom property. You can specify the margin either as a percentage of the window size (which gives the best flexibility for when the widow is resized) or as a number of pixels (px), inches (in), millimeters (mm) or centimeters (cm), points (pt), or picas (pc). For web pages, pixels are frequently used, although inches or centimeters may be easier to think about.

The following example, which you would use in a style sheet, sets all four margins for the p element:

```
p { margin-left: 0.5in; margin-right: 0.5in;
    margin-top: 0.25in; margin-bottom: 0.15in }
```

If you need to specify all the margins for an element, you can also use the margin property and specify the margins in a clockwise order starting from the top: top, right, bottom, and then left. The following example sets a top margin of 0.75 inches, a right margin of 0.5 inches, a bottom margin of 0.25 inches, and a left margin of 0.5 inches for the h5 element. The result is more concise but arguably harder to read:

```
h5 { margin: 0.75in 0.5in 0.25in 0.5in }
```

## SET LINE HEIGHT

To control the amount of vertical space that an element occupies, you can set the line height (also called "leading") by using the line-height property and specifying the measurement as a multiple of line spacing, a number of measurement units (such as points, pixels, inches, or millimeters), or a percentage of the space normally allotted to the font size or object.

> If you've ever longed to be able to call on extra assistance... at any time of the day or night... without the need to hire, train, and fire... without worry, hassle, or significant expense— then our virtual services are exactly what you need.
>
> Our fully-trained, highly motivated staff members can be up and running with your specific business needs within hours... either onsite or off. Whether you need an assistant, a supervisor, or a top-level manager, we can provide an experienced staff member with the skills and expertise you require.

Figure 8-4: **Applying a first-line indent and changing the line height can greatly change the appearance of an element.**

Setting an exact line height in points is useful in precise layouts. The following example sets the line height to 24 points:

```
.spaced { line-height: 24pt }
```

Figure 8-4 shows the effect of changing line height and applying a first-line indent.

# Prevent a Background Graphic from Being Tiled or Scrolling

As discussed in Chapter 4, you can add a background graphic to an element using the background attribute in the element's tag. If the graphic isn't large enough to occupy the entire background, however, the browser will *tile*, or repeat, the graphic automatically, so make it big enough. Tiling tends to spoil the effect of a background graphic.

To prevent tiling, use the background-image property in the appropriate style to place the graphic, and then specify the background-repeat property with the value no-repeat to prevent the graphic from repeating. The following example, which uses an embedded style sheet, applies the graphic named avs.jpg in the images folder as the background image and prevents it from being tiled:

```
<style>
    body { background-image: url(images/avs.jpg);
        background-repeat: no-repeat }
</style>
```

To fix a background graphic so that it remains in the same position in the browser window even when the web page is scrolled, add the background-attachment property and specify the value fixed. The following example continues the previous example and fixes the background graphic in place:

```
<style>
    body { background-image: url(images/sunset.jpg);
        background-repeat: no-repeat;
        background-attachment: fixed }
</style>
```

**TIP**

Note the syntax for specifying the background graphic: url tells the browser that the parentheses contain the location of the graphic file.

**NOTE**

If you do want to repeat a background graphic, set the background-repeat property to repeat, repeat-x, or repeat-y. The repeat value makes the graphic repeat as many times as is necessary to fill the space, from left to right and from top to bottom. The repeat-x value makes the graphic repeat horizontally as many times as is necessary to reach the other side of the space. The repeat-y value makes the graphic repeat vertically as many times as is necessary to reach the bottom of the space.

To control where the background graphic appears, set the background-position property:

- **Horizontal placement. Choose** left, center, or right.
- **Vertical placement. Choose** top, center, or bottom.

For example, to position the background graphic in the center of the web page:

```
<style>
    body { background-image: url(images/sunset.jpg);
        background-repeat: no-repeat;
        background-attachment: fixed;
        background-position: center center }
</style>
```

## Create a Floating Layout with CSS

Instead of using frames to display different information in different areas of a web page (as discussed in Chapter 7), you can create a *floating layout* by using CSS. To do so, you use the float property to set the appropriate part of the text to float to the left or right, as needed. This enables you to position elements side by side and create boxes and columns as needed.

The float property has three settings.

- left    Moves the element to the left and makes content wrap around its right side.
- right    Moves the element to the right and makes content wrap around its left side.
- none    Turns off floating for the element so that it appears in its normal position.

### UNDERSTAND HOW A FLOATING LAYOUT WORKS

To set up a floating layout, you define the sections of the web page that you want to float, and then apply the appropriate float setting to them.

You can float a graphic as it is, because it occupies a chunk of space, but for text-based content, you need to divide it up into sections. Here's how you do that:

- Use the <div> tag to cordon off the content you want to put into one area of a page.
- Add a class or id to each <div> section so that you can refer to it easily.
- Set the float property for that class or id to position the <div> section.

**TIP**

It's often helpful to sketch out your web page before you start creating it. Use either a piece of paper or the online equivalent—for example, a drawing program (such as Paint on Windows) or a word processor (such as Microsoft Word). Give a simple but descriptive name to each section—leftcolumn, header, and so on—so that you can easily identify them in your HTML document and your CSS document.

Figure 8-5: *The sample page as a single-column layout.*

## CREATE A TWO-COLUMN FLOATING LAYOUT

To create a simple two-column floating layout:

1. Create the HTML page as usual. This example uses a simple page, whose code is shown here and which appears in Figure 8-5:

```
<?xml version="1.0" encoding="utf-8"?>
<!DOCTYPE html PUBLIC "-//W3C//DTD XHTML 1.0
Transitional//EN"
        "http://www.w3.org/TR/xhtml1/DTD/xhtml1-
transitional.dtd">
<html xmlns="http://www.w3.org/1999/xhtml" xml:
lang="en" lang="en">
<head>
    <meta http-equiv="content-type" content="text/
html; charset=utf-8" />
    <title>Acme Virtual Services: How We Can Help
You</title>
</head>
<body>
    <h1>Acme Virtual Industries: How We Can Help
You</h1>
    <img src="images/team_leaders.jpg" alt="Acme
Team Leaders" width="200px" />
    <p><em>Our trained staff are standing ready to
help your business.</em></p>
    <h2>The Easy Way to Get a Helping Hand... in
Moments</h2>
    <p>If you've ever longed to be able to call
on extra assistance... at any time of the day or
night... without the need to hire, train, and
fire... without worry, hassle, or significant
expense&#8212;then our virtual services are
exactly what you need.</p>
    <p>Our fully-trained, highly motivated staff
members can be up and running with your specific
business needs within hours... either onsite or
off.</p>
    <p>Whether you need an assistant, a
supervisor, or a top-level manager, we can provide
an experienced staff member with the skills and
expertise you require.</p>
</body>
</html>
```

2. Use `<div>` tags to divide the `<body>` section into two divisions, one for the left column and one for the right column. Give each column a simple id: leftcolumn and rightcolumn. The listing shows the `<div>` tags in bold.

```
<body>
    <h1>Acme Virtual Industries: How We Can Help You</h1>
    <div id="leftcolumn">
    <img src="images/team_leaders.jpg" alt="Acme Team Leaders"
width="200px" />
    <p><em>Our trained staff are standing ready to help your
business.</em></p>
    </div>
    <div id="rightcolumn">
    <h2>The Easy Way to Get a Helping Hand... in Moments</h2>
    <p>If you've ever longed to be able to call on extra
assistance... at any time of the day or night... without the
need to hire, train, and fire... without worry, hassle, or
significant expense&#8212;then our virtual services are exactly
what you need.</p>
    <p>Our fully-trained, highly motivated staff members can
be up and running with your specific business needs within
hours... either onsite or off.</p>
    <p>Whether you need an assistant, a supervisor, or a top-
level manager, we can provide an experienced staff member with
the skills and expertise you require.</p>
    </div>
</body>
```

3. Change the width of the `<img />` tag so that it occupies 100% of the column it's in rather than using a fixed measurement. This will let the graphic resize with the browser window.

```
<img src="images/team_leaders.jpg" alt="Acme Team Leaders"
width="100%" />
```

4. Add the style sheet reference to the header.

```
    <title>Acme Virtual Services: How We Can Help You</title>
    <link rel="stylesheet" type="text/css" href="acme_two_cols
.css" />
</head>
```

**NOTE**

Instead of floating rightcolumn to the left and making it wrap to leftcolumn, you could float it to the right. This would increase the amount of space between the columns.

**TIP**

If you're having trouble getting your wrapped elements to appear in the right places, add a different-colored border to each rule so that you can see where its limits are.

## QUICKSTEPS

### CREATING A THREE-COLUMN FLOATING LAYOUT

To create a three-column floating layout, use a similar technique to that for the two-column floating layout, but create a center column as well (see Figure 8-7). Follow these general steps:

1. In the HTML file, create a separate <div> section for each of the three columns.

2. Assign each <div> section a unique id—for example, leftcolumn, centercolumn, and rightcolumn.

3. Create a style sheet that defines three rules for the columns. Here's an example:

```
/* Acme Virtual Industries
   three-column style sheet,
   acme_three_cols.css */
#leftcolumn { float: left;
              width: 18%;
              padding: 2% }
#centercolumn { float: left;
                width: 55% }
#rightcolumn { float: left;
               width: 18%;
               padding: 2% }
```

4. Attach the style sheet to the HTML file. This example uses a different style sheet name than the two-column layout, so you'll need to update the <link> in the HTML file to point to the three-column style sheet.

5. Create a style sheet as described earlier in this chapter and add the CSS rules. The following listing shows all the style sheet needs to create the columns, but in practice, your style sheet will normally include formatting for the text elements:

```
/* Acme Virtual Industries two-column style sheet,
acme_two_cols.css */
#leftcolumn { float: left;
              width: 35% }
#rightcolumn { float: left;
               width: 60% }
```

6. Save the changes to the style sheet, and then display the HTML page. The picture and its caption now appear on the left, with the main text on the right, as shown in Figure 8-6.

*Figure 8-6: **The sample page with a floating layout applied.***

## CAUTION

While What You See Is What You Get (WYSIWYG) applications such as Dreamweaver enable you to create floating layouts quickly, the layouts may not always be perfect. Always test your layouts in a browser or three to avoid awkward surprises.

## QUICKSTEPS

### OVERRIDING STYLE SHEETS IN YOUR BROWSER

Style sheets have many advantages, but with unsuitable desktop or browser settings, they may produce pages that are hard to read. Most browsers enable you to override some aspects of style sheets. You may want to use these techniques not only for easier viewing of some web pages you visit, but also to check how your own web pages look when your style sheets are not (or not fully) in effect.

#### APPLY YOUR OWN STYLE SHEET IN INTERNET EXPLORER

Internet Explorer lets you apply your own style sheet to all web pages you visit; this style sheet overrides any style sheet that each web page is using. You can also choose to ignore the colors, font styles, and font sizes specified on web pages.

1. Start Internet Explorer or switch to it.

2. Click the **Tools** menu button and then click **Internet Options**. The Internet Options dialog box appears.

Continued . . .

Figure 8-7: *You can create a three-column layout by adding a center column.*

### PREVENT FLOATING WITH THE CLEAR PROPERTY

To prevent an element from being floated, you can set the clear property of an object. The clear property has four values, as explained in Table 8-3.

| VALUE | MAKES THE ITEM |
|-------|----------------|
| left  | Move below left-floated objects but wrap around right-floated objects |
| right | Move below right-floated objects but wrap around left-floated objects |
| both  | Move below both left- and right-floated objects |
| none  | Wrap around objects floated either left or right |

Table 8-3: *Values for the clear Property*

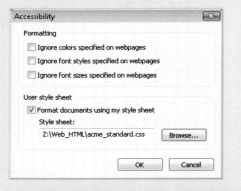

## QUICKSTEPS

### OVERRIDING STYLE SHEETS IN YOUR BROWSER *(Continued)*

3. On the General tab, click **Accessibility**. The Accessibility dialog box appears.

4. Select the **Format Documents Using My Style Sheet** check box, click **Browse**, select the style sheet in the Open dialog box, and click **Open**.

5. If you want to ignore colors, font styles, or font sizes, select the appropriate check boxes in the Formatting area.

6. Click **OK** and then click **OK** again.

### USE DEFAULT FONTS AND COLORS IN FIREFOX

Firefox lets you choose your own default font or default color instead of those specified in a web page's style sheet.

1. Start Firefox or switch to it.

2. On Windows, click the **Tools** menu and then click **Options**. The Options dialog box appears. On the Mac, click the **Firefox** menu and then click **Preferences**. The Preferences window opens.

3. Click the **Content** button at the top of the window to display the Content tab.

*Continued . . .*

---

For example, you can add to the page a footer that runs all the way across the page, as shown in Figure 8-8. To do so:

1. In the HTML document, create a division containing the footer's content, and give it a unique id (the example uses pagefooter as the id).

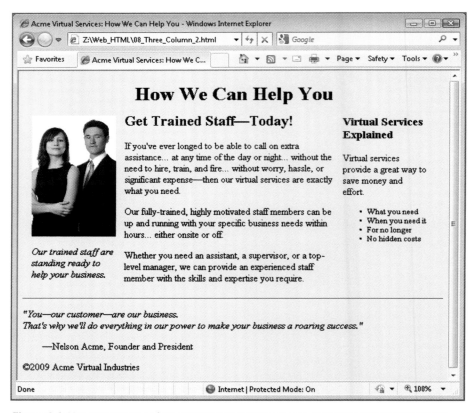

*Figure 8-8:* **You can use the** clear **property to create an area that runs across the whole page.**

## UICKSTEPS

### OVERRIDING STYLE SHEETS IN YOUR BROWSER *(Continued)*

4. In the Fonts & Colors area, click **Advanced**. The Fonts dialog box appears.

5. Choose the fonts you want to use.

6. Clear the **Allow Pages To Choose Their Own Fonts, Instead Of My Selections Above** check box.

7. Click **OK** to close the Fonts dialog box.

8. Back on the Content tab of the Options dialog box, click the **Colors** button. The Colors dialog box appears.

9. Choose the colors you want to use.

10. Clear the **Allow Pages To Choose Their Own Colors, Instead Of My Selections Above** check box.

11. Click **OK** to close the Colors dialog box.

12. Click **OK** (Windows) or the **Close** button (Mac OS X) to close the Options dialog box.

### APPLY YOUR OWN STYLE SHEET IN SAFARI

Safari also lets you apply your own style sheet. Follow these steps:

1. In Windows, click the **Edit** menu and then click **Preferences**. The Preferences dialog box appears. On the Mac, click the **Safari** menu and then click **Preferences**. The Preferences window opens.

2. Click the **Advanced** button to display the Advanced preferences.

3. Click the **Style Sheet** drop-down menu, click **Other**, and use the resulting dialog box to choose the style sheet.

4. Click the **Close** button to close the Preferences dialog box or Preferences window.

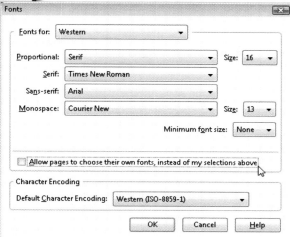

2. In the style sheet, create a rule for the footer that sets the float property to left and the clear property to both. Set the width property to 100% to make the footer run all the way across the page. Here's an example that also puts a top border on the footer so that you can see the area it occupies:

```
#pagefooter { float: left;
              border-top: 1px
blue solid;
              clear: both;
              width: 100% }
```

3. Save the style sheet, and then display the HTML page.

## How to...

- *Configure Web Options in the Office Applications*

- *Understanding How the Office Applications Use HTML*

- *Adding the New Web Page and Web Page Preview Commands to the Office Applications*

- *Start a New Web Page in Word*

- *Create Hyperlinks*

- *Check How a Page Will Look*

- *Remove Sensitive Information from the Document*

- *Save Word Documents as Web Pages*

- *Choosing Suitable Web File Formats*

- *Remove Office-Specific Tags from a Word Document*

- *Using Word to Create HTML Elements*

- *Create Web Pages from Excel Workbooks*

- *Create Web Pages from PowerPoint Presentations*

# Chapter 9

# Creating Web Pages Using the Microsoft Office Applications

If you have one of the versions of Microsoft Office 2007, you can use the Office applications' built-in features for saving documents in web-page format. These features enable you to put Word documents, Excel spreadsheets, and PowerPoint presentations on to a website or an intranet site in a format in which they can be viewed using a browser.

## Get Ready to Create Web Pages in the Office Applications

Before you start using the Office applications to create web pages, configure web options in each of the applications that you plan to use. These options control how the applications create web pages. Once you've specified the options you

**TIP**

Microsoft Office 2003 for Windows, Microsoft Office 2008 for Mac, and Microsoft Office 2004 for Mac have similar features. In Office 2003, choose **Tools** and then choose **Options** to open the Options dialog box. In Office for the Mac, press ⌘+COMMA or choose **Preferences** from the application's menu (for example, choose **Word** and then choose **Preferences**) to open the Preferences dialog box (which contains the options).

**NOTE**

You must set the web options separately for each of the Office applications. The changes you make in one application don't affect the settings in the other applications.

**NOTE**

The General tab appears in the Web Options dialog box for Excel and PowerPoint on Windows; it doesn't appear for Word. The Office for the Mac applications have fewer options, which this chapter does not discuss in detail.

want for web pages, you probably won't need to change them. If you do need to change them for a particular file, you can do so when you're saving the file as a web page.

You also need to know how the Office applications handle HTML. This section explains that topic too.

## Configure Web Options in the Office Applications

The web options vary among the applications, but Word, Excel, and PowerPoint have the same core set of options, which are discussed in this section. The options that are substantially different for one or another of the applications are discussed separately in the section for that particular application later in this chapter.

### DISPLAY THE WEB OPTIONS DIALOG BOX

To configure web options, first display the Web Options dialog box.

1. Open the application for which you want to configure web options. For example, if you want to set options for Word, click the **Start** button, click **All Programs**, click **Microsoft Office**, and then click **Microsoft Office Word 2007**.

2. Click the **Microsoft Office** button (the Office-logo button in the upper-left corner), and then click the **Options** button. For example, click the **Word Options** button in Word or the **Excel Options** button in Excel. The Options dialog box appears.

3. In the category list on the left, click **Advanced**, and then scroll down to the bottom of the dialog box.

4. Click the **Web Options** button. The Web Options dialog box for the application appears.

5. Choose options as discussed in the following subsections, click **OK** to close the Web Options dialog box, and then click **OK** to close the Options dialog box.

### CHOOSE GENERAL TAB OPTIONS FOR EXCEL

Choose options as follows on the General tab for Excel (see Figure 9-1):

1. Select the **Save Any Additional Hidden Data Necessary To Maintain Formulas** check box to make Excel save in the web page any hidden data that is required for

## UNDERSTANDING HOW THE OFFICE APPLICATIONS USE HTML

The Office applications use HTML for creating web content, automatically applying all necessary tags when you save a file in one of the web formats. The applications use standard tags (such as those discussed in the rest of this book) for creating standard HTML elements (such as headings, paragraphs, and tables) that will be displayed by a web browser, and custom, Office-specific tags for saving Office application-specific data in a web-compatible format.

This combination of standard and custom tags enables the Office applications to save an entire Word document, Excel workbook, or PowerPoint presentation. Saving all the information like this is called *round-tripping:* saving a file with all its contents, formatting, and extra items (such as customizations and Visual Basic for Applications code) so that the application that created the file can reopen it with exactly the same information and formatting as when it saved the file.

Round-tripping enables you to create HTML documents instead of documents that use the standard Office file formats (for example, the Word Document format, the Excel Spreadsheet format, or the PowerPoint Presentation format). But always remember that the Office-specific data is saved along with the HTML data. Any visitor to your website can view the entire source code for a web page, including any Office-specific data, by using a View Source command.

Word enables you to remove the Office-specific tags from a web page you save (see "Remove Office-Specific Tags from a Word Document," later in this chapter). You may also choose to use Word to create specific HTML elements that you then paste into your standard HTML editor, where you can then integrate them with the code you create manually. (See the "Using Word to Create HTML Elements" QuickSteps, later in this chapter.)

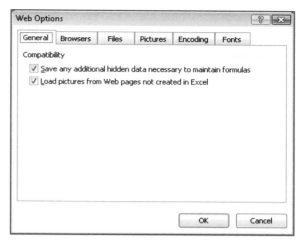

*Figure 9-1: **For most purposes, you should select both the options on the General tab of the Web Options dialog box for Excel.***

maintaining the formulas in the worksheets shown in the web page. Excluding any relevant hidden data will prevent the formulas from working correctly.

2. Select the **Load Pictures From Web Pages Not Created In Excel** check box to make Excel include graphics from non-Excel sources in the web pages you create from Excel. Including such graphics helps to keep your worksheets complete. The usual reason for clearing this check box and omitting graphics from other sources is that the graphics will not be available in the web pages.

### CHOOSE GENERAL TAB OPTIONS FOR POWERPOINT

Choose options as follows on the General tab of the Web Options dialog box for PowerPoint (see Figure 9-2):

1. Select the **Add Slide Navigation Controls** check box if you want the presentation to include controls for navigating among slides. Usually, having the controls is beneficial, but you may decide that your presentations don't need them; if so, clear this check box. If you include the controls, use the Colors drop-down list to choose the text color and background color you want for the controls—for example, White Text On Black or Browser Colors.

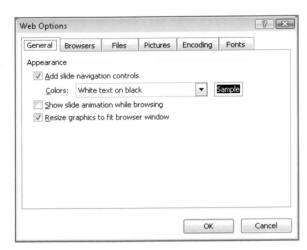

Figure 9-2: *The General tab of the Web Options dialog box for PowerPoint enables you to add slide navigation controls, display slide animations while the viewer is browsing, and automatically resize graphics to fit the browser window.*

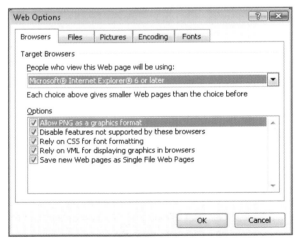

Figure 9-3: *The Browsers tab of Word's Web Options dialog box lets you specify the types of browsers for which you want your web pages to work correctly.*

2. Clear the **Show Slide Animation While Browsing** check box unless you want the presentation to include animations when the viewer is browsing from slide to slide.

3. Select the **Resize Graphics To Fit Browser Window** check box to make the presentation automatically resize its graphics so that they fit within the browser window. This makes the presentation easier to view and so is usually a good idea.

### CHOOSE BROWSERS TAB OPTIONS

The Browsers tab lets you choose which features to use in your web pages based on the browsers you're expecting to view them. Figure 9-3 shows the Browsers tab of the Web Options dialog box for Word, which offers one more option than for Excel and PowerPoint. Table 9-1 explains the options and shows for which browsers they're turned on (with the check box selected) or off (with the check box cleared).

The best way to select the options is to click the **People Who View This Web Page Will Be Using** drop-down list and select the earliest browser version that you want to support. The choice you make in this drop-down list automatically selects the relevant check boxes in the Options group box. You can then select or clear check boxes manually to fine-tune the choices you've made.

As of this writing, the most sensible option is to select **Microsoft Internet Explorer 6 Or Later** in the People Who View This Web Page Will Be Using drop-down list. Now that Internet Explorer has moved on to version 8 and the other market-leading browsers—Firefox (25 percent), Safari (10 percent), Google Chrome (around 1 percent), and Opera (around 1 percent)—support CSS, VML, and PNG, there's little point in choosing the earlier settings anymore.

### CHOOSE FILES TAB OPTIONS

On the Files tab of the Web Options dialog box, choose options for controlling how each Office application handles filenames and file locations in the web pages you create, and specify whether to use Office as the default editor for web pages created by the Office applications. Figure 9-4 shows the Files tab of the Web Options dialog box for Word, which has the most extensive set of options for files.

| OPTION | EXPLANATION | IE 3, NAVIGATOR 3 | IE 4, NAVIGATOR 4 | IE 4 OR LATER | IE 5 OR LATER | IE 6 OR LATER |
|--------|-------------|-------------------|-------------------|---------------|---------------|---------------|
| Allow PNG As A Graphics Format | Enables web pages to contain graphics in the PNG format. All current browsers can display PNG graphics. | Off | Off | Off | Off | On |
| Rely On CSS For Font Formatting | Uses Cascading Style Sheets for font formatting. | Off | On | On | On | On |
| Rely On VML For Displaying Graphics In Browsers | Uses Vector Markup Language for displaying graphics. | Off | Off | Off | On | On |
| Save New Web Pages As Single File Web Pages | Uses the Single File Web Page format for saving new files. | Off | Off | On | On | On |
| Disable Features Not Supported By These Browsers | (Word only.) Turns off HTML features the browsers don't support. | On | On | On | On | On |
| Save An Additional Version Of The Presentation For Older Browsers | (PowerPoint only.) Creates a version of the presentation that's viewable in Internet Explorer 3, Internet Explorer 4, Netscape Navigator 3, or Netscape Navigator 4. | On | On | Off | Off | Off |

*Table 9-1: **Options on the Browsers Tab of the Web Options Dialog Box***

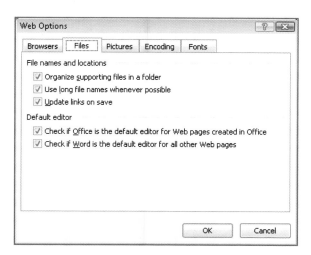

*Figure 9-4: **The Files tab of the Web Options dialog box contains a different set of options for Word, Excel, and PowerPoint. This is the Files tab for Word.***

Word, Excel, and PowerPoint for Windows all include the following options (the Office applications for Mac have different options):

- Select the **Organize Supporting Files In A Folder** check box if you want the application to save graphics and other separate elements in a folder that has the same name as the web page plus "_files"—for example, the web page named "products.html" receives a folder named "products_files" automatically. The application automatically creates a file named "filelist.xml" that contains a list of the files required for the web page.

- Clear the **Use Long File Names Whenever Possible** check box to prevent the application from creating long filenames that include spaces, which may not be compatible with the web server you're using. It's best to keep filenames short and to use underscores instead of spaces when you need to separate parts of the filename.

- Select the **Update Links On Save** check box if you want the application to automatically check each link and update any information that has changed each time you save the file. In most cases, this automatic updating is helpful.

**NOTE**

Word documents, Excel worksheets, and PowerPoint presentations keep all their text and embedded elements (such as graphics) in the same file. Linked items, such as graphics or automation objects from other applications, are kept in separate files.

**CAUTION**

Keeping the supporting files together in a folder is usually helpful because you can move the web page and its supporting files easily to another folder. If you clear the **Organize Supporting Files In A Folder** check box, the Office applications save the graphics and other separate elements in the same folder as the web page. This behavior tends to make your folders harder to manage, as you cannot see at a glance which supporting files belong to which web page. However, if you do not have permission to create new folders in the folder in which you are saving your web pages, you may need to clear the **Organize Supporting Files In A Folder** check box so that the Office application does not attempt to create new folders for your web pages.

**TIP**

If you're creating an intranet site whose visitors will all use monitors with a higher resolution than 800 × 600, you can choose a higher resolution. Similarly, if you're designing a website for small-screen computers (such as handheld computers), choose a lower resolution, such as 640 × 480 or even 544 × 376.

- Select the **Check If Office Is The Default Editor For Web Pages Created In Office** check box if you want Internet Explorer to check if the Office applications are your default HTML editors for web pages created by the Office applications when you click the Edit button in Internet Explorer. Clear this check box if you want to be able to use another application to edit the web pages you've created with the Office applications.

The Files tab in the Web Options dialog box for Word also includes the Check If Word Is The Default Editor For All Other Web Pages check box. Select this check box if you want to use Word as your default HTML editor for web pages created either using Word or using applications other than the other Office applications. (Excel will still be the default editor for web pages created using Excel, and PowerPoint for web pages created using PowerPoint.) Clear this check box if you want to use another HTML editor as the default.

### CHOOSE PICTURES TAB OPTIONS

On the Pictures tab of the Web Options dialog box (shown here), choose options for the pictures you include in your web pages.

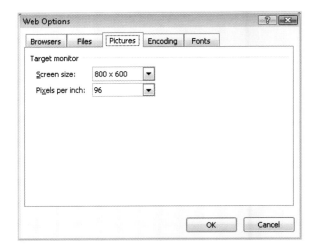

- In the Screen Size drop-down list, select the minimum resolution that you expect most visitors to your website to be using. For most websites, the best choice is 800 × 600, a resolution that most current computers support (including even the smallest netbooks).

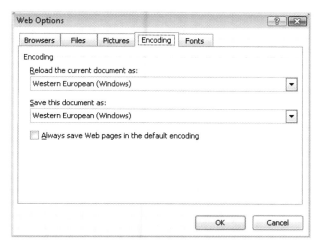

Unicode is a scheme for representing characters on computers. For example, a capital A is represented by 0041 in Unicode, and a capital B is represented by 0042. *UTF-8* is the abbreviation for Universal Character Set Transformation Format 8-Bit. *ISO* is the short term used to denote the International Organization for Standardization.

- In the Pixels Per Inch drop-down list, select the number of pixels per inch (ppi) to use for pictures in your web pages. The default setting is 96 ppi, which works well for most pages. You can also choose 72 ppi or 120 ppi. This drop-down list does not appear in the Web Options dialog box for PowerPoint.

### CHOOSE ENCODING TAB OPTIONS

The Encoding tab of the Web Options dialog box (shown here) lets you specify which character-encoding scheme to use for the characters in your web pages. The Office for Windows applications in North America and Western Europe use the Western European (Windows) encoding by default. This works well for most purposes, but you may prefer to choose Western European (ISO) for compliance with the ISO-8859-1 standard or Unicode (UTF-8) for compliance with the Unicode standard. Similarly, the Office for Mac applications use the Western European (Macintosh) encoding as the default; as with Windows, you may want to change to Western European (ISO).

Select the encoding you want in the Save This Document As drop-down list. Then, if you always want to use this encoding, select the **Always Save Web Pages In The Default Encoding** check box. Selecting this check box disables the Save This Document As drop-down list.

The Reload The Current Document As drop-down list at the top of the Encoding tab lets you reopen the current document using a different encoding. This can be useful when you need to check how the document looks when encoded differently.

### CHOOSE FONTS TAB OPTIONS

The Fonts tab of the Web Options dialog box offers the following options:

- Use the **Character Set** list box to specify the character set you want to use for your pages. Use the **English/Western European/Other Latin Script** item unless you need to create pages in another character set, such as Hebrew or Arabic. You need to make sure that the character set you choose is available for the encoding you're using, so don't make changes here unless you know what you're doing.

## QUICKSTEPS

### ADDING THE NEW WEB PAGE AND WEB PAGE PREVIEW COMMANDS TO THE OFFICE APPLICATIONS

Word, Excel, and PowerPoint include a Web Page Preview command that you can use to see how your document will look as a web page. But this command doesn't appear in the Ribbon or on the Microsoft Office button menu, so you need to add it to the Quick Access toolbar before you can use it.

Similarly, both Word and Excel have a Save As Web Page button for saving an unsaved document or workbook as a web page, and Word has a New Web Page command that you can use to start a new web page. You have to add these buttons to the Quick Access toolbar, too.

Follow these steps:

1. Open the application you want to change.

2. Click the **Microsoft Office** button, and then click the **Options** button to open the Options dialog box.

3. In the left column, click the **Customize** item to display the Customize screen. Figure 9-5 shows the Customize screen for Word with customization underway.

4. Make sure the Customize Quick Access Toolbar drop-down list shows **For All Documents (Default)**.

5. In the Choose Commands From drop-down list, choose **Commands Not In The Ribbon**. The list of commands appears in the list box below the drop-down list.

6. Scroll down to the Web Page Preview command.

*Continued . . .*

- Use the **Proportional Font** drop-down list and its **Size** drop-down list to specify the proportional font and font size to use for your pages.

- Use the **Fixed-Width Font** and its **Size** drop-down list to specify the monospaced font and font size.

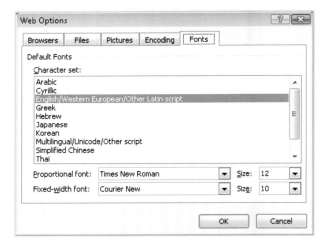

After you finish choosing settings in the Web Options dialog box, click **OK** to close the dialog box, and then click **OK** to close the Options dialog box.

# Create Web Pages in Word

After choosing suitable web options, you're ready to start creating web pages in Word. The first step is to start a new web page. You can then add text and hyperlinks and check how the page will look. If you're creating a web page from an existing document, you will need to remove any sensitive information from it and then save it as a web page.

## Start a New Web Page in Word

You can now create a new document in Word and add content to it like this:

1. Start Word, if it is not already running, or switch to Word.

### ADDING THE NEW WEB PAGE AND WEB PAGE PREVIEW COMMANDS TO THE OFFICE APPLICATIONS

*(Continued)*

7. Click the **Web Page Preview** command, and then click the **Add** button to add it to the list box on the right. You can then click it in that list box and use the up-arrow button or down-arrow button to reposition it on the Quick Access toolbar.

8. For Word or Excel, scroll up to the **Save As Web Page** button, click it, and then click the **Add** button to add it to the list box on the right.

9. For Word only, scroll the left list box up to the **New Web Page** button. Add this button to the Quick Access toolbar and reposition it if you want to.

10. Click the **OK** button to close the Options dialog box.

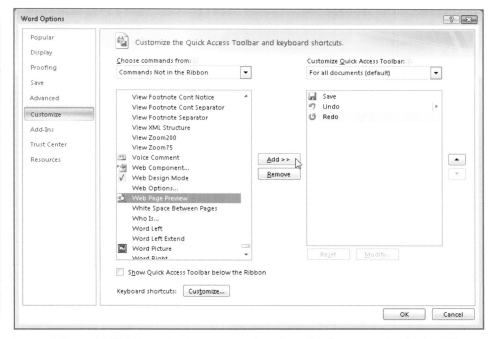

Figure 9-5: *Put the Web Page Preview command on the Quick Access toolbar in the Office applications so that you can preview your web pages.*

### NOTE

Instead of starting a new web page from scratch in Word, you can create a web page by opening an existing Word document, Excel workbook, or PowerPoint presentation. Click the **Microsoft Office** button menu, click **Save As**, and then click **Other Formats** to save it in a web format. See "Save Word Documents as Web Pages," "Create Web Pages from Excel Workbooks," and "Create Web Pages from PowerPoint Presentations," all later in this chapter, for details.

2. Click the **New Web Page** button on the Quick Access toolbar. You will need to add this button to the Quick Access toolbar, as described in the QuickSteps, "Adding the New Web Page and Web Page Preview Commands to the Office Applications."

3. Create content on the page by using standard Word techniques. For example:

   ● To enter text, type it as usual.

   ● To apply a style, click the **Style** drop-down list on the Formatting toolbar, and then click the desired style name.

   ● To apply direct formatting (for example, bold or italic), select the text to which you want to apply it, and then click the appropriate button on the Formatting toolbar.

4. Save the document as described in the section "Save Word Documents as Web Pages," later in this chapter.

# Create Hyperlinks

The process of inserting a hyperlink is the same in each of the Office applications, so it is discussed here. The example shown is from Word. To insert a hyperlink, display the Insert Hyperlink dialog box by following these steps, and then follow the steps in the subsection that discusses the type of hyperlink you want to create:

1. Open the file in which you want to create the hyperlink. For example, start Word and then open the document.

2. If you want the hyperlink to use existing text or a graphic as the object the user will click, select that text or graphic. If not, position the insertion point where you want the hyperlink to appear.

3. Click the **Insert** tab on the Ribbon, go to the **Links** group, and then click the **Hyperlink** button. The Insert Hyperlink dialog box appears (see Figure 9-6).

4. Complete the hyperlink with one of the following sections, depending on whether you want to create a hyperlink to an existing file or web page, a place in the current document, a new document, or an e-mail address.

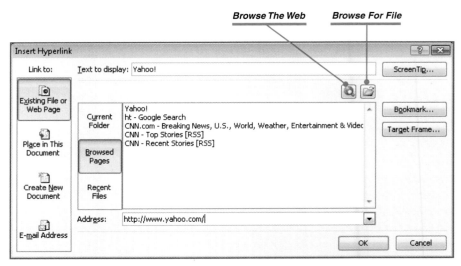

Figure 9-6: *The Insert Hyperlink dialog box enables you to create hyperlinks to web pages, places within the same file, files, or e-mail addresses.*

## CAUTION

If Internet Explorer is not your default browser, the Browse The Web button will not work correctly. Clicking the button opens your default browser, but when you return to the Insert Hyperlink dialog box, the Office application tries to get the URL from Internet Explorer rather than from your default browser. Instead, browse to the web page in your default browser, copy the address from the address bar, and then paste it into the Address box in the Insert Hyperlink dialog box. In the Office for Mac applications, you will need to use copy-and-paste in any case.

## CREATE A HYPERLINK TO AN EXISTING FILE OR WEB PAGE

To create a hyperlink to an existing file or web page:

1. In the Link To column, click the **Existing File Or Web Page** button if it is not already selected.

2. Navigate to the file or web page in one of these ways:

   - Click the **Browse For File** button, use the resulting Link To File dialog box to select the file, and then click the **Open** button. The Office application automatically enters the URL in the Address text box.

     –Or–

   - Click the **Browse The Web** button to make Windows open or activate an Internet Explorer window, browse to the page to which you want to link, and then switch back to the Insert Hyperlink dialog box. The Office application automatically enters the URL in the Address text box.

     –Or–

   - Click the **Current Folder** button to display the current folder. Click the **Browsed Pages** button to display a list of web pages you've browsed recently. Click the **Recent Files** button to display a list of local files you've worked with recently.

     –Or–

   - Select the address from the Address drop-down list.

3. Change the default text in the Text To Display text box to the text you want displayed for the hyperlink. (This is the text that the user clicks to access the linked page. If you have selected text on your web page, it will appear here.)

4. To add a ScreenTip to the hyperlink, click **ScreenTip**, type the text in the Set Hyperlink ScreenTip dialog box, and then click **OK**. The ScreenTip gives the user extra information about the link before they click it.

*Figure 9-7: The Office applications enable you to link to a particular place in the destination document—for example, to a bookmark in a Word document (left), a cell or range in an Excel worksheet (right), or a slide in a PowerPoint presentation.*

5. To make the hyperlink connect to a particular anchor in the document rather than simply to the beginning of the document, click **Bookmark** and choose the anchor item in the Select Place In Document dialog box (see Figure 9-7). You'll need to have placed the bookmark or anchor in the document beforehand.

6. Click **OK**. The Office application inserts the hyperlink.

### CREATE A HYPERLINK TO A PLACE IN THE CURRENT DOCUMENT

To create a hyperlink to a place in the current document:

1. In the Link To column, click the **Place In This Document** button (see Figure 9-8).

2. Change the default text in the Text To Display text box to the text you want displayed for the hyperlink. (This is the text that the user clicks to access the linked page and is the text you first selected, if you did so.)

3. To add a ScreenTip to the hyperlink, click **ScreenTip**, type the text in the Set Hyperlink ScreenTip dialog box, and then click **OK**.

4. Click **OK**. The Office application inserts the hyperlink.

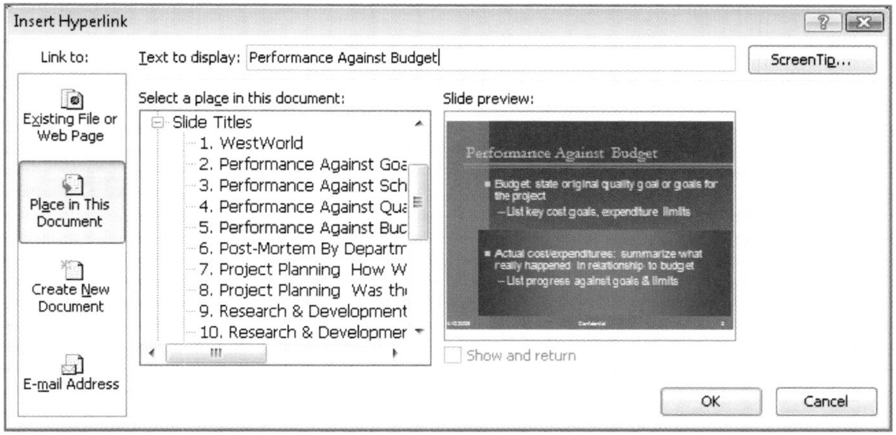

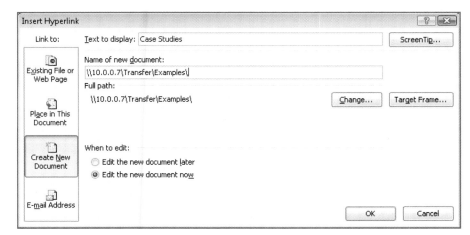

Figure 9-8: *The Place In This Document area of the Insert Hyperlink dialog box enables you to quickly link to an anchor in the same document.*

Figure 9-9: *When you need to link to a new document, Office lets you create the new document immediately. This helps ensure that the new document is saved with the correct name and location, reducing the possibility of error.*

## CREATE A HYPERLINK TO A NEW DOCUMENT

To create a hyperlink to a new document:

1. **Create New Document** button (see Figure 9-9).

2. Type the filename and extension in the Name Of New Document text box. Look at the path in the Full Path area and make sure it shows the folder you want. If necessary, click the **Change** button; use the Create New Document dialog box to specify the folder, filename, and extension; and then click **OK**.

3. Change the default text in the Text To Display text box to the text you want displayed for the hyperlink. (This is the text that the user clicks to access the linked page and is the text you first selected, if you did so.)

4. To add a ScreenTip to the hyperlink, click the **ScreenTip** button, type the text in the Set Hyperlink ScreenTip dialog box, and then click **OK**.

The Office applications automatically create a hyperlink when you type a URL, e-mail address, or a network path in a document and then press **SPACEBAR**, **TAB**, **ENTER**, or a punctuation key. If you find this behavior awkward, you can turn it off: Click the **Microsoft Office** button, and then click the **Options** button. Click the **Proofing** category, and then click the **AutoCorrect Options** button. In the AutoCorrect dialog box, click the **AutoFormat As You Type** tab, clear the **Internet And Network Paths With Hyperlinks** check box, and then click **OK** to close each dialog box.

5. By default, the Office application selects the Edit The New Document Now option button. If you prefer not to open the new document for editing immediately, select the **Edit The New Document Later** option button.

6. Click **OK**. The Office application inserts the hyperlink and creates the document.

### CREATE A HYPERLINK TO AN E-MAIL ADDRESS

To create a mailto hyperlink that starts a message to an e-mail address:

1. In the Link To column, click the **E-mail Address** button (see Figure 9-10).

2. Type the e-mail address in the E-mail Address text box (or click it in the Recently Used E-mail Addresses list box), and type the subject for the message in the Subject text box.

3. Change the default text in the Text To Display text box to the text you want displayed for the hyperlink. (This is the text that the user clicks to access the linked page and is the text you first selected, if you did so.)

4. To add a ScreenTip to the hyperlink, click the **ScreenTip** button, type the text in the Set Hyperlink ScreenTip dialog box, and then click **OK**.

5. Click **OK**. The Office application inserts the hyperlink.

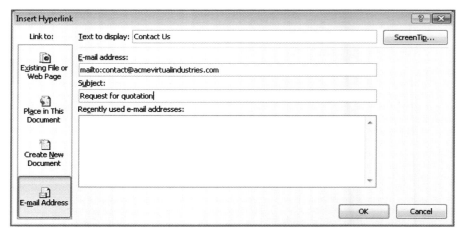

Figure 9-10: *The Insert Hyperlink dialog box lets you quickly create a mailto hyperlink to a recently used e-mail address.*

# Check How a Page Will Look

Before you save an Office document as a web page, you may want to use Web Page Preview to check how it looks.

**1.** If the document is not already open, open it in the appropriate application. For example, open a Word document in Word.

**2.** Click the **Web Page Preview** button on the Quick Access toolbar. (You will need to add this button to the Quick Access toolbar, as described in the "Adding the New Web Page and Web Page Preview Commands to the Office Applications" QuickSteps, earlier in this chapter.) The application creates a temporary file containing the page in a web format and then displays the page in Internet Explorer. Figure 9-11 shows an example.

**3.** After viewing the web page, click the **Close** button (the X button) to close the Internet Explorer tab or window.

# Remove Sensitive Information from the Document

When creating a web page that you will place on a website (as opposed to a site on a local network), make sure you remove the personal information and sensitive data that the Office applications automatically include by default in documents. To remove this information:

**1.** Start the application and open the document that you will turn into a web page.

**2.** Click the **Microsoft Office** button, highlight **Prepare**, and then click **Inspect Document**. The Document Inspector dialog box appears. This dialog box contains different options for the different applications, but the basic idea is the same: to let you remove any potentially sensitive information. Figure 9-12 shows the Document Inspector dialog box for Word.

**3.** Select the check box for each category of information you want to remove from the document.

**4.** Click the **Inspect** button. The application checks the document and updates the dialog box to show which items it found (see Figure 9-13).

**5.** Click the **Remove All** button for each category of sensitive information you want to remove. If necessary, click the **Reinspect** button to inspect the document again to make sure all the dangerous data has been stripped out.

*Figure 9-11:* **Web Page Preview enables you to identify problems with your web pages (such as the squished image here) before you save them in an HTML format.**

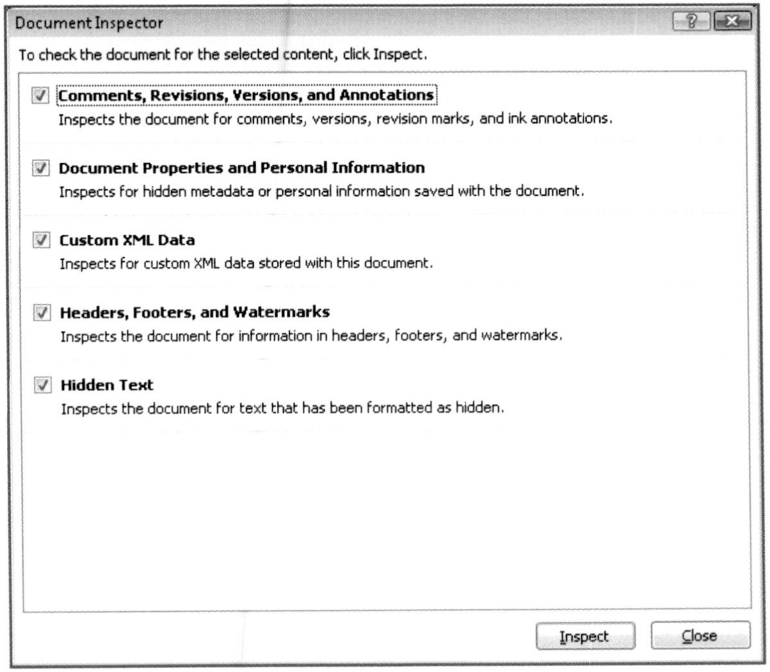

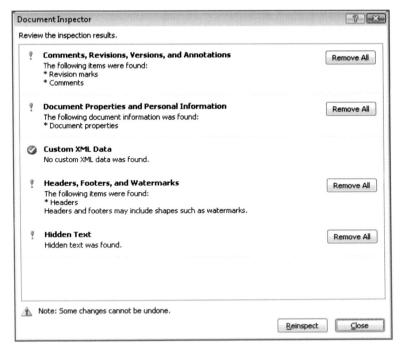

Figure 9-12: *Use the Document Inspector dialog box to check a document for sensitive information before you publish it as a web page.*

Figure 9-13: *Click the Remove All button for each category of document information you want to remove.*

6. Click the **Close** button to close the Document Inspector.

7. Click the **Save** button on the Quick Access toolbar to save the document.

## Save Word Documents as Web Pages

To save an existing Word document as a web page:

1. Start Word if it is not already running, or switch to it.

2. Click the **Microsoft Office** button, click **Open**, select the existing document you want to save as a web page, and then click **Open**. Alternatively, click the **Microsoft Office** button, and then click the document on the Recent Documents menu. The document opens.

## QUICK**FACTS**

### CHOOSING SUITABLE WEB FILE FORMATS

Word, Excel, and PowerPoint each offer two or more HTML formats to choose from; so before you save a file in HTML, make sure you understand how the formats differ from each other and which format is suitable for which purposes.

Word, Excel, and PowerPoint each offer the Single File Web Page format and the Web Page format. Word also offers the Web Page, Filtered format.

#### WEB PAGE FORMAT

The Web Page format creates an HTML file that contains the text contents of the document along with a separate folder that contains the graphics for the document. This makes the web page's HTML file itself smaller, but the page as a whole is a little clumsy to distribute because you must distribute the graphics folder as well. The folder is created automatically and assigned the web page's name followed by _files. For example, a web page named Products.html has a folder named Products_files.

Files in the Web Page format use the .htm and .html file extensions. These files also use Office-specific tags to preserve all of the information the file contains in an HTML format.

#### SINGLE FILE WEB PAGE FORMAT

The Single File Web Page format creates a web archive file that contains all the information required for the web page—all the text contents and all the graphics. Use the Single File Web Page format to create files that you can easily distribute.

Files in the Single File Web Page format use the .mht and .mhtml file extensions. These files use Office-specific tags to preserve all of the information the file contains in an HTML format.

*Continued . . .*

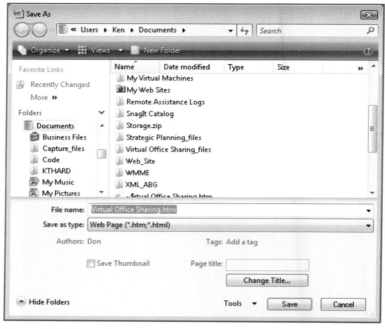

*Figure 9-14: Word's Save As dialog box for saving web pages includes the Page Title area and the Change Title button.*

3. Click the **Save As Web Page** button on the Quick Access toolbar. The Save As dialog box appears.

4. In the Save As Type drop-down list, select the file format you want to use (see the "Choosing Suitable Web File Formats" QuickSteps in this chapter for a discussion of the available formats). For example, choose Web Page. Word displays the web page-related controls (see Figure 9-14).

5. Choose the folder in which to save the web page.

6. In the File Name text box, type the filename. If you want to use the .html extension instead of the .htm extension (for a file in either the Web Page format or the Web Page, Filtered format) or the .mhtml extension instead of the .mht extension (for a file in the Single File Web Page Format), type the extension as well.

## CHOOSING SUITABLE WEB FILE FORMATS *(Continued)*

### WEB PAGE, FILTERED FORMAT

The Web Page, Filtered format is available only in Word. Like the Web Page format, this format creates an HTML file that contains the text contents of the document along with a separate, automatically named folder that contains the graphics for the document. However, this format removes Office-specific tags from the document.

Removing these features reduces the size of the file, which is a good idea when you just want HTML. This is great when what you need is a web page without Word-specific features or advanced formatting. The disadvantage is that the file loses Word items such as document properties, template links, and VBA code, so this format is not useful for when you need to round-trip complex documents—that is, save them in web-page format and then bring them back into Word without losing any data or meta data.

Files in the Web Page, Filtered format use the .htm and .html file extensions.

---

7. Check the title displayed in the Page Title area. (You may see no title.) To change the title, click the **Change Title** button, type the new title in the Set Page Title dialog box, and then click **OK**.

8. Click **Save**. Word saves the document as a web page.

9. If you've finished working with the document, click the **Microsoft Office** button, and then click **Close**. If you've finished working with Word, click the **Microsoft Office** button, and then click **Exit *Application*** (where *Application* is the application's name).

# Remove Office-Specific Tags from a Word Document

As discussed earlier in this chapter, Word uses custom HTML tags to store the Office-specific data required to save the entire Word document in an HTML format. Saving this Office-specific data is good if you want to be able to edit the document in Word with all the features present, but you don't need this extra data when you're using Word on a one-time basis to create pages for your website.

To remove the tags from a document, follow these steps:

1. Follow the steps in the previous section, but choose the **Web Page, Filtered** format in the Save As Type drop-down list in the Save As dialog box.

2. When you click **Save**, the Microsoft Office Word dialog box shown here appears, telling you that Office-specific tags will be removed. Click **Yes**.

## USING WORD TO CREATE HTML ELEMENTS

If you choose not to use Word as your main HTML editor, you may still want to use Word to create some HTML elements so that you can include them in your web pages.

1. Start Word if it is not already running.

2. Open an existing document or create a new document that contains the desired content.

3. Save the Word document in one of the HTML formats.

4. View the resulting page in your browser.

5. View the source code of the web page. For example, in Internet Explorer, click the **Page** menu button and then click **View Source**.

6. Select the code for the element you want to copy, and then issue a Copy command (for example, press **CTRL+C**).

7. Switch to your HTML editor, position the insertion point, and then issue a Paste command (for example, press **CTRL+V**).

8. Close Word and your browser if you have finished working with them.

3. Depending on the browser settings you have chosen in the Web Options dialog box, you may also see warnings about features that will be removed from the Word document. Click **Continue** if you want to proceed anyway; click **Cancel** if you want to choose another format.

# Create Web Pages from Excel and PowerPoint

Word is great for creating web pages, but if the data you want to use on a web page is part of a workbook, you'll want to work from Excel instead. Similarly, you can create web pages from presentations by using PowerPoint.

## Create Web Pages from Excel Workbooks

Excel lets you save a selected part of the workbook, a worksheet, or the entire workbook as a web page, with or without interactivity. Usually, however, what you'll want to do is "publish" a copy of part of the workbook, of a worksheet, or of the entire workbook, because the Publish dialog box offers more features and flexibility for web pages.

To save an Excel workbook, worksheet, or part of a worksheet as a web page:

1. Start Excel if it is not already running, or switch to Excel.

2. Open the existing worksheet, or create a new worksheet, add content, and save it.

3. If you want to save a worksheet rather than a workbook as a web page, select that worksheet. If you want to save a range from a worksheet as a web page, select that range.

4. Click the **Save As Web Page** button on the Quick Access toolbar. The Save As dialog box appears (see Figure 9-15).

5. In the Save area, select the **Entire Workbook** option button if you want to save or publish the entire workbook. Select the **Selection** option button if you want to publish the active worksheet or the selected range. When a range is selected, the Selection option button lists the range (for example, "Selection: $A$1:$H$15"); if no range is selected, the Selection option button reads "Selection: Sheet."

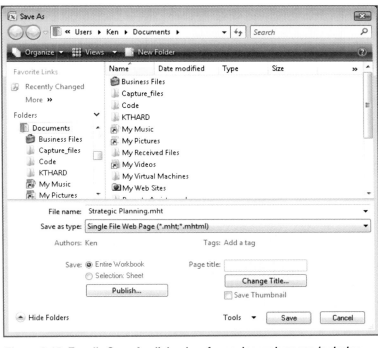

Figure 9-15: *Excel's Save As dialog box for saving web pages includes controls for publishing the workbook, worksheet, or selection.*

## NOTE

Files saved in the Web Page format can use the .htm extension or the .html extension. Files saved in the Single File Web Page format can use the .mht extension or the .mhtml extension.

6. Use the Address box and the main list box to specify the folder in which to save the web page.

7. In the Save As Type drop-down list, select the file format you want to use—for example, Web Page (*.htm, *.html). See the "Choosing Suitable Web File Formats" QuickSteps for a discussion of the available formats.

8. In the File Name text box, type the filename. If you want to use the .html extension instead of the .htm extension or the .mhtml extension instead of the .mht extension, type the extension.

9. Click **Publish**. The Publish As Web Page dialog box appears (see Figure 9-16).

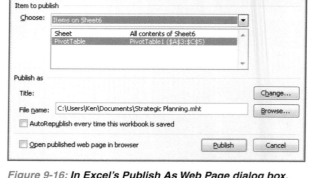

Figure 9-16: *In Excel's Publish As Web Page dialog box, choose whether to republish the web page automatically each time you save the workbook.*

**NOTE**

The AutoRepublish Every Time This Workbook Is Saved option is convenient for making sure the web page is always up-to-date, but use it only if you have a permanent and fast connection to the site on which you're publishing the web page.

**NOTE**

Internet Explorer may display the information bar, telling you that it has restricted the file from showing active content that could access your computer and prevented the spreadsheet from being displayed. To view the spreadsheet, click the information bar, click **Allow Blocked Content**, and then click **Yes** in the Security Warning dialog box.

10. Use the Choose drop-down list and list box in the Item To Publish section to specify which item to publish. If necessary, change the item selected in the Choose drop-down list. If you select the Range Of Cells item, Excel displays a Collapse Dialog button. Click this button to collapse the dialog box to its title bar, select the range in the worksheet, and then click the **Collapse Dialog** button again to restore the dialog box.

11. Check the title (if any) displayed in the Title text box. To change it, click the **Change** button, type the new title in the Set Title dialog box, and then click **OK**.

12. Check the path and filename in the File Name text box. If necessary, type a change, or click **Browse**, specify the folder and filename in the Publish As dialog box, and then click **OK**.

13. Select the **AutoRepublish Every Time This Workbook Is Saved** check box if you want Excel to automatically publish this web page again each time you save the file.

14. Select the **Open Published Web Page In Browser** check box if you want Excel to display the web page in Internet Explorer so that you can check it. This is usually a good idea, because it helps you pick up any errors that occur when you publish the web page.

15. Click **Publish**. Excel publishes the web page and (if you selected the Open Published Web Page In Browser check box) displays it in Internet Explorer.

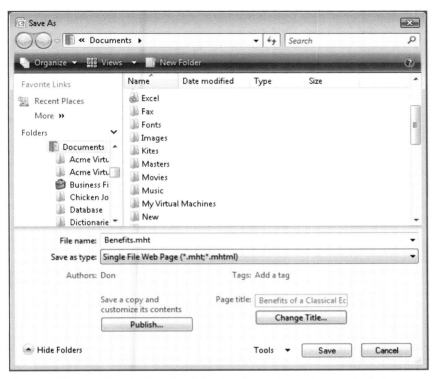

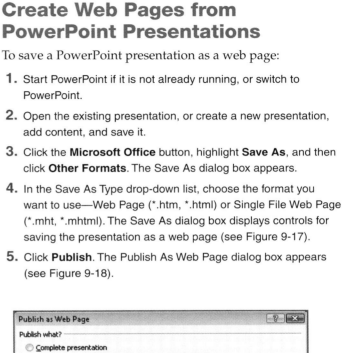

Figure 9-17: *PowerPoint's Save As dialog box for saving web pages includes a Publish button and a Page Title text box.*

# Create Web Pages from PowerPoint Presentations

To save a PowerPoint presentation as a web page:

1. Start PowerPoint if it is not already running, or switch to PowerPoint.

2. Open the existing presentation, or create a new presentation, add content, and save it.

3. Click the **Microsoft Office** button, highlight **Save As**, and then click **Other Formats**. The Save As dialog box appears.

4. In the Save As Type drop-down list, choose the format you want to use—Web Page (*.htm, *.html) or Single File Web Page (*.mht, *.mhtml). The Save As dialog box displays controls for saving the presentation as a web page (see Figure 9-17).

5. Click **Publish**. The Publish As Web Page dialog box appears (see Figure 9-18).

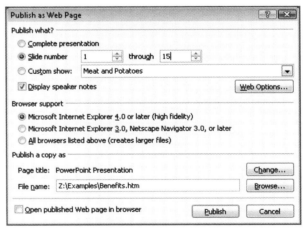

Figure 9-18: *The Publish As Web Page dialog box lets you choose which parts of the PowerPoint presentation to publish and which browsers to support.*

## TIP

Web presentations created with the Microsoft Internet Explorer 4.0 Or Later setting work for most current and recent web browsers.

## NOTE

Internet Explorer may display the information bar, telling you that it has restricted the file from showing active content that could access your computer and prevented the presentation from being displayed. To view the presentation, click the information bar, click **Allow Blocked Content**, and then click **Yes** in the Security Warning dialog box.

## TIP

PowerPoint presentations tend to include many graphics for elements, such as background, bullets, or lines, as well as any graphics that you include manually. If a graphic is missing, the presentation may display no image, a blank placeholder for the image, or a red X.

6. In the Publish What? section, choose which part of the presentation to publish: the complete presentation, a range of slides, or a custom show that you've defined. (If the presentation contains no custom shows, the Custom Show option button is unavailable.) Select the **Display Speaker Notes** check box if you want to include speaker notes with the slides.

7. In the Browser Support section, select the **Microsoft Internet Explorer 4.0 Or Later** option button, the **Microsoft Internet Explorer 3.0, Netscape Navigator 3.0, Or Later** option button, or the **All Browsers Listed Above** option button.

8. Check the title displayed in the Page Title readout. To change it, click the **Change** button, type the new title in the Set Page Title dialog box, and then click **OK**.

9. Check the path and filename in the File Name text box. If necessary, type a change, or click the **Browse** button, specify the folder and filename in the Publish As dialog box, and then click **OK**.

10. Select the **Open Published Web Page In Browser** check box if you want PowerPoint to display the web page in your default browser so that you can check it.

11. Click the **Publish** button. PowerPoint publishes the page and (if you so chose) displays it in Internet Explorer.

## How to...

- *Understand the Basics of Forms*
- *Define the Form Structure*
- *Understanding the method Attribute*
- *Add Fields to the Form*
- *Complete a Form*
- *Letting Visitors Upload Files*
- *Create a Form That E-mails Its Contents to You*
- *Understand the Different Categories of User Events*
- *Dealing with Script Threats*
- *Show When a Page Was Last Updated*
- *Redirect the Browser to Another Page*
- *Verify That a Form Is Filled In*

# Chapter 10
# Using Forms and Scripts

This chapter shows you how to create forms to collect information from visitors to your website, either using a script on a web server or (more simply) via e-mail.

You'll also learn how to add scripts to your pages to perform useful actions. For example, you can show when a page was last updated, redirect the browser to another page, or verify that the visitor has completed the required fields on a form.

## Create Forms

To enable people who visit your web pages to provide you with information, you create a form that the visitors can fill in. For example, you might:

- Implement a logon form to ensure that all visitors to certain parts of your website had registered (and perhaps paid a subscription)
- Provide a signup form for an e-mail newsletter or a hard-copy catalog
- Allow visitors to upload pictures or other files to you

## Understand the Basics of Forms

A web form is a web page that contains *fields*, areas in which a visitor can enter information or select from a set of predefined options. When a visitor accesses the form, the browser displays the web page as usual, including the form's fields. The visitor can interact with the fields—for example, by typing text into a text field, by selecting a check box or one option button in a group of option buttons, or by choosing an item from a drop-down list.

When finished with the form, the visitor clicks a command button that submits the form, usually by running a Common Gateway Interface, or CGI, script written in a programming language such as Perl.

For a form to work, you must:

- Create a form that contains the appropriate fields for your purpose
- On the web server, set up a script that will handle the information the visitor enters in the form
- Include in the form the appropriate HTML instructions for the script that will process the form

This process is much more complex than simply creating a web page and copying it to your web host's server, but most web hosts provide easy-to-use scripts for a variety of common form uses. So before you start to plan or create any forms, check which script capabilities your ISP or web host provides for your type of account. (Typically, different types of user accounts have different levels of scripts available—usually, the more you pay, the more scripts you get.)

## Define the Form Structure

Before starting to create your form as described in this section, decide the purpose of the form and establish which information it will collect. Divide that information into suitable fields.

For example, if you plan to create a database with the information the form gathers, keep the first and last names separate rather than placing them together

**TIP**

Many websites also offer form scripts, so it's worth searching for what you need. Your web host may also provide forums for users to share code, techniques, and advice.

10

in a single field. Similarly, separate address information into several fields, as in the example later in this chapter. Separating both the name and address allows you to sort by each of the components so you can sort by last name, by city, by ZIP code, and so on.

To start a form:

1. Open Notepad or your HTML editor, and start a new web page. For example, if you have created the skeleton of an HTML document, as suggested earlier in this book, open that file, and then save it under a different name. Otherwise, create the following document skeleton, and then save it under a name of your choice:

```
<?xml version="1.0" encoding="utf-8"?>
<!DOCTYPE html PUBLIC "-//W3C//DTD XHTML 1.0 Transitional//EN"
        "http://www.w3.org/TR/xhtml1/DTD/xhtml1-transitional
.dtd">
<html xmlns="http://www.w3.org/1999/xhtml" xml:lang="en"
lang="en">
<head>
<title></title>
</head>
<body>
</body>
</html>
```

2. Click in the body where you want to start the form, and then type the beginning of the opening <form> tag:

```
<form
```

3. Type the action attribute and specify the name (and, if necessary, the location) of the script that you want to use for returning or processing the data that the visitor enters in the form. The following example uses the script named register.php stored in the /cgi-bin/ folder:

```
<form action="cgi-bin/register.php"
```

4. Type the method attribute and specify the value get or post, as appropriate. (See the "Understanding the method Attribute" QuickFacts for an explanation of the difference between get and post.) For example:

```
<form action="cgi-bin/register.php" method="get">
```

5. Optionally, type the name attribute and specify the name you want to assign to the form. The name is not necessary unless you want to be able to access your forms via

## NOTE

For the action attribute, you will need to enter the name and location of a script that is available to you—a script that your web host provides for you, a script that you have downloaded from another location on the Web and have installed on your website, or a script that you have developed yourself. If you simply follow the example shown in this section, your form will not work, unless you just happen to have a script called register.php stored in a folder named /cgi-bin/.

### UNDERSTANDING THE METHOD ATTRIBUTE

For the method attribute, you will need to specify either get (to send the form data to the script specified by action) or post (to send the form data in the HTTP header). Whether you need to specify get or post depends on the script you're using.

Generally, you use get when you're collecting or retrieving data, and use post when you need to store the data, e-mail it, or otherwise manipulate it. For security reasons, you should use post rather than get for product order forms.

get assembles the content of the form into a text string called a *querystring*, which is added to the URL in the address box of the next page loaded in the browser, separated by a question mark. Each field in the querystring is separated by an ampersand (&), each space is replaced by a plus sign (+), and the name of each field is followed by a space and the field's value.

For example, if you visit a site, type <u>Jane Ramirez</u> in the text box named textbox1, and click the Submit button, the querystring ?textbox1=Jane+Ramirez&mybutton=Submit is added to the URL in the address box.

The advantage of get is that if the visitor bookmarks the page, the querystring is saved in the bookmark, so he or she can return directly to the result of the form. The disadvantage is that displaying the form contents in the address bar can be a security problem.

post does not add the querystring to the address bar, so it avoids the potential security problem; that's why it's better for product order forms. The disadvantage of post is that the visitor cannot bookmark the result of the form.

scripts, but you may find that assigning names to your forms helps you to distinguish one from another:

```
<form action="cgi-bin/register.php" method="get"
    name="registration"
```

6. Type the closing angle bracket to complete the <form> tag:

```
<form action="cgi-bin/register.php" method="get"
    name="registration">
```

7. On a new line, type the closing </form> tag:

```
</form>
```

8. Between the <form> and </form> tags, enter the text and fields for the form, as discussed in the following sections.

## Add Fields to the Form

After creating the basic structure for the form and specifying the action and method to take, add text boxes, drop-down lists, check boxes, and command buttons to the form as needed. Also add any text or other objects (for example, graphics) that the form needs, using tags as usual.

### ADD A SINGLE-LINE TEXT BOX

To add a single-line text box:

1. Place the insertion point at the appropriate position between the <form> and </form> tags, and press **ENTER** to create a new line.

2. Type a label for your field to identify it to the user. For example, type <u>First Name</u>.

3. Type the beginning of an <input/> tag, a space, the type attribute, an equal sign, double quotation marks, text, and double quotation marks:

```
<input type="text"
```

4. Type a space, the name attribute, an equal sign, double quotation marks, the name that you want to assign to the text box, and double quotation marks:

```
<input type="text" name="firstname"
```

5. Type a space, the size attribute, an equal sign, double quotation marks, the desired width for the text box, and double quotation marks. This is the number of characters

## TIP

Setting the type attribute to text makes the <input/> tag display a single-line text box.

## NOTE

You do not need to use double quotation marks when specifying numeric values, such as those for the size attribute and the maxlength attribute.

## TIP

If the text box is for the visitor to enter a password or other information that should be shielded from prying eyes, use type="password" instead of type="text" for the <input/> field. When a visitor types in the box, it displays an asterisk or bullets for each character rather than the character itself. Don't assign a default value to a password text box because it will appear as asterisks or bullets rather as text.

Login Name: psmith492

Password: ••••••••|

## NOTE

Throughout a form you will want to add text for titles, labels, and instructions, which is nothing more than typing the text. The next several sets of steps discuss how to create form fields and leave you to add your own text outside of the fields. You'll see an example of how text is used for titles and labels in the concluding section "Complete a Form."

that can be displayed in the text box (the user can enter more than this number—up to the number specified by the maxlength attribute, which is explained next):

```
<input type="text" name="firstname" size="20"
```

6. If you want to display default text in the text box, type a space, the value attribute, an equal sign, double quotation marks, the default text, and double quotation marks:

```
<input type="text" name="firstname"
    size="20" value="Type your first name here"
```

First Name: Type your first name

Last Name: Type your last name

7. If you want to limit the amount of text that the visitor can enter, type a space, the maxlength attribute, an equal sign, double quotation marks, the maximum number of characters, and double quotation marks:

```
<input type="text" name="firstname"
    size="20" value="Type your first name here"
    maxlength=20 />
```

### ADD A MULTILINE TEXT BOX

Single-line text boxes are convenient for getting short pieces of text from your visitors, but if you want them to be able to express themselves more freely, use a multiline text box instead.

To add a multiline text box:

1. Place the insertion point between the <form> and </form> tags, and press **ENTER** to create a new line.

2. Type the beginning of a <textarea> tag:
```
<textarea
```

3. Type a space, the cols attribute, an equal sign, and the number of columns that the text box should occupy. This is roughly the number of characters that will appear across the width of the text box (this is equivalent to the size attribute for the <input/> tag):
```
<textarea cols="40"
```

4. Type a space, the rows attribute, an equal sign, and the desired number of rows for the text box:
```
<textarea cols="40" rows="10"
```

**5.** Type the closing angle bracket for the <textarea> tag, any default text you want to appear in the text box, and the closing <textarea> tag:

```
<textarea cols="40" rows="10">Please type your message here.</
textarea>
```

### ADD A DROP-DOWN LIST

If you need to enable visitors to select one item from a number of items, use a drop-down list. To add a drop-down list:

**1.** Place the insertion point at the appropriate position between the <form> and </form> tags, and press **ENTER** to create a new line.

**2.** Type the beginning of the <select> tag:

```
<select
```

**3.** Type a space, the size attribute (which specifies the number of lines visible in the list), an equal sign, double quotation marks, 1, and double quotation marks, and the closing angle bracket.

```
<select size="1">
```

**4.** Press **ENTER** to start a new line.

**5.** Type the beginning of the <option> tag, a space, the value attribute, an equal sign, double quotation marks, the identifying number that will signify that the visitor chose this item, and double quotation marks. For example, to create the first item:

```
<option value="1"
```

**6.** Type the closing angle bracket of the <option> tag, the text that you want to appear for the item in the drop-down list, and the closing </option> tag. For example, to create the list item AL:

```
<option value="1">AL</option>
```

## TIP

By default, the browser displays the first item in the drop-down list. To make the browser display another item, add the selected attribute to the opening <option> tag for the appropriate item—for example, <option value="3" selected>United States</option>. Setting the default item is particularly useful when you have a long list of items in which the item the visitor is most likely to choose does not appear first. (Alternatively, you can rearrange the list to put the most likely item or items first.)

## NOTE

If you do not specify text for the value attribute of a check box, it receives the value "on" if it is selected.

---

**7.** Repeat steps 4-6 to create as many list items as you need. The following code shows an abbreviated example:

```
<option value="1">AL</option>
<option value="2">AK</option>
<option value="3">AR</option>
<option value="4">AS</option>
<option value="5">AZ</option>
<option value="6">CA</option>
<option value="7">CO</option>
<option value="8">CT</option>
...
<option value="58">WI</option>
<option value="59">WY</option>
```

**8.** Type the closing </select> tag to end the drop-down list. When the user clicks the down arrow of the drop-down list, the entire list will be displayed.

### ADD A CHECK BOX

For presenting options that are not mutually exclusive, use check boxes. To add a check box:

**1.** Place the insertion point at the appropriate location between the <form> and </form> tags, and press **ENTER** to create a new line.

**2.** Type the beginning of an <input/> tag, a space, the type attribute, an equal sign, double quotation marks, <u>checkbox</u>, and double quotation marks:

```
<input type="checkbox"
```

**3.** Type a space, the name attribute, an equal sign, double quotation marks, the name that you want to assign to the check box, and double quotation marks:

```
<input type="checkbox" name="Catalog"
```

**4.** Type a space, the value attribute, an equal sign, double quotation marks, the identifying text that will signify that the visitor chose this item, and double quotation marks.

```
<input type="checkbox" name="Catalog" value="Catalog"
```

**5.** Type a space, the id attribute, an equal sign, double quotation marks, the identifier name for this check box, and double quotation marks:

```
<input type="checkbox" name="Catalog" value="Catalog"
id="catalog"
```

**6.** If you want the check box to be selected by default, type a space followed by
<u>checked="checked"</u>:

```
<input type="checkbox" name="Catalog" value="Catalog" id="catalog"
    checked="checked"
```

**7.** Type the slash and closing angle bracket for the <input/> tag:

```
<input type="checkbox" name="Catalog" value="Catalog" id="catalog"
    checked="checked"/>
```

**8.** On the next line, type the beginning of a <label> tag that will display the text that
appears next to the check box:

```
<label
```

**9.** Type the for attribute, an equal sign, double quotation marks, the check box's id name,
double quotation marks, and a closing angle bracket:

```
<label for="catalog">
```

**10.** Type the text that you want to appear next to the check box, followed by the closing
</label> tag:

```
<label for="catalog">Send a Catalog</label>
```

> ☑ Send a Catalog    ☐ Add to Mailing List

**NOTE**

Option buttons are also known as *radio buttons,* because
on a conventional radio, only one station can be selected
at a time.

## ADD OPTION BUTTONS

Option buttons enable a visitor to choose among two or more mutually
exclusive options. Only one option button in a group of option buttons can be
selected at any one time; selecting an option button clears all the other option
buttons in the group.

To add a group of option buttons:

**1.** Place the insertion point at the appropriate location between the <form> and </form>
tags, and press **ENTER** to create a new line.

**2.** Type the beginning of an <input/> tag, a space, the type attribute, an equal sign, a pair
of double quotation marks, <u>radio</u>, and another pair of double quotation marks:

```
<input type="radio"
```

**3.** Type a space, the name attribute, an equal sign, a pair of double quotation marks, the
name for the group of option buttons, and another pair of double quotation marks:

```
<input type="radio" name="customertype"
```

**4.** Type a space, the id attribute, an equal sign, double quotation marks, the identifier name for this radio button, and double quotation marks:

```
<input type="radio" name="customertype" id="customer"
```

**5.** Type the closing slash and angle bracket for the <input/> tag:

```
<input type="radio" name="customertype" id="customer"/>
```

**6.** On the next line, type the beginning of a <label> tag that will display the text that appears next to the option button:

```
<label
```

**7.** Type the for attribute, an equal sign, double quotation marks, the option button's id name, double quotation marks, and a closing angle bracket:

```
<label for="customer">
```

**8.** Type the text that you want to appear next to the option button, followed by the closing </label> tag:

```
<label for="customer">Existing Customer</label>
```

**9.** Repeat steps 1 through 8 to add each of the other option buttons to the group. Use the same name attribute for each of the option buttons (see the accompanying Note).

**10.** Optionally, to make one of the option buttons selected by default, add the checked attribute to it and set the value to checked:

```
<input type="radio" name="customertype" id="customer"
    checked="checked"/>
```

○ Existing Customer  ⊙ New Customer

## ADD COMMAND BUTTONS

The controls discussed so far in this chapter let visitors interact with your forms, enter text, and make choices; but to enable them to take an action, you must add one or more command buttons. At the very least, you must add a button for submitting the form. It's often a good idea to include a button that resets the form, clearing all the options chosen or data entered in its fields.

To add a submit button:

**1.** Place the insertion point at the appropriate position between the <form> and </form> tags, and press **ENTER** to create a new line.

## NOTE

The name attribute associates the option buttons with each other, making them a group. If you assign a different value to the name attribute for the different option buttons in the group, they will be independent of each other and will not function correctly. To create two different groups of option buttons, use a different name value for the buttons that belong in each group.

## NOTE

To create a reset button, follow these steps, but use type="reset" instead of type="submit", and assign the button a value such as <u>Reset the Form</u> or <u>Clear All Fields</u>.

**2.** Type the beginning of an `<input/>` tag, a space, the type attribute, an equal sign, a pair of double quotation marks, <u>submit</u>, and another pair of double quotation marks:

```
<input type="submit"
```

**3.** Type a space, the value attribute, an equal sign, a pair of double quotation marks, the name for the button, another pair of double quotation marks, and the closing slash and angle bracket for the `<input/>` tag:

```
<input type="submit" value="Submit Feedback"/>
```

## Complete a Form

The following listing shows the complete code for the sample form shown in Figure 10-1, except that part of the list of states and possessions is omitted for conciseness.

```
<h1>Customer Feedback</h1>
<form action="feedback.php" method="get">
<p>First Name: <input type="text" name="firstname"
    size="20" value="Type your first name here"
    maxlength="20"/>
</p>
<p>Last Name: <input type="text" name="lastname"
    size="20" value="Type your last name here"
    maxlength="20"/></p>
<p>Address 1:
<input type="text" name="address1"
    value="Address line 1" size="40"/>
</p>
<p>Address 2:
    <input type="text" name="address2"
        value="Address line 2" size="40"/>
</p>
<p>City:
    <input type="text" name="addresscity"
        value="City" size="17"/>
     State: <select size="1">
    <option value="1">AL</option>
    <option value="2">AK</option>
    <option value="3">AR</option>
    <option value="4">AS</option>
    <option value="5">AZ</option>
    <option value="6">CA</option>
    <option value="7">CO</option>
    <option value="8">CT</option>
```

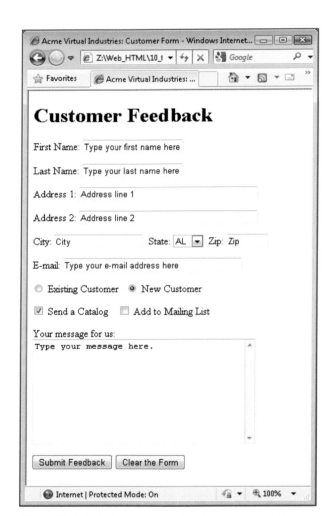

*Figure 10-1: Include a reset or clear button on your forms so that visitors can easily clear the information they've entered in the form if necessary.*

## LETTING VISITORS UPLOAD FILES

Depending on the types of forms you create, you may sometimes need to let visitors upload files to you. For example, if you accept visitor input for your site, you might need to let visitors upload pictures; if you sell software, you may need to allow visitors to upload configuration files to you so that you can diagnose problems.

To enable visitors to upload files:

1. Place the insertion point at the appropriate position between the <form> and </form> tags, and press **ENTER** to create a new line.

2. Type the beginning of an <input/> tag, a space, the type attribute, an equal sign, a pair of double quotation marks, <u>file</u>, and another pair of double quotation marks:

   ```
   <input type="file"
   ```

3. Type a space, the name attribute, an equal sign, a pair of double quotation marks, the name for the upload controls, and another pair of double quotation marks:

   ```
   <input type="file" name="upload"
   ```

4. Type a space, the size attribute, an equal sign, a pair of double quotation marks, the approximate width of the text box in the upload controls, another pair of double quotation marks, and the closing angle bracket for the tag:

   ```
   <input type="file" name="upload"
   size=60 />
   ```

Figure 10-2 shows the resulting upload controls in a form.

No matter which types of files you receive, check them for viruses before opening them by using an antivirus program such as Norton AntiVirus (www.symantec.com), McAfee VirusScan (www.mcafee.com), or the free Avast (www .avast.com) with up-to-date virus definitions. Even files as apparently harmless as JPEGs can contain malware.

```
<option value="9">DC</option>
<option value="10">DE</option>
<option value="11">FL</option>
<option value="12">FM</option>
<option value="13">GA</option>
<option value="14">GU</option>
<option value="15">HI</option>
<option value="16">IA</option>
<option value="17">ID</option>
<option value="18">IL</option>
<option value="19">KS</option>
<option value="20">KY</option>
<!-- Other states omitted here for brevity -->
<option value="58">WI</option>
<option value="59">WY</option>
</select>
 Zip:
<input type="text" name="addresszip"
    value="Zip" size="5" maxlength="5"/>
</p>
<p>E-mail:
    <input type="text" name="email"
        value="Type your e-mail address here"
        size="40"/>
</p>
<p><input type="radio" name="customertype"
    id="customertype"/>
    <label for="customertype">Existing Customer</label>
      <input type="radio"
        name="customertype" id="newcustomer" checked="checked"/>
        <label for="newcustomer">New Customer</label></p>
<p><input type="checkbox" name="Catalog"
    value="Catalog" id="catalog" checked="checked"/>
    <label for="catalog">Send a Catalog</label>
      
    <input type="checkbox" name="MailList"
        value="MailList" id="maillist"/>
    <label for="maillist">Add to Mailing List</label></p>
<p>Your message for us:<br />
    <textarea cols="40" rows="10">Type your message here.
    </textarea></p>
<p><input type="submit" value="Submit Feedback"
    name="submit" align="middle" id="submit"/>
    <input type="reset" value="Clear the Form" name="clear"
align="left"/></p>
</form>
```

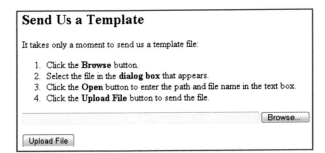

**Send Us a Template**

It takes only a moment to send us a template file:

1. Click the **Browse** button.
2. Select the file in the **dialog box** that appears.
3. Click the **Open** button to enter the path and file name in the text box.
4. Click the **Upload File** button to send the file.

[                                    ] Browse...

[ Upload File ]

**Figure 10-2: Use an** <input/> **tag with** type="file" **to create upload controls in a form. The visitor clicks the Browse button to display a dialog box that makes it easy to select a file on a local drive.**

**NOTE**

The type attribute file gives you a text box field with a Browse button (on Windows) or a Choose File button (on the Mac). The user can enter a path and filename in the field, or click the button, which opens the standard system dialog box used to locate and select a file, which, in either case, will be uploaded to the server running your web page.

**NOTE**

As with the simple text box, the size attribute does not limit the number of characters the user can enter; rather, it only specifies the size of the text box that displays them.

# Create a Form That E-mails Its Contents to You

If your web host doesn't supply an easy-to-use script that fulfills your needs, you can easily create a form that e-mails its contents to you. This is a quick and easy method of returning the contents of the form, but you have to expose an e-mail address, which may be gathered by either live visitors or spiders crawling the Web. Either way, the e-mail address may end up on a spam list—so use an address that you can abandon without disrupting your main lines of communication.

To create a form that e-mails its contents to you:

**1.** Type the beginning of the opening <form> tag:

```
<form
```

**2.** Type the action attribute, an equal sign, a pair of double quotation marks, mailto: and the e-mail address, and another pair of double quotation marks:

```
<form mailto:"customers@acmevirtualindustries.com"
```

**3.** Type a space, the method attribute, an equal sign, a pair of double quotation marks, post, another pair of double quotation marks, and the closing angle bracket for the <form> tag:

```
<form mailto:"customers@acmevirtualindustries.com" method="post">
```

**4.** Create the remainder of the form as described earlier in this section.

If the visitor is using Internet Explorer, clicking the command button to submit an e-mail form may display a warning (such as that shown here) that the form will be submitted via e-mail and without encryption, revealing the visitor's e-mail address to you. The visitor can choose whether to proceed with submitting the data or canceling the submission.

Visitors using Firefox or another browser that uses the Mozilla codebase (such as Camino) will typically see a message started automatically in their default e-mail application and will be able to choose between sending it manually and canceling it without sending it. The message will not be sent automatically.

# Use Scripts in Your Web Pages

A script is a list of commands written in a *scripting language* (a type of programming language) that is used to automate activity. Various scripting languages can be used on web pages, but the most widely used as of this writing is JavaScript.

Scripting can be highly complex—but you can also use short and straightforward scripts to add interactivity to your web pages and make them perform actions that HTML alone cannot perform. This section introduces you briefly to scripts and shows you examples of some simple actions that you can perform with JavaScript without learning much of the language. If you find these actions useful, you may choose to learn more about JavaScript so that you can use it more fully. Consult a book such as *JavaScript: A Beginner's Guide* (McGraw-Hill, 2009) for detailed information.

To tell the browser that you're using a script rather than HTML codes, you enclose the script between an opening <script> tag and a closing </script> tag. Inside the opening <script> tag, you use the type attribute to specify the scripting language in which the script is written—in this case, JavaScript:

```
<script type="text/JavaScript">
</script>
```

## Understand the Different Categories of User Events

A script runs because it is triggered by the visitor (or the visitor's browser) taking an action. Such an action is called an *event*, simply meaning that something definable happened. Table 10-1 explains the most widely used user

| EVENT NAME | EVENT OCCURS WHEN |
|---|---|
| **BROWSER-GENERATED EVENTS** | |
| onload | The browser starts to load a web page |
| onunload | The browser starts to leave the web page (because the visitor has told it to load another web page) |
| onerror | An error occurs in a script that the browser is trying to run |
| onabort | The visitor stops the current page from being loaded (for example, by clicking the Stop button) |
| **MOUSE EVENTS** | |
| onmousemove | The visitor moves the mouse pointer in the browser window |
| onmouseover | The visitor moves the mouse pointer so that it is over a particular element—for example, the visitor moves the mouse pointer over a graphic |
| onmouseout | The visitor moves the mouse pointer so that it leaves the element in question—for example, the visitor moves the mouse pointer off the graphic again |
| onclick | The visitor clicks an element on the web page |
| ondoubleclick | The visitor double-clicks an element on the web page |
| onmousedown | The visitor clicks the mouse button on an element and keeps pressing the mouse button |
| onmouseup | The visitor releases the mouse button that he or she has been holding down |
| **KEYBOARD EVENTS** | |
| onkeypress | The visitor presses and releases a key (in other words, performs a normal keystroke action) |
| onkeydown | The visitor presses a key and holds it down |
| onkeyup | The visitor releases a key that he or she has been holding down |
| **FORM FIELD EVENTS** | |
| onsubmit | The visitor clicks the submit button on a form |
| onreset | The visitor clicks the reset button on a form |
| onselect | The visitor selects an option button, a check box, or a menu item |
| onchange | The visitor types in a text box or clicks a different option button, check box, or menu item |
| onfocus | The visitor moves the focus to a form field—for example, by clicking in a text field before typing in it |
| onblur | The visitor moves the focus away from the form field in question |

*Table 10-1: User Events for Scripts*

## DEALING WITH SCRIPT THREATS

JavaScript can be used to perform malicious actions against the will of the visitor to a web page, so some people prevent their browsers from executing JavaScript. Some browsers also block scripts by default on the grounds that they might be malicious.

On Windows, Internet Explorer usually displays the information bar to warn a visitor about active content such as JavaScript. To use the script, the visitor must click the information bar, and then click **Allow Blocked Content**, as shown here.

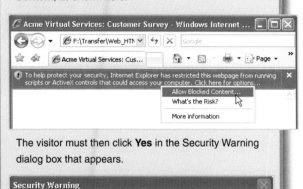

The visitor must then click **Yes** in the Security Warning dialog box that appears.

If your pages rely on JavaScript and the browser doesn't execute it, the pages will not work properly. Consider warning users that they will need to enable JavaScript in order to view your pages successfully. Alternatively, provide a version of your site that doesn't use JavaScript so that users can view your site without it.

events that you can use in your scripts, divided into categories. The following events are usually the most useful:

- The onclick event is useful for performing actions when the visitor clicks an element on a web page—for example, a link.

- The onsubmit event is useful for checking that all required fields in a form have been completed before it is sent for processing.

- The onmouseover and onmouseout events are used for implementing effects such as an image rollover: As the mouse moves over it, an existing graphic is replaced by another graphic; when the mouse moves off the graphic's area, the original graphic is restored.

- The onselect event can be used to automatically select, clear, or make available other check boxes, option buttons, or menu items affected by the current choice.

# Show When a Page Was Last Updated

Some of the pages on your site are likely to change frequently. If they do, you may want to show visitors when the pages were last updated so that the visitors will know whether the pages contain new information since their last visit. While you can include the date as text and change it manually each time you change the page, it's much easier to use a short script that inserts the date and time on which the page was last modified—or, more accurately, when it was last saved to the web server.

The following example uses the document.lastModified statement to provide the date and time the page was saved, and the document.write statement to add explanatory text before and a period after:

```
<script type="text/JavaScript">
    document.write("This page was last modified on ")
    document.write(document.lastModified)
    document.write(".")
</script>
```

This page was last modified on 05/08/2009 20:29:18

The onload and onunload events are widely used by unscrupulous websites to display pop-up windows containing material that most visitors would probably not have chosen to view. Because of this usage, many browsers enable users to block the display of such automatically generated windows. Even if these windows are not blocked, avoid using them, as they frequently produce negative reactions from visitors.

## Redirect the Browser to Another Page

You can use JavaScript to redirect the browser to another page:

```
<script type="text/JavaScript">
    window.location="http://www.acmevirtualindustries.com"
</script>
```

## Verify That a Form Is Filled In

If you create forms, you may need to verify that the required fields are filled in before you allow a visitor to submit the form. You can use a script to check the contents of the fields.

The following example shows the code for a web page (see Figure 10-3) that includes a short script that performs basic validation on the two text boxes, simply ensuring that neither is empty.

```
<?xml version="1.0" encoding="utf-8"?>
<!DOCTYPE html PUBLIC "-//W3C//DTD XHTML 1.0 Transitional//EN"
        "http://www.w3.org/TR/xhtml1/DTD/xhtml1-transitional
.dtd">
<html xmlns="http://www.w3.org/1999/xhtml" xml:lang="en"
lang="en">
<head>
    <meta http-equiv="content-type" content="text/html;
charset=utf-8" />
    <title>Acme Virtual Industries: Preferred Customer Login</
title>
<script type="text/javascript" language="JavaScript">
    function verify(loginform)
        {if (loginform.login.value=='')
            {alert('Enter your login name.'); return false;}
        if (loginform.password.value=='')
            {alert('Enter your password.'); return false;}
        return true}
</script>

</head>
<body>
<h1>Preferred Customer Login</h1>
<p>Please log in to access the Preferred
```

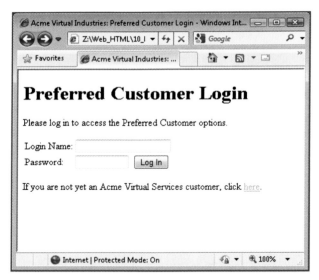

**Figure 10-3: This page uses a short script to check that the Login Name and Password text boxes contain entries before the form is submitted.**

**TIP**

You can also use the document.write statement to display other information in a web page. For example, the document.write(document.title) statement displays the page's title, the document.write(location.href) statement displays the file name of the active web page, and the document.write(document.referrer) statement displays the name of the web page that referred the browser to the current web page.

**NOTE**

You can also redirect the browser by using an http-equiv meta tag, as discussed in Chapter 1. The advantage of the meta tag is that it will not trigger a script warning; however, some browsers enable you to block meta refreshes, which prevents such redirection from working. If you use a meta tag to redirect the browser, provide an explanation in the redirecting page of where the browser is being sent, along with a link that the visitor can click manually if the meta refresh is disabled.

```
    Customer options.</p>
<form method="post" action="login.cgi"
    onsubmit="return verify(this);">
<table border="0">
    <tr>
        <td>Login Name:</td>
        <td colspan="2"><input type="text"
            name="login" size="20"/></td>
    </tr>
    <tr>
        <td>Password:</td>
        <td><input type="password" name="password"
            size="10"/></td>
        <td><input type="submit" value="Log In"/></td>
    </tr>
</table>
</form>
<p>If you are not yet an Acme Virtual Services customer,
    click <a href="new_cust.html">here</a>.</p>
</body>
</html>
```

The form itself contains two text boxes (input type="text"), one named login and the other named password, and a submit button that bears the text "Log In." The onsubmit event in the <form> tag specifies that when the form is submitted (in other words, when the visitor clicks the Log In button), the script returns the value of the function named verify for the current object (onsubmit="return verify(this);").

The code within the <script> and </script> tags in the document header does the following:

● States that the script language used is JavaScript

● Declares a function named verify and specifies that the object it works on is loginform

● Compares the value (the contents) of the text box named login on the form named loginform (loginform.login.value) to an empty string (' '). If there is a match, the alert statement displays a message box telling the visitor the problem and returns the value false, preventing the form from being submitted.

- Compares the value (the contents) of the text box named password (loginform.password.value) to an empty string (' '). If there is a match, the alert statement displays a message box (shown here) telling the visitor the problem and returns the value false, again preventing the form from being submitted.

If both the login text box and the password text box contain text, the function returns the value true, which allows the form to be submitted.

  code, 49
&shy; code, 49

## A

absolute links, 82, 83
Adobe Dreamweaver, 17
aligning elements, 56
   graphics, 70
   tables, rows, and cells, 110–113
   text, 148
alternative text, 68–69, 129
   adding to a frame page, 127
anchor element, 83, 84
Apache, 33
Arachnophilia, 16
asymmetrical Internet connections, 33
attributes
   action, 185
   align, 48, 56, 110–113, 148
   alt, 15
   bgcolor, 115, 116
   cellpadding, 109–110
   cellspacing, 109–110
   class, 143
   color, 61
   colspan, 114
   content, 20
   href, 17, 84
   id, 142–143
   maxlength, 187
   method, 185, 186
   name, 20, 133, 185–186
   noresize, 129
   nowrap, 108
   rowspan, 114
   rules, 105
   scrolling, 129
   size, 61
   style, 62, 63, 64, 66

   valign, 113
   whitespace, 48
audio
   delivery methods, 94–95
   formats, 94
   links for downloading, 95
   links for playing, 95–96
   streaming, 33

## B

background color, 64–65
blinking text, 64
blogging services, 37
body, 8
boldface, 58
borders, 64, 65–66
   applying to graphics, 72
   frames, 127–128
   tables, 101, 103–105
breaks, 48
browsers
   checking web pages with other browsers,
     23–26, 40
   overriding style sheets in your browser, 155–157
bulleted lists, 50, 51–52

## C

Cascading Style Sheets. *See* CSS
case sensitivity in HTML tags, 5
clients. *See* web clients
clip-art graphics, 69
colors, 40
   background color, 64–65
   type color, 61
comments, 13
compression, 74, 79
connection speed, 32–33
copyright, 69

CSS, 62
   aligning, centering, or justifying text, 148
   controlling font formatting, 146–148
   embedded style sheets, 139
   external style sheets, 136, 138, 140–142
   floating layouts, 151–157
   formatting the first letter of an element, 145
   formatting the first line of an element, 146
   indents, 148
   internal style sheets, 136
   line height, 149–150
   linking multiple style sheets to a web page, 142
   margins, 149
   overriding style sheets, 146, 155–157
   overview, 136–138
   preventing background graphics from being tiled
     or scrolling, 150–151
   selector, 138, 142–145
   style cascade, 137
   style rules, 138–139
   versions, 140
custom uploading, 41
Cyberduck, 42

## D

definition lists, 50, 53–54
dithering, 40
divisions, 48
   using as a selector, 144–145
DNS, 34
DOCTYPE declaration, adding to a web
   page, 6–7
document head. *See* header
documenting your website, 4
Domain Name Service. *See* DNS
domain names
   getting your own, 32
   registering, 34–36
Domain Naming System. *See* DNS

# E

e-mail
    creating a form that e-mails its contents to you,
        194–195
    creating a hyperlink to an e-mail address, 172
    creating an e-mail button, 90–91
    creating links to send e-mail, 88–91
    signature, 76–79
embedding video in a web page, 96
emphasis. *See* italics
eNom, 35
Excel
    creating web pages from Excel workbooks,
        178–180
    General tab options, 160–161
extranets, 31

# F

file extensions, 19
file formats, 176–177
File Transfer Protocol. *See* FTP
FileZilla, 42
Firefox, 23–26
    using default fonts and colors in, 156–157
floating layouts, 151
    preventing with the clear property, 155–157
    three-column, 154–155
    two-column, 152–154
folders
    creating, 4–5
    My Web Sites, 5
    separating content by, 4
fonts, 46–47, 62
    color, 61
    formatting, 60–61, 64
    monospaced fonts, 59
    type size, 60–61
    *See also* formatting

formatting, 14, 46
    aligning elements, 56
    basic structure, 47
    boldface, 58
    borders, 64
    breaks, 48
    divisions, 48
    fonts, 60–61
    headings, 49–50
    hyphens, 49
    inline styles, 62–66
    italics, 58
    keyboard text, 60
    line spacing, 63
    lists, 50–55
    nonbreaking space, 49, 50
    overlining, 63
    paragraphs, 47
    preformatted text, 57
    sample text, 60
    smaller or bigger text, 60
    strikethrough, 59, 63
    subscript and superscript, 59
    underlining, 58, 63
    variable text, 60
forms, 183–184
    adding a multiline text box, 187–188
    adding a single-line text box, 186–187
    check boxes, 189–190
    command buttons, 191–192
    completing, 192–193
    creating a form that e-mails its contents to you,
        194–195
    drop-down lists, 188–189
    letting visitors upload files, 193
    option buttons, 190–191
    structure, 184–186
    verifying that a form is filled in, 198–200
frames, 120–121
    adding alternative text, 127, 129
    borders, 127–128

    creating component documents, 123
    creating using both rows and columns, 126
    creating using columns, 125
    creating using rows, 124–125
    defining height and width, 121–122
    inline, 130–133
    links that change the contents of frames, 133
    margins, 129
    planning web pages with, 121
    preventing visitors from resizing, 129
    scrolling, 129
framesets, 120
    adding component documents, 126–127
    creating frameset documents, 123–124
    nesting, 130
FTP, 41
FTP clients, 41
    transferring websites using, 42–43

# G

GIF files, 75
Go Daddy, 35
graphics
    adding titles to, 72
    aligning, 70
    alternative text, 68–69
    applying borders, 72
    background graphics, 74, 76
    changing the size of, 70–71
    creating or acquiring, 68–69
    in an e-mail signature, 76–79
    imagemaps, 91–93
    inserting, 68
    keeping down file size to load pages faster, 79
    locating, 69
    long description URLs, 70
    positioning with spacers, 73
    preventing background graphics from being tiled
        or scrolling, 150–151
    using to control text appearance, 72

## H

header, 8
headings, 49–50
    adding to a web page, 10–11
hiding elements, 66
horizontal rules, 75–76
.htm, 19
.html, 19
HTML
    defined, 2
    which version to use, 4
HTML 5, defined, 3
HTML editors, 16
HTTP, 27
hyperlinks, 16–18
    creating in Word, 168–173
    creating linked files, 18–19
    to an e-mail address, 172
    to an existing file or web page, 169–170
    to a new document, 171–172
    to a place in the current document, 170
    See also links
hyphens, optional, 49

## I

imagemaps, 91–93
images
    adding pictures to a web page, 14–15
    sizing, 15
indenting, 48, 55–56, 148
    first-line indents, 62
inline frames, 130–133
Internet, defined, 27
Internet Explorer, 23–26
    applying style sheets in, 155–156
Internet Information Services (IIS), 33
intranets, 31, 164

IP addresses, 29
IPv4, 28, 29
IPv6, 28–29
ISO, 165
ISPs, evaluating, 34
italics, 58

## J

JavaScript, 197
    redirecting to another page, 198
    See also scripts
JPEG files, 75

## K

keyboard shortcuts
    assigning to a link, 86
    for saving web pages, 11
Komodo Edit, 16
KompoZer, 17

## L

line breaks, 12–13
line spacing, 63
linked files, creating, 18–19
links
    absolute links, 82, 83
    changing tab order, 86–87
    creating multiple links in a graphic, 91–93
    displaying a ScreenTip for, 87–88
    to download a file, 86–87
    for downloading audio or video files, 95
    graphic links, 82–84
    mailto, 90
    opening in a new window, 86
    to a particular point on a web page, 85–86

for playing audio or video files, 95–96
    relative links, 82–83
    to send e-mail, 88–91
    text links, 82
    within a web page, 84–85
    See also hyperlinks
lists, 50
    bulleted lists, 50, 51–52
    definition lists, 50, 53–54
    nested lists, 54–55
    numbered lists, 50, 52–53
logical style tags, 58
lossy and lossless compression, 74

## M

margins, 149
markup tags. See tags
Markup Validation Service, 22–23, 24
meta tags, 20
    redirecting to another page, 21–22, 199
    reloading pages automatically, 20–21
Microsoft Expression Web, 17
Microsoft Office, 160
    See also Office applications
Microsoft Word. See Word
monospaced fonts, 46–47, 59
moving text, 65–66
My Web Sites folder, 5

## N

naming conventions, 4
navigation, 86–87
nested framesets, 130
nested lists, 54–55
nested tables, 115–116
Network Solutions, 35
nonbreaking space, 49, 50

Notepad
    opening, 5
    opening two or more files at once, 18
    pinning Notepad to Start menu, 6
numbered lists, 50, 52–53

## O

Office applications
    choosing Browsers tab options, 162, 163
    choosing Encoding tab options, 165
    choosing Files tab options, 162–164
    choosing Fonts tab options, 165–166
    choosing General tab options for Excel, 160–161
    choosing General tab options for PowerPoint, 161–162
    choosing Pictures tab options, 164–165
    displaying Web Options dialog box, 160
    how applications use HTML, 161
    removing Office-specific tags from Word documents, 177–178
    Save As Web Page, 166–167, 175–177
    Web Page Preview command, 166, 173, *174*
    *See also* Excel; PowerPoint; Word
optional hyphens, 49
ordered lists. *See* numbered lists
organizing your website, 4
overlining, 63

## P

paragraphs, 47
    adding to a web page, 11–12
Parallells Desktop, 25
PC-emulation programs, 25
physical style tags, 58
PNG files, 74
PowerPoint
    creating web pages from PowerPoint presentations, 181–182
    General tab options, 161–162

previewing a web page, 166, 173, *174*
properties
    font, 146–148
    line-height, 63, 149–150
    margin, 149
    text-align, 148
    text-transform, 63
    visibility, 66
proportional fonts, 46–47
protocols, 41
pseudo-elements, 145–146
public identifiers, 6

## R

redirecting to another page, 21–22, 198
refreshing pages automatically, 20–21
Register.com, 35
relative dimensions, 122
reloading pages automatically, 20–21
robots meta tag, 20
round-tripping, 161
rules, 75–76, 105, 117

## S

Safari, 23–26
    applying style sheets in, 157
screen resolution, 40, 164
ScreenTips, for links, 87–88
scripts, 195
    redirecting to another page, 198
    showing when a page was last updated, 197
    threats, 197
    user events, 195–197
    verifying that a form is filled in, 198–200
scrolling, preventing, 150–151
search engine optimization, 21
search engines, 21
self-closing tags, 12

SEO. *See* search engine optimization
servers. *See* web servers
shopping carts, 33
Single File Web Page format, 176
soft hyphens, 49
source code, viewing, 13
special characters, 49
streaming, 33
strikethrough, 59, 63
strong text. *See* boldface
subscript and superscript, 59
system identifiers, 6

## T

tables
    adding rows and columns, 103
    aligning, 110–113
    applying a background color, 115
    borders, 101, 103–105
    data tables, 98
    grouping cells by rows and columns, 105–108
    layout tables, 98
    nested, 115–116
    overview, 97–98
    padding and spacing, 109–110
    planning, 98
    setting table and cell height, 109
    setting table and cell width, 108–109
    spanning cells over columns or rows, 114–115
    structure, 98–102
    vertical rules, 117
tags, 6, 49, 59
    <!-- -->, 13
    <a>, 17
    <b>, 58
    <basefont>, 61
    <big>, 59, 60
    <blockquote>, 56
    <body>, 8
    <br/>, 12–13, 48

<colgroup>, 107
<dd>, 53–54
<div>, 48, 144–145
<dl>, 53–54
<em>, 58
<font>, 60
<form>, 185
<frameset>, 124, 125, 126
<h1>, 10, 49–50
<head>, 8
<hr/>, 75–76
<HTML>, 7–8
<i>, 58
<img>, 14–15
<kbd>, 60
<li>, 51–52
<marquee>, 65–66
<nobr>, 48
<ol>, 52–53
<p>, 11–12, 47
<pre>, 57, 59
<samp>, 60
<script>, 195
<small>, 60
<span>, 144
<strike>, 59
<strong>, 58
<sub>, 59
<sup>, 59
<table>, 98–102
<tbody>, 106
<td>, 100
<tfoot>, 106
<title>, 9
<tr>, 100
<tt>, 59, 60
<u>, 58
<ul>, 51–52
<var>, 60
case sensitivity, 5
iframes, 131–133

img, 68
meta tags, 20
nesting, 59
self-closing, 12
TCP/IP, 27
text
 blinking, 64
 capitalization, 63
 indenting, 48, 55–56, 62
 line spacing, 63
 moving, 65–66
 preformatted, 57
 *See also* formatting
text links, 82
text paragraphs, adding to a web page, 11–12
tiling, preventing, 150–151
titles, 9, 11
traffic, 31–32

## U

underlining, 58, 63
Unicode, 165
Uniform Resource Locators. *See* URLs
unordered lists. *See* bulleted lists
updates, showing when a page was last updated, 197
uploading, letting visitors upload files, 193
uptime, 32–33
URLs, 29–30
 entering in browsers, 31
 long description URLs, 70
user events, 195–197
UTF-8, 165

## V

validating HTML, W3 Markup Validation Service, 22–23, *24*
versions
 HTML 5, 3
 which HTML version to use, 4

vertical rules, 117
video
 delivery methods, 94–95
 embedding in a web page, 96
 formats, 94
 links for downloading, 95
 links for playing, 95–96
 streaming, 33
View Source Code command, 13
VirtualBox, 25
VMWare Fusion, 25

## W

W3 Markup Validation Service, 22–23, 24
Web, 27
web browsers
 checking web pages with other browsers, 23–26, 40
 overriding style sheets in your browser, 155–157
web clients, 28
web hosts
 amount of space, 31
 amount of traffic, 31–32
 assessing requirements, 30
 audio and video streaming, 33
 choosing a service, 31
 evaluating, 34
 Internet connection speed and uptime, 32–33
 number of accounts, 32
 shopping carts and secure servers, 33
 support for web tools, 33
 your own domain name, 32
Web Page, Filtered format, 177
Web Page format, 176
web pages
 accessing, 29–30
 adding header and body tags, 8
 adding the <HTML> tags, 7–8
 checking with other browsers, 23–26

web pages (*cont.*)
comments, 13
creating from Excel workbooks, 178–180
describing pages with meta tags, 20
formatting, 14
headings, 10–11
images, 14–15
keeping small enough to download quickly, 39
laying out, 77
line breaks, 12–13
linking to a particular point on, 85–86
links within, 84–85
reloading automatically, 20–21
saving, 9, 11
structure, 6–8, 47
text paragraphs, 11–12
titles, 9
viewing, 9–10
viewing the source code, 13
web servers, 28, 33
secure servers, 33
web-authoring applications, 16–17, 37
with built-in FTP, 41
websites, 28
checking on other browsers, 40
making effective, 37–39
planning contents, 36–37
transferring to the Web, 41–43
updating and maintaining, 40–41
Windows Vista
Business Edition, 33
FTP client, 41
Ultimate Edition, 33
Word
creating HTML elements, 178
creating hyperlinks, 168–173
removing Office-specific tags from Word
documents, 177–178
removing sensitive information from a document,
173–175
saving documents as web pages, 166–167, 175–177
starting a new web page, 166–167
Web Page Preview command, 166, 173, 174
World Wide Web. *See* Web

# X

XHTML, defined, 3
XHTML 5, 3
XML, defined, 3